PENGUIN BOOKS

WITNESS TO WAR

Antoinette May is the author of three other books, *Haunted Ladies*, *Different Drummers*, and *Haunted Houses and Wandering Ghosts of California*. Her biographical series "Women Who Paved the Way" is syndicated by Chronicle Features, and she has written a weekly column for the *San Francisco Chronicle*.

WITNESS TO WAR

A Biography of
MARGUERITE HIGGINS

Antoinette May

PENGUIN BOOKS

PENGUIN BOOKS
Viking Penguin Inc., 40 West 23rd Street,
New York, New York 10010, U.S.A.
Penguin Books Ltd, Harmondsworth,
Middlesex, England
Penguin Books Australia Ltd, Ringwood,
Victoria, Australia
Penguin Books Canada Limited, 2801 John Street,
Markham, Ontario, Canada L3R 1B4
Penguin Books (N.Z.) Ltd, 182-190 Wairau Road,
Auckland 10, New Zealand

First published in the United States of America by
Beaufort Books, Inc., 1983
Published by Viking Penguin Inc. 1985

LIBRARY OF CONGRESS CATALOGING IN PUBLICATION DATA
May, Antoinette.
Witness to war.
Bibliography: p.
Includes index.
1. Higgins, Marguerite.   2. War correspondents—
United States—Biography.   3. Foreign correspondents—
United States—Biography.   I. Title.
[PN4874.H478M39   1985]   070.4′33′0924 [B]   84-18950
ISBN 0 14 00.7597 6

Printed in the United States of America by
R. R. Donnelley & Sons Company, Harrisonburg, Virginia
Set in Linotype Times Roman

Page 275 constitutes an extension of this copyright page.

To John Wilson, whose enthusiasm,
know-how, and personal involvement
helped to make this book a reality.

Acknowledgments

This is the story of a reporter and her times. It owes at least as much to those who were her witnesses—Lieutenant General William Hall, Helen and Tom Lambert, James O'Donnell, Ruth Montgomery, and the late Jean Craig Clack, without whose practical assistance and encouragement this biography would not have been possible.

But there were other witnesses as well, many who provided truly invaluable aid and information in gathering the varied skeins of a narrative that spanned more than four decades and three wars. The only possible means of crediting them seems to be alphabetically. Marguerite Higgins, for all her daring and romanticism, was also a pragmatist. I think she would approve. My heartfelt thanks to:

Elie Abel, Ellen Ainsworth, David Alcott, Judy Barden, Catherine Basset, Keyes Beech, Shirley Beedy, Bob Button, Haakon Chevalier, Cherry and Don Cook, Carolyn Davis, Dick Demerest, Bob Donovan, Bernadeen Frankel, Morton Glatzer, Kay and Russell Hill, Toni Howard, Ann Hunter, Lieutenant Colonel George Kelley, Richard Lake, Ted Laymon, Flora Lewis, C.J. Marrow, Alyce McIntyre, General John Michaelis, Carl Mydans, Helen Nathan, David M. Nichol, Mike O'Neill, Major Charles Payne, Eleanor Piel, Ogden Reid, Fred Shaw, Belleveron and Bernard Shapiro, Miriam Sturrier, Jean Louise Talbot, Captain Harry Taylor, John Tebbel, Phoebe True, and Steve White.

Contents

Photographs appear following page 124.

PROLOGUE

The January day at Arlington National Cemetery was as gray as the mood of those gathered. Grim and overcast, its appearance underscored the tragedy. It was sad; funerals always are. But the loss was more abstract: that one so young and so vital could be struck down suddenly and mysteriously.

There had been jokes and stories about "La Belle Higgins" dating from World War II. Journalists had talked of "Maggie"—her "liberation" of Dachau, her sad affair with a hero of the French Resistance, and her ingenious methods of stealing stories. "What Makes Maggie Run?" had been a frequent topic of conversation at press clubs and cocktail parties. It had always been difficult to reconcile the young heroine of those faraway adventures with the Washington superstar she had become.

In one pew sat Robert and Ethel Kennedy. Marguerite had always been close to the Kennedy family; someone once dubbed her the "Madame Recamier" of Camelot. Among the familiar figures seated was Vice President Hubert Humphrey. One rarely saw so many political notables assembled away from the Hill. The military brass was also well represented. Naturally the largest contingency was the Washington press corps, which was out in force, boosted by many from the old *New York Herald Tribune* staff.

A huge wreath had been sent by President Johnson. A bouquet was from Jacqueline Kennedy. Others, some who loved Marguerite best, couldn't be there. Ruth Montgomery was in Egypt and Keyes Beech was in Saigon. Jim O'Donnell was on assignment in Berlin. John and Mary Michaelis were in Turkey. They were all much like Marguerite herself, individuals whose hectic, often tempestuous lives took them to far-off places.

Many of those present were men. Marguerite Higgins was known to have loved not only well but also frequently and for the most part wisely. The controversy that had invariably swirled about her when she was alive promised to be immortal. The turbulence that had always surrounded Marguerite's career—a dazzling climb to the top that left a bitter trail— had produced memories that could never lie buried.

Two small children, unaware of the extent of their mother's fame, listened quietly between their father and grandmother. How proud Marguerite had been of her exquisite son and daughter; how she had delighted in bringing them out to bow and curtsy, say a few polite words, and then disappear with their nurse. Had that busy mother, forever jetting from one trouble spot to another, really ever known her children? How would they remember her in years to come?

The grandmother, another Marguerite, was a young-looking woman with caramel-colored hair and a marked French accent. Today her eyes darted anxiously about the church, as though assuring herself that everything was right. Even in her grief there was a sense of urgency, an air of barely suppressed drama.

Then there was the husband, Lieutenant General Bill Hall, a tall, handsome man, who was years older than Marguerite but well known for his attraction to and for women. What were his thoughts now? There had been a wife and four children before Marguerite. How soon would another woman follow her?

Alone with his thoughts was Peter Lisagor, the distinguished author and columnist, who had been Marguerite's mentor and constant companion during the last difficult years, the man that many were convinced had been more than a friend.

The requiem mass was drawing to a close. The military chaplain had talked about Marguerite's youth, her talent, and her bravery. Soon the legendary reporter who had sat at polished desks in the world's capitals exchanging ideas with Nehru, Khrushchev, Chiang Kai-shek, Franco, and Tito would be laid to rest among the fallen heroes of the wars that she had so ably reported.

How strange it was that this woman who had so often defied death— who had crossed the German lines to beat the United States Army to Dachau and had landed with the marines at Inchon—would succumb to the assault of a tiny insect. A body that had proved immune to the ravages of wars had been destroyed by a rare tropical parasite.

Mourners left the chapel and took their places in the cortege that would take them to the grave site selected for its proximity to John Kennedy's final resting place. Death was a waste for one so young; but this might have been Marguerite's choice—quitting while still ahead.

Marguerite Higgins, woman of fact and legend, would have had little patience with old age. She would have hated the restrictions, the limitations, and the final inevitable relegation to the sidelines. To die young would have been infinitely preferable to a lingering, perhaps undignified exit. She would have wanted to be remembered above all for her vitality and yes, her style, when there would be no Maggie around to tell the story right.

PART I

WHAT MADE MAGGIE RUN

One

Who can say it was not prophetic that Maggie Higgins's parents should meet in a bomb shelter? While the German Big Bertha rocked the Paris street above them, the two attractive and volatile young people were drawn instantly to one another.

For them World War I was a grand adventure. Like characters from a film, they looked the parts assigned them in the drama—a narrative that despite its horror seemed created to fulfill their own fantasies.

Lawrence Daniel Higgins was tall and handsome, with all the charm, the poetry, the dreams, and the restlessness that characterized his Irish ancestry. His parents, the O'Higginses, had fled a life of crushing poverty and prejudice in Ireland, consigning the O' part of their surname to the old sod while en route to California.

Larry was attending law school at the University of California when the war broke out. Looking about at the nearly windowless walls of the library at Berkeley, he felt the Great War beckon—a glorious escape. The headlines were scarcely dry when he enlisted in the French army as an ambulance driver hoping to transfer as soon as possible to the fledgling air force.

As his train clattered across vast deserts, climbed the Rocky Mountains, and then sped through farmland and burgeoning cities, he listened to the long, low whistle. To him it was destiny's voice summoning him to arms. He heard it again on the old sailing ship that took him to Cherbourg. Standing on the damp deck, his excitement heightened by the rise and fall of the vintage vessel as it cut through foam, he thrilled to the sound of the wind as it filled the sails. How fortunate he was to have this grand opportunity to die as every brave man should wish to die—fighting for his country!

Of course, Larry reflected dreamily, his eyes on the midnight stars, if he didn't get killed, it would be nice to say one day, "Back in nineteen seventeen, when I was an aviator, I used to— "

It would be the fate of Larry Higgins to survive both war and peace. He would tell many stories many times, and his most ardent audience would always be his daughter.

Petite, vivacious and deliciously pretty, Marguerite de Godard (the second in a dynasty of star-crossed Marguerites) was also on her way to Paris. Like Larry, she was a romantic; but she also possessed a pragmatic Gallic streak.

Some thirty years before, the first Marguerite's great beauty had won the heart of an aristocratic young army officer, Georges de Godard, who eloped with her to the outrage of his titled parents. The couple had three daughters before young de Godard died of a rare tropical disease contracted while fighting with the French colonial forces in what would one day be known as Vietnam.

A few months later his widow accidentally shot herself in the foot while hunting. The wound became infected and Madame de Godard died of blood poisoning. The Count and Countess de Godard, never having accepted their commoner daughter-in-law, would have nothing to do with the orphaned children. It remained for the dead mother's impoverished family to rescue them from an orphanage. At sixty-three, Grandmother Piguet went to work as a postmistress to support the young girls.

Even at three, the message was clear to little Marguerite: A pretty face was not enough to protect one from the risks of living. It was a philosophy that she would pass on to her own daughter one day.

When World War I broke out the enterprising beauty, by then in her late teens, left her family in Lyons and hurried to Paris where she knew the scarcity of men had opened many doorways to women who possessed the courage to enter them.

The city that awaited Larry and Marguerite was a far cry from the prewar capital of gaiety and fashion. Motorcars and carriages had all but vanished. Boulevards were virtually deserted as pedestrians scuttled from one side of the street to the other between sporadic artillery barrages. Yet like most of the young men and women who had converged on the fabled city, neither was disturbed by scarcities. Champagne still flowed freely. Candlelight parties lasted beyond dawn. Who knew or even cared what time it was? Thick black curtains shut out the lightening sky as well as the gunnery flashes. Each tasted and gloried in an independence never before known while searching always for something more.

Fantasy collided with destiny the night Marguerite and Larry took shelter in the metro. While great shells pounded away above them, the crowd adapted in varying ways to the cavernous subway station. Somewhere a woman sobbed hysterically. Elsewhere a drunk retched. A crippled veteran of the Franco-Prussian War whistled "La Marseillaise" while a group of American doughboys sang "The Whiffenpoof Song" and passed a bottle.

As the shelling continued and the air below ground grew increasingly foul, Larry decided to forsake the camaraderie and comparative safety of the shelter. Stepping over a poker game, he turned toward the stairway. It was then that he spotted a familiar face, that of an American Red Cross nurse. Beside her another woman caught his eye, a delicate blonde with bright blue eyes and dainty, piquant features. The animated play of expression across her pert face stopped for an instant as their eyes caught and held. The young aviator pushed his way toward the two women through the crowd.

The eventual union of Larry and Marguerite was as highly charged as the circumstances of their meeting. The dashing American adventurer, the spirited mademoiselle—it was inevitable that they would love and marry. Welding two very strong personalities into a permanent union was more challenging than either then could have imagined. The spark was always there, sometimes a glittering display of fireworks; at other times angry, raw, and searing.

The focal point of their love and the panacea for their disillusionment was their only daughter.

Two

Marguerite Higgins once described Hong Kong, the city of her birth, as a sparkling, multifaceted gem of mysteriously shifting colors, a place where one risks enchantment.

She might have been speaking of herself.

Like the city, the woman was a study in contrasts. Sometimes there was the rough-and-tumble Maggie, a tough, hard, aggressive woman who lived like a man, insisting that men's rules work for her; she demanded, and received, equality. At other times there was the gentle, soft-voiced Marguerite—feminine, elegant, and fragile as a painted fan.

She was born September 3, 1920. Maggie learned Chinese from her amah, formal French from her mother, and a liberal dose of soldier French from her father. Her international head start was fated; but as a child she was confused and hurt by the differences that eventually would set her apart from those whose acceptance she most desired.

Larry was never meant for the discipline required of a law student. After the war ended there was a short stint at the Sorbonne and then a job with the Pacific Mail Steamship Company.

The exotic East cried out for exploration. Happily the young couple settled into a game of playing house. Life was still an adventure, with the real world held in abeyance. An assistant freight manager's salary went comparatively far in the oriental city. There was a pretty hillside apartment with a commanding view of the harbor.

When little Marguerite was born an amah was added to the ménage, who like the ecstatic parents was devoted to the child. The baby resembled an exquisite doll with curly blonde hair and eyes like two great blue sapphires.

All were panic-stricken when the six-month-old infant contracted malaria. The doctor's prescription was a trip to Dalat, a mountain resort in what would be known as Vietnam. What Mrs. Higgins thought about taking her ailing child to the country where her father had died of a tropical fever is unknown, but the family went. Maggie recovered.

The occasion was the beginning of a lifetime of journeys. First there were the yearly sea voyages to France where the much adored child was petted and fussed over by her aunts, Tante Genevieve, who had become a vintner in Lyons, and Tante Juliette, who had succeeded her grandmother as postmistress. In Hong Kong, on the stately ocean liners that took her to the Continent, and in France, Maggie was an instant attention getter. Her dainty blonde charm and quick, clever ways were a constant source of pride and pleasure to her parents, who were certain that they had spawned the brightest, most beautiful child in the world.

Surrounded by so much admiration and unconditional love, Maggie may well have shared their opinion. Her careless confidence, though, was short lived. The Higginses Hong Kong idyll ended when the time came to begin Maggie's formal education. There was a tearful farewell to the amah and another ocean voyage, this time to California.

Chabot Court was brand new in 1925, a middle-class cul-de-sac nestled just below the Oakland foothills. The people who were buying the one- and two-story bungalows were mostly young families. Had the term upwardly mobile been in vogue then the label would have fit neatly.

Ownership of one of the more modest homes cost Larry, now working as a stockbroker, far more than the carefully saved money. It marked the death of a dream. After Paris and Hong Kong his wife, too, may have found the sleepy suburb, approached by crossing railroad tracks, something of a culture shock. Later Maggie's more affluent schoolgirl friends would describe the area as bleak. Initially, at least, the Frenchwoman attempted an optimistic view. However small, the house represented land, an asset she held in high esteem. To her, Chabot Court was merely a stepping-stone.

Soon the tiny house was filled with pictures of France, of Larry in his pilot's uniform, of Marguerite in her wedding gown, and of the elaborate Catholic wedding ceremony itself. Marguerite was eager to take the mock Spanish hacienda with its stucco-and-tile construction and make it her own. Those who entered the dwelling recognized immediately that the residents were different, intriguing people.

Years later in her autobiography, *News Is a Singular Thing*, Maggie described the neighborhood as one that had enough sense to be bored by the limitations imposed by its genteel poverty and the genteel morality on which it relied in order to have some grounds for feeling superior to those who broke free from the norm. This was Chabot Court as Larry and Marguerite must have perceived it, particularly during the depression years. The desire to break the mold, to transcend the norm was strong in both. It was a legacy that matured in their daughter as she grew to womanhood. Maggie's controversial personality embodied the dreams, the drives, and the frustrations of her parents as well as a fierce autonomy of her own, a need that would become an obsession banishing any appeal that a traditional, comfortable life might have had.

Today Maggie's Chabot Court peers feel none of this disdain. After more than fifty years, they recall the neighborhood as a snug harbor filled with children close to the same age, a tiny enclave where it was safe to skate or play tag on the street and where neighbors were genuinely interested and caring of one another.

The initial isolation Maggie felt when she was tormented by the neighborhood children because she was "different" did fade. She adapted to Chabot Court as did her parents. Larry with his radiant charm and Irish blarney was known to have achieved some success as a stockbroker. Mrs. Higgins's Gallic flashes of temperament were accepted with amused tolerance. Their daughter, with the beginnings of a reporter's objectivity, saw the neighbors taking her mother up as they might folk dancing. She was foreign and "quaint." The Higgins family had become the fashion. Of course they adored it; but always for Maggie there were bouts of loneliness, a sense of the alien that despite all her charm would set her ever so slightly apart.

The popular admonition, "Don't send the children to church, take them," was lost on the Higgins family. Larry preferred lazing his way through the Sunday paper while listening to sporting events on the radio. His wife spent Sunday preparing elaborate, gourmet dinners. Both took their affiliation with the Catholic church lightly but insisted upon the traditional forms for their daughter.

The solution was to entrust Maggie's religious education to a neighbor, Mrs. Emma Craig. "Mother and I would pick Maggie up faithfully every Sunday morning," Jean Craig recalled. "Mrs. Higgins's contribution was to create adorable frilly little dresses for Maggie to wear.

The dresses were so short that her panties showed. Mother and the other ladies thought the effect anything but cute. They were shocked. When people stopped us on the way to church to ooh and ah over how precious Maggie looked, Mother was annoyed and embarrassed. Usually she ended up dragging us down the block and into the sanctity of the church. Finally a delegation of mothers called on Mrs. Higgins to explain that Maggie's clothes were just too 'Frenchified' for an Oakland mass. 'Ooh la!' she exclaimed in surprise 'The hems, they will come down.' And they did.

"Once Maggie had made her Communion the parental pressure to attend church was off, but by that time she had her own reasons for going. There was always one altar boy or another that appealed to her. Maggie developed an eye for boys very early."

Weekly church attendance was the beginning of a lifetime friendship between Maggie and Jean, who was three years older. "I often went home with her after mass," Jean remembered. "Marguerite Senior—that's how most of us referred to Mrs. Higgins—would have something marvelous simmering on the stove but the domesticity stopped there. I'd never seen anyone like her—the highest heels, the blondest hair. It was hard to think of her as someone's mother. Larry was exciting and so handsome. Sometimes he'd tell us about his adventures in the Lafayette Escadrille. There were pictures of him all over the house, always in uniform, standing beside one of those tipsy, tilting bamboo-tailed planes that he used to fly. Adults usually appear old to a child, but they always seemed very young. I remember them as though it was yesterday ... Maggie's mother carrying a cocktail on a silver tray out to the backyard where Larry would be lounging on a swing listening to a ball game on his portable radio. They were a strange, glamorous family, unlike any I'd ever known—or ever would know."

"Your father has lost his job!"

Maggie stared in disbelief at her mother. It was October 1929. Only a few days before she had celebrated her ninth birthday. As the implications of the words sank in, her recently acquired sense of security and acceptance crashed about her as surely as the stock market had crashed. She listened coolly, her young face impassive.

"It was the worst moment of my childhood," she recalled later, "the day when I began to worry about how I would earn a living when I grew up." It was a fear that remained with her always.

Having been herself a child of few privileges, Mrs. Higgins was determined that one way or another her daughter would have everything. At various times the adoring but demanding mother was certain that her offspring would be the best scholar, the best ballerina, the best violinist, and finally the best journalist the world had ever known. Little Marguerite's potential was unlimited. It was a matter of deciding which of the many alluring possibilities to choose.

In this area, at least, mother and daughter were in agreement. Both Marguerites were ambitious and energetic. What the younger may have lacked in talent, she made up in drive and ambition. It remained for the elder to see to it that she had the opportunity to perform in the grand arena of life.

After a few frantic months of making the rounds, Larry was able to secure a job as manager of the Oakland branch of the National Bankitaly Company. The position sounded far more impressive than the salary, which was hardly enough to finance the type of education his wife had in mind for Maggie, much less the music and ballet lessons. To compensate, Mrs. Higgins began teaching French. Her first pupils were the neighborhood children on Chabot Court.

Emboldened by her neighborhood success, Mrs. Higgins approached the prestigious Anna Head School. She would be delighted to teach French there in exchange for a scholarship for her daughter. The offer was duly considered and accepted.

Despite its exclusivity, the Anna Head School was an ugly place. The massive, block buildings were grayish brown and grim. Looking up at the austere structure and knowing that she was surrounded by some of the richest girls in California, Maggie may have seen herself as a latter-day Jane Eyre, plucky and determined to make her way in the great world. Others then and later perceived her more as Becky Sharp, the little girl on the make, sexy, sharp tongued, ambitious, and at times too clever for her own good.

A classmate, Portia Lyde, recalled Maggie "standing alone, serious and unsmiling, her pale, short hair blowing in untidy strands about her face, chin shoved stubbornly forward, looking over the rest of us at something beyond that only she could see.

"Hindsight would dictate that even then she had a sense of destiny, which makes good biographical material, but I strongly suspect my image of her may have been colored by later events in her life. There was little doubt even then that she knew she was not like the rest of us. She took herself seriously. She always seemed calm and self-assured but at the same time singularly shy, aloof, detached.

"There was a delightful, light spatter of freckles over the bridge of her nose culminating in a few stray ones on her upper cheeks. The effect, together with her nose, which was short and drifted upward, was great."

Like a schoolmistress in a nineteenth-century novel, Mary Elizabeth Wilson, the principal of the Anna Head School, ran a tight ship. Students wore no lipstick or nail polish and began each school day with chapel services. During the brief break that followed, they were given a ration of bouillon before going on to class.

The girls wore uniforms that had been specially designed by the tennis player, Helen Wills Moody, an alumna. The ensemble consisted of a gray, pleated skirt, a white blouse that remained permanently in place because it buttoned under the crotch, and a gray sweater that Maggie daringly shortened to elbow length—the only girl to do so.

A consummate risk taker even then, Maggie, whose long, curling eyelashes were the envy of the school, one day showed up with them cut to tiny stubs. She had heard that trimming made lashes grow even more luxuriant!

During her freshman year Maggie became best friends with a newcomer, Phoebe True. "We were both bright and motivated," Phoebe recalled, "but I was rebellious, spoiled, and rich. I didn't have as great a stake in making good as Maggie, but we both got excellent grades and were good at athletics. I was sort of a troublemaker and I think she liked that quality in me, while I admired her idealism. I thought of her even then as rather naive and do-goodish. She was strongly motivated to make changes, though all of it was very schoolgirlish."

A boarder, far away from her parents in the East, Phoebe enjoyed spending weekends with the Higgins family. "Maggie's parents were quite unusual and very charming. They were wonderful hosts who made me feel at home," she recalled. "It was fun to go there, but I couldn't miss the violent arguments that frequently erupted between them or the way they pushed Maggie to excel at everything. They obviously adored her, lavishing far more than they could afford; yet always there was this pressure to achieve."

The friendship continued to flourish until a dramatic incident parted the girls in their sophomore year. "The school being what it was, two of the older girls who were very into boys decided to run away. I was restless enough to go with them. An uncle of one of the boys put us up for the night. Nothing happened but there was a tremendous scandal at the school. My family was mobilized. We were brought back and sent to our rooms in utter disgrace.

"Maggie was extremely loyal and passionate about it all. She thought it was terribly unfair and led a kind of demonstration. I think the school was afraid of ground-swell opposition. We were kicked out and I was placed on a train and sent back to my parents in New York. Maggie and I kept up a steady correspondence in the next two years, all the while looking forward to attending college together and joining the same sorority."

The loss of her closest friend underscored Maggie's sense of social isolation. She could never forget the economic gulf that separated her from the others. Then as later she lived on the edge. What she perceived as her need had nothing to do with her reality. She was always driven, frequently envisioning or creating problems that did not—or need not— exist. Although her peers were unaware that she was receiving a scholarship, Maggie could never forget it.

There were other distinctions that established a wider gulf than money. One of these was religion. Maggie was for seven years a Catholic in a Protestant school. A budding intellectual, she was quick to ask value questions. Why do you think this? How can that be? What about—? Less analytical classmates parroted Maggie's efforts to probe and debate to their mothers, who were threatened by this seeming challenge to family beliefs. Friendships were subtly withdrawn, leaving Maggie baffled and hurt.

Alice McIntyre, who was three years younger than Maggie, admired her from a distance. A student of Mrs. Higgins, Alice was charmed by the Frenchwoman from the first time she saw her handwriting. "It was so large!" Alice recalled. "I'd never known anyone who wrote so dramatically. It looked so exciting, so foreign. I immediately adopted the style and felt freed from the oppressions of a Puritan heritage. Mrs. Higgins was a friendly, tolerant teacher who inspired me to the extent that I wound up a French translator, among other things.

"Unlike the rest of our parents, Mrs. Higgins had escaped the Victorian influence. There was no Calvinist heritage, no Anglican reserve, no Quaker transcendentalism. Instead there was that Old World grace and accommodation that the Puritans found so unredeemably terrifying and our Anna Head mothers viewed as distinctly alarming. They spoke of Mrs. Higgins with pinched lips that implied that she was not quite a lady.

Our fathers who'd been in World War I still referred to 'those Frenchies, ooh! la! la!' so naturally mothers thought twice about inviting Mrs. Higgins to join in their social activities.''

Maggie's ''immoral'' French blood carried a stigma that was as disturbing as her questioning Catholicism. It seems unlikely that one as young as she could have pinpointed the cause of the others' reserve, yet it is certain that Maggie felt the effect and was stung by it.

Tom Byther, the son of longtime friends of the Higginses, was Maggie's frequent escort to Anna Head dances. ''Those girls are so rich,'' he confided to his mother. ''They know they're somebody from the moment they're born. They might all wear school uniforms in the daytime but they go home to mansions. Maggie's kind of funny. I never know what she'll say next. Sometimes she's snippy to *them*.''

It was as though the young teenager anticipated rejection, or worse yet, condescension. Rather than allow that, she erected a wall about herself. No one would be allowed to ever feel sorry for her or to perceive her other than as an equal. Better to be disliked than to be a victim, she seemed to have decided early on, and never wavered from the choice.

If Larry and Marguerite were not a social asset to their daughter, they enriched her life in other, more subtle ways. Alice McIntyre noted, ''Like most immigrants, Mrs. Higgins absorbed information through her child. She recognized the girl's intelligence and accepted her ideas and actions uncritically. I doubt that there are many mothers who react this way, particularly if their daughters are as beautiful and naturally sexy as Maggie. It's a crisis for mother and daughter when the latter comes of age and starts saying, 'Move off the earth, Mother, I'm *it* now.' Mrs. Higgins never seemed to experience that struggle. I never had the sense of the Wicked Witch wanting to put Snow White to sleep the moment she proved fairest. Mrs. Higgins appeared comfortable with this superior beauty on her hands. Replacing the Victorian nonsense that the rest of us had to cope with was a Frenchwoman's matter-of-fact awareness that a girl ultimately becomes a nubile young woman.

''Then there was Larry. I remember standing with Maggie in the tile foyer of that stucco house. Maggie was asking her mother for permission to do something. As she hesitated, Mr. Higgins entered. He took off his hat and topcoat, revealing a redheaded Irishman with smiling, blue eyes. I was shaken, embarrassed. He just didn't look like a father should look—solemn, gray, authoritarian. He seemed more like some unreliable person that you could actually *talk* to, entirely too young and handsome to be someone's *father*. It was easy to imagine him taking a French bride with no thought of what anyone would say.

"My sinful longing to remain in that house with Mr. Higgins forever was swiftly proven improbable. Maggie's eyes had taken on a shining glow the instant he entered the house. She was asking his permission with the happy assurance of one who knows in advance what the answer will be. Finishing her plea, she turned away for an instant, then looked back at him. I'd noticed that sidelong glance countless times. No other girl at Anna Head used her eyes with such a devastating effect. But what I saw then was much more—a visible streak of blue flame searing across space to encounter the adoring humor in the man's eyes. An angel flying between would have been electrocuted. My fantasies of Mr. Higgins died instantly—Maggie had him in her pocket! She and I went off, who knows where, and that was that."

There was no quasi-sexual relationship implied in Alice's anecdote. Father and daughter adored one another; the mother eliminated the potential Electra complex by tolerantly stepping aside and allowing her child to grow up on center stage. Maggie enjoyed a power over her father that might have been as much the product of her French mother's example as Larry's loving encouragement.

Maggie was free from several conventional constraints. "She was the only girl I ever heard bad-mouth her mother in six years at Anna Head's," Alice said. "The rest of us had been so conditioned to remember who we were that we were paralyzed with respect for our powerful, proper parents. Only Maggie felt free to level a complaint. What a complaint! I can hear her now: 'My mother had to give me her big fanny! Damn her!' I can still remember the shock. It was true, too.

"Maggie had a pair of rounded buttocks that was amazingly graceful on her slender, rather narrow frame. They tapered to a willowy waist, a long rib cage and well-shaped breasts, sloping shoulders, long, delicate arms and legs. Her body was beautiful in a way that was not then publicly considered in American culture. World War II hadn't defined women as sex objects by the center fold. We had Bette Davis not Betty Grable, Hepburn but not Monroe. I only knew that she looked wonderfully agreeable in her gym bloomers and possessed the coordination of a dancer."

If she could not compete financially with heiresses such as Phyllis Hill of the Hills Brothers Coffee family or Diana Dollar of the Dollar Steamship family, Maggie could and did hold her own with grades and athletic prowess. She was a natural competitor who hated to lose. This intensity was tolerated, resented, or admired, depending on one's viewpoint.

Alice McIntyre recalled Maggie on the school basketball court. "It would be dusk and she would be all alone, practicing basket after basket, perfecting her form, honing her skill after years of playing the game well. Her bloomers were light blue, her short-sleeved shirt and sneakers white, her hair spun gold. She leaped and leaped, swinging the ball first low, then lifting it up, up for a ringer, then leaping higher and higher on her springy legs with intensity and concentration that made her glow in the dark."

Alice would later become an editor at *Esquire*. She and Maggie came to know one another at a Girl Reserve camp in the Sierra Nevada Mountains. In the evenings the girls sat around the camp fire, talking. In this sylvan setting far from the influences of boys or parents, they were inspired to cultivate ambitions of their own. They discussed careers as a means of serving the world and were inspired and imbued with idealism. Surrounded and protected by the dense pine forest, the young women were encouraged to reflect and to speak out. At evening's end they stood before the flickering fire, swaying gently, arms locked as they sang.

After one such night Alice experienced a revelation. Returning to Oakland the next evening she chanced to sit next to Maggie on the train. Tentatively the younger girl ventured, "Do you know there's nothing that can't be thought of into infinity?"

"Of course," Maggie replied and then looked at her closely, eagerly, "do you?"

Alice nodded solemnly. Relief poured over her that someone understood.

Maggie smiled her encouragement, dissolving the enormous gulf between senior and freshman. "Some day I'm going to know about everything, even the stars," she said. The two sat for a long time in silence, watching the stars as the train rattled down the mountain toward home.

Away from school Maggie lived a kind of internal life, escaping the rapidly accelerating family problems through dreams and novels. To evade the nagging parents who sought with increasing persistence to find their own lost dreams in her, she once ran away for two days, taking with her enough food and water for herself and her dog, Foxy. More often she found release in fantasies of grand adventures. Maggie was very much her father's daughter, liking nothing better than to listen to the war stories he liked nothing better than to tell. Maggie hung on every word.

"My plane had two guns," he'd say, his eyes lighting as though he described a lost sweetheart. "One was mounted on the fuselage and fired through the propeller with a CC gear to keep from hitting it. The other was mounted on the top wing and fired above the propeller. Later I got a Camel joystick with triggers fixed so I could fire both guns with one thumb if I needed to."

Air war could get personal. "You're certain that each lead bullet or antiaircraft shell has your name on it," he told her. "When you fire, you don't just aim toward Berlin and wait for a report. You wait until you're right on top of a Hun's tail and then you open up and see your tracer bullets going past him or into him and if you get him you see him go spinning down in flames. But then, he's been practicing, too, and is ready to do a half roll as soon as you start your dive. Just do a sloppy turn and expect to hear bullets sing your swan song."

"But what about the antiaircraft guns?" Maggie would prompt.

"Oh, they were easy to fool if you were quick enough," Larry would reply. "A burst sounded like a loud cough. As soon as I'd hear it, I'd start zigzagging. The burst you hear won't hurt you. The sound's a warning. The battery has you in its range. The next one will be close until you sideslip, zoom, turn, or throttle down. Then he fires where you should have been but aren't."

Larry described the pyrotechnic effects. "The Huns used shrapnel that burst black, the Allies used high explosives that burst white. An Austrian naval battery used a shell that burst pink. Nearly scared the hell out of me the first time I saw it."

Back on the ground the pilots lived well. Larry told of a cook who made eggs Benedict, a bartender who fixed cocktails, poured champagne or Napoleon brandy, and a valet who brought hot water each morning.

Larry's tales of glamour and glory differed greatly from the scenes depicted by Hemingway and Remarque—Maggie's favorite writers—but as she listened and read, her own fascination for war grew and with it a sense of personal destiny, a drive and a certainty, that transcended adolescent fantasy.

Tension mounted in the Higgins household, caused by personality conflicts and Marguerite's increasing independence, which triggered ever more frequent drinking bouts and violent arguments. On one occasion Larry, clad only in his shorts, chased his daughter down the street. On another he hurled a two-foot-high silver golf trophy at her. It crashed through the front window. Mrs. Higgins then effectively switched the spotlight to herself by fainting.

Arguments and the ensuing fainting spells were not reserved for the home. As Mrs. Higgins sagged and finally thumped to the floor, Maggie would quietly excuse herself, returning with ammonia. Neighbors, unused to this type of domestic drama, thought her a strange, unfeeling child. Then, as later, her detachment was a form of self-defense. Though classmates considered Maggie a brain who received top grades with no effort, this was not the case—an A average was necessary to retain her scholarship at Anna Head. She had become a professional bookworm whose air of casual confidence was actually grace under fire. The violent arguments at home did little to ease her case.

Jean Craig remembered one time when Mrs. Higgins directed her anger at Maggie, who remained icily polite. "When the inevitable fainting spell occurred, Maggie merely stepped over her and beckoned me to do the same. Leading me into her bedroom, she closed the door firmly and began to talk. What about? Oh, boys probably. All the girls on Chabot Court were mad about Carl Ferguson, the handsomest boy on the block. Naturally he chose Maggie."

Three

It was the time of the tall, frosty zombie, the rumba, and Snow White. These were the last summer months of 1937. Maggie was about to enter the University of California at Berkeley.

Mrs. Higgins was busy cutting, pinning, and stitching. Her creations, culled from the pages of *Vogue,* were nothing less than sensational. Maggie would have a wardrobe equal to any of the young heiresses who would be going through rushing with her. But of course she would join a sorority! All the Anna Head girls did. Young Marguerite could hardly be the exception. The necessary money would come somehow. It always did.

Standing patiently while her mother pinned the rich fabrics (cannily acquired at bargain sales) about her, Maggie listened intently to radio reports of the missing Amelia Earhart. The aviatrix had long been a heroine of hers. Now it appeared that she and her wonder plane had dropped into the sea—what a tragic end to such an adventurous life. Of course forty *was* old, the sixteen year old philosophized. Earhart had done so much, experienced so many things; perhaps she was ready to die.

Turning slightly as Mrs. Higgins, mouth filled with pins, directed her, Maggie thought of the reporters who had flocked to the South Pacific to cover the mysterious disappearance. What a story! Suppose one was to actually find her . . . that's the kind of journalist I'll be, she determined, making headlines, not just writing them. Maggie's ambitions had focused on journalism during her sophomore year at Anna Head. As always she intended to be the very best.

In the meantime another exciting world beckoned. The fittings were interrupted by numerous phone conversations. Phoebe True had returned from New York and would be entering the University of California with Maggie. She and Ellen Ainsworth, another close friend from the Anna Head School, were swept along with Maggie in the thrilling anticipation of sorority life. Every detail of their numerous outfits had been compared and minutely discussed. It was essential that each ensemble be perfect for its designated occasion. The three girls, plus two other classmates from the high school, had agreed upon their selection.

"I knew nothing about sororities," Phoebe recalled years later. "I didn't know a 'good' one from a 'bad' one. Maggie and the other Anna Head girls were my guides as to which one to pick. We debated for hours. Parenthetically I can say it's ridiculous, but in those days you absolutely did it. There was no question. Maggie was no different. She was just as eager and anxious to join as the rest of us. As I recall, Alpha Phi was regarded as Number Three then. We didn't even consider trying for the top two because we all wanted above all else to stick together."

A record-breaking heat wave did nothing to dampen the excitement, which was almost unbearable. A round of receptions, luncheons, and teas, eagerly attended, was just as avidly dissected. Many of the affairs included mothers of the rushees, who were also closely assessed by sorority and alumnae. It was a heady, exciting time. If Maggie had any doubts regarding her acceptability to Alpha Phi she kept them to herself. Her grades were among the highest of any of the incoming freshmen. Her high school record was full of triumphs, for she had been extremely active in sports and other school activities. Her clothes had been wisely chosen. She chatted easily and confidently with the older girls who seemed so gracious, so full of wit and charm. How delightful it would be when she and the other Anna Head graduates became a part of this scintillating world.

But she did not. Of all the Anna Head girls, Maggie was the only one blackballed. "It was a terrible, devastating thing," Phoebe remembered. "Maggie's shock and subsequent depression is difficult to describe. 'Why?' we all speculated. The most plausible explanation was her parents. It wasn't their lack of money. In the next four years I saw many middle-class girls pledge. As much as I personally liked Maggie's parents, I could see that they were different. Mrs. Higgins just wasn't proper enough. She wore such high heels with no stockings and her hair was obviously bleached. You can't imagine how she stood out amongst all those terribly proper ladies. Then, too, there were the stories of Larry's drinking.

"It was a terrible thing to happen to Maggie. She prided herself on her individualism but still wanted desperately to be part of the 'in' crowd. For a while I thought of refusing to join in protest, but the pressure was just too strong. I tried to compensate by inviting Maggie to lunch at the Alpha Phi house as often as possible. Before long I got called in. There were rules against having outsiders too often, particularly an outsider who'd been blackballed as undesirable. It was embarrassing and sad. Just how sad is difficult—if not impossible—to comprehend now."

The force of the experience caused Maggie to go even deeper into herself. One woman remembered her clearly as a freshman. Pretty, self-contained, sitting alone in the library while other girls sat in softly giggling groups. "We became friendly acquaintances because we were both alone," she recalled. "Though we never knew one another well, I remember her clearly after all these years. She was so self-sufficient, so totally herself. We talked about literature and writing, never gossip. She simply wasn't interested. Maggie was intensely individual, complete within herself."

For a time Maggie attempted to adjust to her disappointment. She joined Gamma Phi Beta, a sorority in which her friend Jean Craig was an active member. Though not as "social" as Alpha Phi, the Gamma Phis were attractive and active. Jean was warm and supportive as always. The house, only a year old, with its square modern lines, big windows, and white stucco facade was a striking departure from the Tudor-style structures that lined Channing Street.

The sorority scrapbook records Maggie's efforts in a series of faded newspaper pictures and articles. There is a shot of Maggie wearing a demure little dress with a white Peter Pan collar and a bodice that looks as though it had been pasted on. She holds a large shamrock, a reminder of the Shamrock Luncheon, which was the first sorority freshman event of the year. Another picture shows her as the newly elected vice-president of the (five-thousand-member) sophomore class, the look of frank admiration on the face of the new president, Bob Williams, frozen in time. Maggie wears a long brocade gown with a short bolero jacket cut to display a tiny waist. Still another photograph shows her tea dancing at the St. Francis Hotel in San Francisco. A final picture and story announce that Miss Marguerite Higgins will entertain the freshman and sophomore members of Gamma Phi Beta and their dates at a party in her home prior to the Spring Formal at the Claremont Hotel.

Marge Simenson remembered her at this time. "I don't suppose I'd have joined Gamma Phi Beta if it hadn't been for her. I was so impressed by her at rushing. I remember how she fixed me with those big, blue eyes and said in her soft voice, 'You will come back, won't you?' "

All the Gamma Phi Betas were aware of the force of those china blue eyes and that sweet, breathy voice. They were aware, too, that behind the feminine fragility was determination. Maggie achieved top grades and attracted boys with equal ease.

Maggie Higgins was the ideal sorority girl—for as long as she chose to be. Her desire to play the sorority game, possibly to show the Alpha Phis just what a social asset she could be, diminished as the months passed and newer, more heady opportunities revealed themselves.

Disappointment had served only to heighten her competitive instinct, boredom had increased her restlessness, and defeat had given impetus to an emergent bitchy streak. Early in her freshman year Maggie, a science and letters major, joined the staff of the university paper, the *Daily Californian*. Almost immediately she realized that the *Daily Cal* provided an arena far more appropriate to her temperament, talent, and aspirations. This time there could be no possibility of failure.

The *Daily Cal*, published entirely by students, was considered one of the finest university papers in the country. It not infrequently scooped the metropolitan papers on local issues. Assuming a liberal stance at a time of general social unrest, the newspaper challenged the status quo through editorials and investigative reporting. When the staff ran pieces examining the living conditions of migrant laborers, they were undermining the agricultural power base that helped to maintain the state university system. Reverberations to the university president, Robert Sproul, were almost instantaneous: "Can't you shut those kids up?" Sproul's reactions were equally prompt. Staff members listened to the outraged executive as the editor held the phone a foot from his ear.

Not surprisingly there was strong pressure both on and off campus to bring the newspaper under the wing of the newly formed journalism department. The student staff was highly wary of this, fearing that their prized autonomy would be lost.

Proud of their clout but also aware of their increasingly precarious position, members of the *Daily Cal* staff were clannish and protective.

They were dedicated and idealistic and expected the same qualities from incoming freshmen. They took themselves and their paper seriously. Many freshmen had no previous high school journalism experience, but they were welcomed and assigned a junior student as a supervisor who explained the ins and outs of campus procedures, the best means of obtaining stories, and how to establish and maintain sources. Ethics as well as journalistic techniques were strongly emphasized. University departments were divided into beats. Since some were more significant than others, they were rotated so that each novice reporter would have a crack at the more challenging stories.

The mentor and rotation systems were the foundation of the paper. If a newcomer survived the freshman cuts, he or she moved up to sophomore status with more interesting assignments and occasional by-line stories. The paper was a pyramid with aspirants working toward the senior positions of editor, managing editor, or city editor. As in the manner of newspapers, many were called and few chosen.

Into this stylized hierarchy stepped Maggie Higgins, a young woman described as having the seductive innocence of Daisy Mae masking a razor-sharp mind. She did not then nor would she ever understand the value of team effort. She was not above cutting corners, batting her large blue eyes or even shedding a few tears if she could perceive an advantage. Winning was everything.

Did Maggie set out to deliberately undermine the system or to take advantage of the youthful idealism that made it work? Was she even sensitive to its existence? These are questions hotly debated by former staff members after more than forty years.

One thing is certain: The *Daily Cal* atmosphere was heady. Maggie was excited by the predominantly radical nature of the staff and challenged by the value questions being debated. Wasn't capitalism responsible for the stock market crash that had cost her father his job? Was it not at least indirectly responsible for his drinking and the seeming inadequacies of her childhood? Should some have so much and others nothing? All around her were new doors waiting to be opened.

Maggie was eager to rush through those doors, to discover her own answers and share them with the world through her writing. A warm friendship had formed between Maggie and Haakon Chevalier, a French professor and an avowed Communist. Chevalier was a brilliant writer and an outspoken social critic. He was an intimate of such liberals as

Lillian Hellman and Lincoln Steffens. Considering Maggie "one of the bright lights on campus," Chevalier counseled her, loaned her books, and invited her to his informal salon. On one occasion she met and talked with Steffens, one of the great muckraking journalists. The notice and encouragement she received was an affirmation of her abilities and a challenge to achieve more.

On a somewhat more personal level she was challenged by Stanley Moore, a charismatic and extremely handsome teaching aide in the philosophy department. Although a scion of a wealthy, socially prominent Piedmont family, Moore was a Communist. Like many of her peers, Maggie was dazzled by him. Sensing his attraction to her, she flirted openly, but he remained unmoved.

Others were far more susceptible. There were any number of volunteer male advisers on the *Daily Cal* staff who were only too happy to advise Maggie on news-gathering techniques and to critique her stories. They remembered her as an "innocent little girl with a great-looking bottom." Maggie was quick to capitalize on her initial impact. Here was a different kind of "in" crowd and a far more significant one than she had encountered before. She was certain that the university paper was the first rung in the ladder leading to a brilliant career.

By the end of Maggie's sophomore year, her sorority sisters began to notice a marked change in her. Not only was she crying out against the system and the inequities that it spawned, but also she had discovered Bertrand Russell and free love.

"If two people really care for one another, what difference does a piece of paper make?" she was fond of demanding of the Gamma Phis, who regarded this hardly original question as pretty heady stuff. "Going all the way" secretly was one thing—openly discussing it was another. "No wonder the boys like her so well," the coeds muttered disapprovingly, "but will they come back?"

The trouble was they did.

Maggie knew that she wanted power in the world as well as in bed. Men had been created for her pleasure as much as she for theirs, and she had no compunction about taking it. She was learning the games of love and war and rapidly reaching the conclusion that the cards were stacked in favor of pretty, young women who were realistic enough to understand their own appetites. The other coeds bitterly resented the edge that her audacity and awareness gave her.

Tom Byther, Maggie's childhood friend who had been frequently warned by his father about "a man's responsibility," found Maggie disconcerting. "She's just all over me, Dad," he complained. Maggie also had complaints. Byther, a well-groomed young man, favored the suits and ties worn by the other members of his fraternity. Maggie had begun to rebel against conformity of all kinds. The two friends drifted apart.

Miriam Byther, Tom's mother, remembered Maggie as the darling moppet of previous years and was disappointed by the emerging woman. "She was a bright, attractive girl, but her wit could be snippy. She had a reputation among the boys. Little Marguerite was dangerous. Her mother complained to me often, 'She's always been her father's daughter, but now *he* doesn't even have her confidence.' "

Raynie Reid, a young liberal with a reputation as a lady-killer, who worked in the business office of the *Daily Cal*, was better suited to Maggie's new life-style. Of the many men she dated during these years, classmates remembered him best. The two were seen together everywhere, sometimes talking and arguing intensely, at other times kissing passionately. "Maggie was an outrageous flirt," a contemporary recalled. "She drove him crazy. In the past he'd always had the upper hand. Now it was she who called the shots. He wanted an exclusive relationship. Maggie's eye was inclined to wander, yet it always returned to Raynie. At the time he seemed to offer the fire and intensity she sought."

During an era when the conduct code for coeds was strictly defined, Maggie broke all the rules. When others were dutifully signing in by 2:30 A.M. and attending chaperoned house parties, she and Raynie went off on a three-week vacation to Mexico.

It's significant that Maggie's first by-line story for the *Daily Cal* was a two-part account of political unrest, which appeared February 2, 1940. Its title was "Mexico: No Bed of Roses." In this, her first excursion into foreign reporting, she frequently uses the pronoun we. Was it the editorial we or a personal statement of her daring adventure? Some of the *Daily Cal* women as well as the Gamma Phis felt that Marguerite went out of her way to flaunt her sexual relationships.

Equally distasteful to the sorority was the change in Maggie's appearance. Gradually the bandbox queen turned scruffy, sometimes wearing one red sock and one white, at other times barefoot. While most people were trying to hold things together and pretend that the depression had changed nothing, Maggie was demanding change.

One evening as the girls sat before a glowing fire in the lounge of the Gamma Phi Beta house, they listened with varying degrees of interest to Winston Churchill's call to arms. The crackle of the overseas broadcast made the man and his message seem very far away; but some wondered if this would be a tiny spark that could spread and destroy the carefree gaiety of campus life and the gracious forms so carefully maintained.

After Churchill's address, the large wooden radio played a favorite Glenn Miller tune. The young women drifted into conversational groups. Someone much closer to home had already begun to challenge, if not to actually undermine, the way things were and the way they were meant to be.

"If only someone could talk to her," they lamented. Unfortunately Jean Craig, Maggie's one close friend in the house, had been graduated. "Let's face it," one insisted. "We're too tame for her. She doesn't belong here. She hasn't for months."

Not only was there the question of Maggie's suspected Communism, her messy appearance, and her open affair with Raynie Reid, but there was also a matter of an unpaid bill to the sorority house. This was carrying protest too far.

Mary Louise Lyman, the sorority president, felt particularly sorry about the conflict. She and Maggie had been friends since childhood. Yet there was no question of allowing Maggie to remain in the sorority. The motto made it very clear: *Remember who you are and what you represent*.

Mary Louise recalled an exchange of confidences that had taken place years before. "What do you want from life?" Maggie had asked with the intensity of a thirteen year old.

"Serenity," she had replied after some thought.

Maggie had been shocked. "Oh, no! Not me! I want fame and excitement!"

Mary Louise smiled ruefully. Well, really, what was a sorority pin compared to that?

The pin was ultimately returned to the Gamma Phis after a heated debate between the sorority board and Maggie's champion, Jean Craig. Maggie didn't even bother to attend the hearing. Her mind was on other things.

Maggie solved her resultant roommate problem by finding an attractive apartment and selecting two dynamic women to share it. Like her,

Eleanor Piel and Berdeen Frankel were highly ambitious, career-oriented women. Eleanor, a transfer student, reported on Berkeley affairs for the UCLA *Bruin*. She was a prelaw student with sights already set on criminal law and would one day practice in New York. Although newly arrived on campus, she had already created a niche for herself in student politics and was dating the student body president.

''In the beginning I must have seemed somewhat important to Maggie because she went out of her way to charm me,'' Eleanor said. ''I was flattered, a bit enthralled by her magnetism and the air she had of being in the center of everything: It was powerful, exciting, and at first a little overwhelming. One very vivid memory comes to mind: Maggie sitting up in bed—a Murphy bed that let down in the middle of the living room—*flirting* with me. She flirted with women just as avidly as with men and could be marvelously effective. Invariably she wanted a task done or information of some kind.

''Maggie had a fresh, pretty look that somehow concealed the fact that she rarely bathed. She would come home at night and simply drop her clothes on the floor. The next morning she'd put them back on. Every few days her mother would come by, pick up the dirty clothes, and replace them with clean ones—that she'd drop in the same place on the floor!

''One evening I held a political strategy meeting—a professor was under fire from the Establishment and our group had rallied round him. It was absolutely off limits to the press and Maggie knew this. She crashed the meeting anyway and wrote about it. Somehow, angry as I was, it didn't destroy our association, but it did underscore my original impressions. Maggie was fascinating to observe, fun to be around, but not to be trusted. She simply didn't operate from the same place as the rest of us.''

Berdeen Frankel, a premed student later to become a San Francisco psychiatrist, thought of Maggie initially as a benefactor. ''I met her in my freshman year,'' she said. ''I needed work badly and she appeared, seemingly out of nowhere, and told me about a great job as a waitress at the women's faculty club. Then, as later, she impressed me as being very savvy, political, sophisticated. After that she would drift in and out of my life, always smiling, busy, confident. I was pleased when she invited me to parties and I generally went. Life was exciting around Maggie; she made it that way. Later, when she asked me to share an apartment, I was flattered. I thought Maggie would be an ideal roommate. As it turned out, she was a very interesting one.

"Ignoring the social and hygienic amenities that most women take for granted saved her all kinds of time for things she considered far more important. Periodically it occurred to her that we were doing all the work around the apartment. Then she'd try to make it up to us her way. She'd have a big party, spend the day cooking marvelous food, invite interesting people—movers and shakers—and introduce us as the guests of honor. At the same time it would never occur to her to clean up the apartment beforehand. She obviously assumed that she and her surroundings would be accepted as is.

"Others have described Maggie as ruthless, but I never saw her that way. There was nothing small, petty, or cruel about her. She took the most direct route to whatever she wanted, making up her own rules as she went along. If someone was inadvertently hurt, I'm sure she was sorry, assuming that she was even aware of it.

"Within her circle Maggie was always the leader, taking charge in a gentle, quiet way. It was she who determined how a thing would go, when it would end. Generally she was charming enough to convince you that it was for your own good or even your own idea. There was a sweet, almost childlike quality about her that was extremely seductive. In the late nineteen fifties when Brigitte Bardot was so popular I was often reminded of Maggie as I'd known her in college.

"In those days we saw her as Daisy Mae—the sloppy appearance, pretty face, long hair falling in waves about her shoulders. Her boyfriend, Raynie Reid, was the perfect Li'l Abner—tall, brawny, lots of thick, dark hair. He was crazy about her. She took the lead in that relationship as she did in all others. She led, he followed.

"It was Eleanor and I who became close friends, who sat up late at night exchanging confidences. Maggie was never a confider. She'd have dreadful arguments with her mother but never referred to them. The woman would call, seemingly quite drunk, and harangue Maggie. I've no idea what it was all about; the conversations were always in French. I just remember Maggie screaming and crying into the phone.

"It was the only time I saw her in anything but total control of her emotions. She was always detached—afraid of close intimacy, I think. There was no question but that she intended to accomplish a great deal and felt that she had to do it all by herself. Rules never stopped her, nor conventions. She just quietly, smilingly, went her own way, oblivious to the expectations of others.

As the time approached for filling the key slots on the *Daily Cal* in her junior year, Maggie campaigned aggressively. Perhaps, she speculated, the sorority brouhaha would work to her advantage. "Those women are persecuting me for my liberal views," she confided to several men on the staff. No one took her claims seriously.

If Maggie was no longer playing the sorority game, neither was she keeping to the rules of the *Daily Cal*. From the beginning she had made a strong impression on the staff. She was a stunning girl, eager, competitive, with a gift for concentration and a knack for getting people to open up to tell their stories. As time passed her competitive instinct dominated all other qualities.

Reporters who followed Maggie in the rotation system complained that she sucked dry all sources. Far worse, it was discovered that she had threatened department heads, convincing them that she was their only pipeline to the *Daily Cal*. Equally detrimental to staff morale and the integrity of the paper, Maggie ignored her duties as mentor to the incoming freshmen. Other juniors dutifully holding office hours on Sunday afternoons discovered their attendance to be twice the normal size. The overflow was comprised of novices originally assigned to Maggie. "Why didn't you take this problem to Higgins?" harassed editors would ask. "She's always too busy," was the usual reply, or sometimes, "She might steal the story."

Maggie's contemporaries were shocked and eventually bitter. The *Daily Cal* staff was a close-knit group, like a family. "The paper was our life," one woman recalled. "With Maggie's talent and drive, her tenure on our school paper probably made very little difference in her career; but it seemed vitally important then. She was a good reporter but made her colleagues very uneasy." Such an assessment would be repeated many times in years to follow.

The tragedy was that while she was desperately struggling to achieve, Maggie was undergoing many personal crises. Her rebellion against what she considered the trappings of capitalist society had brought about a rift between her and her parents. Far more serious, however, was the unwanted pregnancy that Maggie insisted upon aborting, making the back-street arrangements alone and unaided. When Larry inadvertently learned of the event and struck her in a moment of drunken anger, the breech was widened further.

"I'm so lonely," she once confided to another reporter on the paper. "I could tell she was sincere," the woman recalled, "but how could I respond with any warmth when I was literally sitting on my notes for fear she'd steal the story? It wouldn't have been the first time.''

By the fall of 1940 the free countries of Europe—Norway, the Netherlands, Belgium, France—had toppled like ninepins. The gallant evacuation of Dunkirk was in reality a disaster. While 335,000 were saved, virtually the entire British Expeditionary Force was lost.

Speaking out in his brandy-harsh voice, Winston Churchill exhorted the world: ''We shall defend our island whatever the cost may be. We shall fight on the beaches, landing grounds, in the fields, in the streets, and on the hills. We shall never surrender and even if, which I do not for a moment believe, this island or a large part of it were subjugated and starving, then our empire beyond the seas, armed and guarded by the British fleet, will carry on the struggle until God's good time, the New World, with all its power and might, sets forth to the liberation and rescue of the Old.''

Maggie, flirting with the Young Communist League as well as its more attractive male Communist members, was not sympathetic. The *Daily Cal* leadership was predominantly liberal and pacifist. She cast her lot there, passing out literature that urged readers to consider England's treatment of the Irish and suppression of 165 million Hindus.

Tensions ran high on October 3, 1940 when Maggie joined with others to speak in protest of the draft at a mass meeting just outside Sather Gate on the Berkeley campus. The event was possibly the most important in her life thus far. Maggie had given much thought to what she would say. Several men assisted her with her speech, each believing himself to be her only adviser. Actually Maggie had selected the best passages from each and then added her own touches.

Phoebe True and Ellen Ainsworth, Maggie's old friends from the Anna Head School, watched in horror and fascination as she stood before the jeering crowd. ''It was terrible,'' Phoebe recalled. ''Her tiny, ineffective voice struggling to be heard made it even worse. In retrospect, I think she was great to speak out for what she believed. Many of us shared her views; but, I, at least, was too busy being popular to do anything about them. At the time I thought she was weird to make a spectacle of herself.'' The two young women stood stunned, unable to believe that this was their golden girl transformed into a creature who was actually inciting a large, angry crowd to abuse her. Some people even threw rotten tomatoes. ''It was a little like watching the crucifixion of a friend turned martyr,'' Phoebe said.

Larry Higgins learned that his daughter was scheduled to speak at a leftist demonstration and attended out of curiosity. At first he stood hidden in the crowd, but as he watched his beautiful but disheveled daughter speak out for her beliefs he came forward and dropped fifty cents in the collection box. If he could not approve the cause, he was touched at least by her courage.

By the end of 1940 Maggie was sure she had earned her spurs. Certain of receiving a senior position on the newspaper staff, she discussed her upcoming appointment candidly. It was assured. There was no question as to her effort or ability. A feminist column that she had pioneered had brought much favorable comment. It ranged from a discussion of Frances Perkins, Secretary of Labor, to the efforts of the university home economics department to improve the quality of food at San Quentin.

The long-anticipated announcement proved a crushing disappointment. Maggie was passed over for editor, managing editor, and city editor. Her job as night editor was low in the hierarchy. It was a bitter blow that took her totally by surprise.

In the past, during times of deep personal stress, Maggie's control had slipped. There had been occasional tears over criticism, a threat of resignation when she felt that her work or her methods were disapproved. This time there were no tears or threats. Shocked and bewildered, Maggie withdrew still further into her shell.

She fulfilled her term as night editor competently and quietly. The final semester of her senior year was a period of waiting. There was an ardent proposal from Raynie Reid, the young man who had shocked Maggie's friends by lounging around her apartment in his bathrobe. Raynie was generally regarded as strong and silent; Maggie saw him as weak. He was not enough of an achiever to suit her.

Of the many men she had met on campus, she still admired Stanley Moore, the elusive teaching aide who had stimulated her philosophical bent as a freshman. She met Stanley often at lectures and liberal gatherings. He had watched her with admiring, appraising eyes and sometimes challenged her remarks with a half-mocking manner that Maggie found exciting. Moore appeared to be going places. He had received his doctorate in philosophy the year before and was now teaching at Harvard.

Home for the summer holiday, he chanced to meet Maggie on the street. "What next?" he asked.

"I'm going to New York."

"Ahhh, the big time. Perhaps I'll call you."

Raynie Reid stayed behind in California.

In 1941 Maggie was graduated cum laude with a degree in letters and science. Her class's slogan seems curiously appropriate: *They knew what they wanted*. Maggie's yearbook picture shows an eager smile, with eyes that reveal the impatience of someone only waiting to make an unforgettable mark on the world.

PART II

GIRL
REPORTER

Four

In August 1941, Marguerite, newly graduated and just one month short of her twenty-first birthday, arrived in New York with seven dollars and one suitcase. The mistakes of the past—if indeed they were mistakes—had been shrugged off. The *Daily Cal* was kid stuff. Now she was playing for real. So she had lost out on a popularity contest; all the more reason to succeed where it really counted.

She was determined to get a newspaper job and ultimately become a foreign correspondent. Only this could offer the total stimulation she craved, the challenge of being in a perpetual race with one's competitors, with history, and even with time itself. It was a race that would occupy the next twenty-five years of her life.

Doors slammed. City editors growled. L. L. Engelking, city editor of the *New York Herald Tribune*, a Texan and a rebel, was probably impressed by the audacity of the California girl who had no money or connections. He held out a slim promise: "*Maybe* later."

How was she to survive in the meantime? Maggie decided to become a student once more. The life-style was tailor-made. She could live on nearly nothing, honing her skills still further while continuing to hunt for a job. A master's degree from the Columbia School of Journalism offered the kind of clout needed to supplement her *Daily Cal* experience. Just four days before the term was to begin Maggie managed to get accepted.

Years later Dean Carl Ackerman was to describe the phenomenon at a memorial service held by the Overseas Press Club following Marguerite's death. Early one morning Ackerman recalled being informed by his secretary that a girl named Higgins was in the outer office requesting admission to the school.

He sent word out to the young woman that all eleven places allotted to women in the graduate school had been filled. Hours later, as he prepared to leave for lunch, his secretary advised him that Miss Higgins was still sitting outside waiting for him to appear.

Ackerman patiently explained the rules to her, but Marguerite was persistent. Finally he sent her to the dean of women with the promise that if she could talk her way past that formidable barrier he would admit her to his famed journalism class.

As he was leaving his office late that day he noticed that the dean's office door was open. There was Marguerite sitting at the desk, busily typing forms. He gaped at the girl in amazement. She had made it.

Of course it was not quite so simple. The dean of women had firmly informed Marguerite that acceptance was practically impossible: High school and college records had to be in the registrar's hands within the next four days accompanied by five letters of recommendation.

"Thank you for explaining the procedure," Marguerite replied. She flashed the dean a brilliant smile, excused herself, and raced to the telephone. Her hands trembled as she placed the collect call to Larry. The records had to be obtained and airmailed at once. Five academicians had to be contacted immediately and persuaded to recommend her and to send those recommendations by telegraph.

Once the myriad Columbia applications were filled out there was nothing left for her to do but wait and will—will that the weather, always a hazard in those early airmail days, would be good, will that Larry's increasing drinking problem would not prevent his prompt action, will that her former professors were impressed enough by her ability to come through for her. Haakon Chevalier she was certain of; but the others?

The weather across the country continued fair and mild. Larry acted immediately, his Irish charm rising to the challenge. Telegrams containing glowing recommendations flowed in—despite the fact that one initially irate professor had been awakened at 2:00 A.M.

Within four days Ackerman got a call from the bursar's office. "Your Miss Higgins has been accepted by the dean of women, by you, by the registrar, by everybody. Now she's here in my office and says she hasn't any money. What are you going to do?"

What did Ackerman do? He allowed Marguerite to persuade him to send a telegram to her parents asking for tuition. Once more Larry came through with the required amount. Marguerite supplemented the rest of her needs by doing public relations writing for the university.

The class in which she found herself was to be an illustrious one. Among the students were Elie Abel, later to become dean of the school, chief diplomatic correspondent for NBC and London bureau chief for the *New York Times*, and Flora Lewis, eventual Paris bureau chief for the *New York Times* and columnist on foreign affairs.

Abel, who became Chandler professor of communications at Stanford University, recalled Marguerite and Flora as "the golden girls, both from California—one north, one south—both blonde, attractive, talented, and competitive."

For a time it looked as though the two women would share an apartment. "Maggie had her heart set on living in Greenwich Village," Flora remembered. "I was dubious. Columbia was so far uptown. I liked the convenience of being close to campus and knew the rents were cheaper up there. Maggie was so excited about the Village, she knew she could find something great. As it turned out, she located an apartment almost immediately and showed me about with great enthusiasm. To me it was dreadful; tiny, grimy. All Maggie saw was 'atmosphere.' She wouldn't compromise. To her, the Village was where the action was. So it meant getting up earlier to get to class. What was an extra hour's sleep?"

The two women would meet and compete many times in years to come. Flora recalled Maggie as being persistent, hard driving, and energetic. "Once we were given a class assignment to write an editorial on a given subject. Somehow Maggie got to the library ahead of all the rest of us and checked out every available resource on the topic. It was typical of her, yet I feel that people critical of Maggie and her so-called dirty tricks forget just how hard it was in those days to be a woman in a man's world. The odds were enormous. Even women were against you. They could be so cruel in such subtle ways. How many times I've gone to parties and had women, *women* say 'you know men are really smarter, really better at the difficult, complicated things.' Ambition was a dirty word then. Careers were just something you fooled around with until the right man came along. Maggie didn't know that game. She was earnest and played for keeps."

Elie Abel, whose career also paralleled Marguerite's for many years, agreed that they were "competitors from the egg." He remembered her well from the first days at Columbia. "She talked like a shy little girl with the voice of a small child, which heaven knows she was not. It was obvious from the beginning that she had her eye on the main chance and it paid off. She was the first in the class to attain professional success. It was never enough for her to just do a good job. She had to stick it in your eye.''

That Marguerite had obvious advantages in her uphill climb was noted by John Tebbel, a Columbia faculty member: "Even in a class full of stars, she stood out. Maggie was positively dazzling, with a blonde beauty that hardly concealed her equally dazzling intelligence. She was all hard-edged ambition. In those days women had to be tougher to succeed in journalism, a male-dominated and essentially chauvinist[ic] business, and Maggie carried toughness to the outer edge, propelled by driving ambition, which was soon apparent to us all.

''I was one of those who directed the activities of the newsroom, in which every Thursday the class, divided into two competing staffs, covered the New York news. Like any regular reporter, students were assigned to real stories and their efforts later assessed in a critique by the class and those late geniuses Robert Garst, city editor, and Ted Bernstein, then head of the copy desk and later assistant managing editor, of the *New York Times*.

''It was a highly competitive exercise and Maggie loved it. She became known to Bob, Ted, and the rest of the newsroom team as a reporter who could get absolutely any story no matter how difficult. Naturally that was a challenge to us, and we tried to think of assignments that would really challenge *her*. One I remember particularly was her assignment to interview Lewis Valentine, then the celebrated police commissioner of New York. We didn't tell her that he was well known on the police beat as a man who didn't meet the press and never gave interviews. Written questions were sent to him. A man as tough as Maggie, we thought. She came back with the interview, and it was so good she sold it. We learned later from amazed police reporters that she had gone in and exerted her compelling sexual charms on the sergeant guarding Valentine's office, got inside, and then charmed Valentine himself into giving one of the few interviews ever extracted from him.

''Maggie did not hesitate to use her formidable sex appeal whenever she thought it would help, and I never heard of anyone who could resist her. Years later my old friend, the late Hal Boyle, described how Maggie would appear at some headquarters where Boyle and other top war correspondents would be sitting around trying to get information from a tight-lipped general and his staff. In short order Maggie would be having dinner with the general, then flying away next morning with a story the others hadn't been able to get. Naturally a lot of them believed she offered more than lowered eyelashes to get the story. I have no idea whether that's true or not, but I'm sure she would have if it had been necessary to get what she wanted. She was charming but absolutely ruthless, a flawless combination of sex and brains.''

'''Engelking told me he wouldn't hire a woman.''

The warning came from Murray Morgan, a classmate who had immediately landed the coveted job of Columbia University correspondent to the *New York Herald Tribune* but was now moving up to a better-paying job on *Time*.

Marguerite scarcely heard him. Morgan had told her of the opening. He had even recommended her for the job. A quick hug and kiss and she was off and running to the *Herald Tribune* building before any of the men in the class heard of the vacancy.

Standing before Engelking (wearing a green coat with mink collar and cuffs, a garment recently purchased— recently enough not to be soiled or wrinkled—for thirty-five hard-earned dollars) she smiled hopefully.

Before he could say a word, she blurted out, ''I know you said you didn't want to hire a woman reporter. But I had to try. I know I could do a good job for you.''

The silence seemed deafening as the large man studied her appraisingly. ''You think you could do it, eh?''

''Yes.'' Marguerite looked earnest, eager, and ever so beguiling. She looked away and then back, her soft, little girl voice wheedling, ''With so many men going off to war, it might be a good idea. . . .''

She trembled inwardly as his silence remained unbroken. Then finally he nodded. ''Do you think you could start today?''

Five

Soon after Marguerite's arrival in New York the long-anticipated call came from Stanley Moore. The two met and became lovers.

Working on special assignment at the *Tribune* one evening, she took advantage of a momentary lull to describe her new life in a letter to her parents.

Dear Mom and Dad,

Tuesday and the long awaited mayorality election has arrived! We're sitting around in the office waiting for election returns to start coming in. We're putting out a special election edition and the whole staff's jittery and excited.

La Guardia should win if the political experts in New York know whereof they speak.

I'm sitting at the city desk and will take the stories over the phone and rewrite them for the edition.

Tomorrow I'm to interview the government representatives of Poland to the National Labor Conference and try to find out some of the bright ideas about economic reconstruction after the war.

Next Monday the School of Journalism is awarding the Maria Cabot Moor prizes in journalism to South American journalists. Following the dinner at the Hotel Astor we're to dress up in our finery (which means my white satin formal) and have a dance there.

The city room's in an uproar. Typewriters click-clacking, election returns piling up.

Next day—well the little flower barely made it but anyway he won! Now about Stanley. You people seem to be very much afraid that I'm in the clutches of a senile old gentleman. So here are some facts to set your minds at ease: tall, black-haired and Irish, Stanley Moore teaches the young in the lore of philosophy. He handles a section at Harvard and also has two tutees at Radcliffe.

Stanley was the youngest and brightest philosopher ever to have graduated from the University of California philosophy department. He was a Phi Beta Kappa and chairman of the forensic commission—debating society—when he was there.

Stanley's family are the Piedmont Stanley Moores. His father was one of California's most famous lawyers, counsel for the Nolans in his time.

Stanley comes down to New York almost every other weekend. He can afford to now because he is earning about $280 a month and does not pay rent or board.

He is a radical and incurably so. We agree on such principles as the best world is one where both Negro and Jew and Rockefeller and Roosevelt have a chance at enough to eat, a chance at assimilating culture and art and happiness or at least a fair share of them—a chance you don't get when working ten hours a day for $12 a week.

I don't think Stanley's radicalism will ever hurt him, for he will always be able to rely on money which he is scheduled to inherit, and furthermore he is too brilliant in my opinion to be discarded by society because of his political beliefs.

With all his streamlining and modernism, Stanley is quite a sentimentalist beneath the surface. His favorite music doesn't show it though for he sticks doggedly to Bach and Beethoven and Mozart. He considers Wagner and Tchaikovsky too sentimental.

He is good for me because he knows so much more than I, though he, like Daddy, has a tendency to bark and be sarcastic. Then I hate him. But he says I'm to 'give him the blast' when he tries to squelch what I have to say with irrelevant quips.

The point is, we agree not to win an argument but to arrive at the truth. And surprisingly enough he really tries, so you see human nature or at least habits can be changed. And I've a theory that people who resort to the 'human nature can't be changed' argument just as a mask for the reality that they are too lazy to change and feel that it's easier to continue in the same old rut and blame it on destiny.

Well, that's the Stanley picture and I hope I've satisfied your curiosities and answered your questions.

Love,
Marguerite

It was a neat summary but by no means all. Early in 1942 Marguerite wrote to her childhood friend Jean Craig, ''Stanley Moore is the most wonderful man in the world, though slightly on the selfish side—that is a selfish refusal to depart from his way of life even if his nine hours of sleep-orderd existence have to be put above everything else.

"He will be drafted in June and though it makes me sick at heart to think of it, I get used to the idea gradually. It is a terrible predicament. I love him more than anyone I have ever known truly. However, I'm not sure I could be a loyal wife and bear up under the persecutions his politics will be bound to subject him to. Especially if he's open about them.

"So perhaps I don't love him so much after all."

She struggled to change the subject or simply move on, having disposed of it. "The snow, soft and dry, puts a concealing mantle over the landscape's rough outlines. The lights sparkling across the river and the world have turned Morningside to blue, white, and gray. I have bought myself some nice white boots in which to galavant through the puddles and snowdrifts. I'm getting so I can brave the near zero weather with scarcely a shiver." Her letter ended with a request for news about the Chabot Court kids.

Three thousand miles from home Marguerite was doing some soul-searching. Although still a liberal, she had begun to question her position. On a holiday visit to Washington, D.C., where her Anna Head chum Ellen Ainsworth was now living, she confided, "I'm sorry I cut myself off. I miss my old friends."

Marguerite was torn. Despite the influence of Stanley and of Haakon Chevalier, who was now on sabbatical and living in Greenwich Village —his home a mecca for all the liberal luminaries of the day—her own scope was broadening. Once again she was considering new possibilities. The war was well under way and Moore, expecting to be sent overseas, was pressing her to marry him. Deeply involved in her own career, she could see inevitable conflicts. Was what he offered the life she truly wanted—the "little woman" supporting and inspiring a radical?

There was little chance for introspection as her pace quickened. Competition was keen at Columbia. Marguerite remained at the top of her class while attempting to work her way onto the *Tribune*'s full-time staff.

Her reportorial breakthrough came typically through her sense of timing, plus fancy footwork and just plain push.

Madame Chiang Kai-shek, a patient at Columbia Presbyterian Medical Center, had declared the press strictly off limits. Undeterred, Marguerite, carrying supplies, followed a nurse into the sickroom. The innocent, eager face and the soft, determined voice won out as they had before and would again. She got her story and eventually the job.

"Dear Mom," Marguerite wrote shortly after, "you are now the mother of the second woman ever to be hired as a straight news reporter on the *Tribune* (circulation 400,000 daily) at least unless I make some dreadful mistake between now and next week. The boss said he would hire me after commencement."

There was no dreadful mistake. In June 1942 Marguerite began full-time employment with the *Herald Tribune*. So resourceful had she been at stringing that the salary of twenty-five dollars a week was actually a cut from what she had received on a free-lance basis. She had been graduated from Columbia with honors and was an alternate to Elie Abel for a traveling fellowship from the Pulitzer School of Journalism.

Advancement from cub status came a few weeks after Marguerite joined the *Tribune* full-time staff when an editor challenged her to interview James Caesar Petrillo.

Petrillo, the head of the musician's union, was demanding that musicians receive a percentage from recordings played over the air or on jukeboxes. His refusal to grant interviews was well known.

Wheedling Petrillo's room number from the Waldorf Astoria telephone operator, Marguerite knocked on his door promptly at 9:00 A.M.

"Who is it?" a gravelly voice demanded to know.

"Miss Higgins," she answered.

The door opened. There stood the feisty labor czar in a bathrobe and striped silk pajamas smoking a cigar. "Who the hell are you?" he roared.

"Marguerite Higgins." She stood before him windblown, pink-cheeked from the cold and excitement.

"Who is Marguerite Higgins?" he asked in a much softer tone.

Later Petrillo admitted that he had originally opened the door thinking she was the maid and had relented and granted the interview because she looked like his daughter.

It was one of many turning points in Marguerite's career.

Marguerite's social life was equally eventful. Though she still looked like Daisy Mae, a far cry from the remote elegance of the fashion models and movie stars then popular, her appearance exerted a strong appeal. She had the "playmate" look that would later make a fortune for Hugh Hefner—young, careless, naive, somehow conveying to every man the impression that if he could only manage to meet and talk with her, she would be easily seduced. The reality was that for all her air of just having tumbled out of bed—which she frequently had—Marguerite was a woman who did her own choosing.

Bob Shaplen, then a *Tribune* reporter, remembered her well. "I was her first boyfriend on the paper, but everyone was drawn to her. Why not? She was sexy, charming, and bright. She could get more carbon on that cute Irish face of hers than anyone I ever knew, but behind that pert, pretty facade was a woman who knew exactly what she wanted. She was very hardworking with a winning and determined way all her own, a damn good reporter—that more than a writer."

Marguerite moved quickly through the city room, momentarily drawn to various men. Some relationships were transitory, others more lasting. She acquired a reputation for being fast; the men of the *New York Herald Tribune* were not known for their discretion. To them, Marguerite was easy. In reality she was too hard for most men to understand or appreciate. She enjoyed men and was challenged by them.

John Watson, an unusually gifted rewrite man, was particularly attractive to her. An Irishman whose charm and quips may well have reminded her of Larry, Watson had a magnificent talent, which was marred by a drinking problem. Perhaps she imagined that she might help him; certainly she knew that she could learn from him.

Their affair was the subject of much speculation and continuing controversy at the *Tribune*. Some staff members thought that Marguerite was using Watson. Others considered him fortunate to have the association. Marguerite found John immensely appealing but was wary of his drinking. She was a far cry from her trusting mother, who had been entranced by a handsome fly-boy who would, she imagined, carry her away to adventure in a foreign land. *This* Marguerite was determined to make her own adventures.

For a time the Byronic Stanley Moore provided one of them. Possibly Marguerite did not allow herself to look beyond the immediate challenge. He was a prize to be captivated and then captured. Classy, charismatic, and adored by so many of the women she perceived as rivals, Moore was the Prince Charming fantasy fashioned during her Anna Head days come to life. Their connection crackled with enough sexual energy to short-circuit her determined autonomy. Here was a man with breeding, totally at ease in a world that Marguerite had only been allowed to visit on a noblesse oblige basis. With Stanley she would never again be the poor girl invited only on a ''look, see how democratic I am'' whim. Not only did Stanley belong, but he was also brilliant, devastatingly handsome, and an apparent wunderkind destined to make waves.

Marguerite was just two months past her twenty-second birthday when she and Stanley returned to California to be married. Jean Craig, her maid of honor, recalled a shopping trip to I. Magnin in San Francisco. ''Our dresses were lightweight wool. None of that froufrou stuff. We were career women. Maggie's was green, mine blue. We felt terribly sophisticated. Then we got to discussing Stanley's mother and something reminded us of Maggie in her little church dresses with the lacy panties. Mrs. Moore would *never* have approved of that. The thought of her reaction started us giggling like schoolgirls.''

Their nervous laughter may well have been an attempt to barricade themselves against the enormity of what was then considered a lifetime decision. One had to step very carefully and still pray for luck. Life for a woman was a mine field: The wrong choice—the wrong man—meant consignment to a seeming eternity of bitterness and regret.

''Stanley may have been a Communist, but his family was extremely conservative,'' Jean recalled. ''It made no difference that Maggie was descended on her mother's side from the Count and Countess de Godard. To Piedmont society—and particularly to Mrs. Moore—she was a nobody.

''The mother of the groom wore black to the ceremony. Later, at a small reception held in the Moores' elegant home, her manner was a study in icy civility. The Catholic Higginses, already upset by the Episcopal service, were stung; but Maggie appeared to think it very amusing. She made quite a fuss over Larry, who had reenlisted in the air force and had come home on leave to give her away. He looked marvelously young in his captain's uniform, handsomer and healthier than he had in years.''

While the guests drank champagne and attempted to ignore the tension between the new in-laws, the newlyweds went upstairs to finish packing. When they descended, Stanley had Marguerite on one arm and a load of books in the other. The seven-day honeymoon in Carmel that would form the bulk of their married life together was about to begin.

Stanley reported to air force training in Texas. Marguerite, retaining her maiden name, returned to the *Herald Tribune*.

A few weeks later Maggie wrote home to her parents:

Aside from the fact that Stanley is gone, my life is pleasant. I privately think that I have the best job in all New York and the nicest apartment. Working is a thousand times easier than school. So I'll have time to cultivate friends and make more of them.

She was continuing to cultivate John Watson and was frequently observed sitting on his lap at Bleeck's, a popular restaurant frequented by movie and theater personalities as well as the *Herald Tribune* crew. Publicly Marguerite made no effort to explain away her infidelity. Privately she shrugged, "Does anyone expect a man to sit around with his legs crossed?" She had no illusions that Stanley would remain celibate if confronted with attractive alternatives.

This is important as I have really not had time to get to know people well. I plan to take Spanish, Russian, and maybe even Chinese lessons. You see I'm still determined to be a foreign correspondent.

It's a splendid feeling to be on the *Herald* staff. My assignments take me all over the city and even out of town. I'm also equipped with the coveted police card as well as a press card. So you see my dreams have come true. I have four or five ideas for magazine articles brewing. I intend to get these out of the way as soon as I can. My finances are in excellent shape. I receive $25 a week and my fixed expenses amount to $65 a month which allows me plenty of leeway.

That's all for now.

Of course that was not all. She and Stanley enjoyed a brief holiday on Nantucket before he was sent overseas. The romantic interlude, on the quaint island with its cobblestone streets, colorful wharf, and proud whalers' mansions, may have marked a turning point in the relationship. Describing the second honeymoon to Phoebe True, her old Anna Head confidante who was now married and living in New York, Maggie told of how they had rented bicycles to explore the historic island. They had picnicked on the beach and strolled the moors, marveling at the deepening colors as summer drew to a close in tones of red, brown, and bronze.

"The trip was wonderful, but I don't think our marriage will last," the bride of eight months admitted.

Phoebe looked at her in shocked amazement. "Why did you marry him?"

"It was the only way I could get him. Stanley's so attractive, once the war's over and he's back in circulation—who knows? Now he belongs to me. One thing I'm sure of—we're not going to have children. I know they absolutely destroy your sex life.''

Phoebe, who had one child and another on the way, was horrified. What had happened to the idealistic schoolgirl? she wondered. ''Now I realize that Marguerite may have been talking to hear herself talk—testing, speaking aloud concepts that she had been weighing in her mind. At the time I thought her cynical and was hurt by her seeming contempt of marriage and motherhood—my life-style. It was all very shocking in nineteen forty-three.''

Before long Stanley, a newly commissioned lieutenant, was sent to Russia. Marguerite, envisioning him with a beguiling parade of ballet dancers palpitating with desire to show their gratitude, was very much in circulation. Phoebe attended *Herald Tribune* parties with her and was immediately aware of her friend's continued involvement with John Watson. ''One part of me rationalized that if she wasn't totally committed to Stanley there was no point in her merely putting in time; the other part continued to be shocked. She was *married*. My feelings were ambivalent. I, too, was young and ambitious. Marguerite's life-style seemed so exciting. I disapproved but still envied her independence.''

Jean Craig, who came east to visit, also remembered the period vividly. Taking a cab directly from Grand Central Station to the *Tribune* office, she entered the noisy city room tentatively, intimidated by the air of organized confusion. Spotting Marguerite across the cluttered room, she noted that although her friend had forsaken the mismatched bobby sox that had distinguished her college days, her stockings were snagged and her nails were broken. ''Even in that scruffy atmosphere, she looked messy,'' Jean remembered, ''but as always those sparkling blue eyes seemed to transcend everything. I felt terribly out of place in my best suit and a hat with a veil and gloves; but Maggie came running over, gave me a big hug, then insisted on taking me around to everybody, including the city editor. They all had to meet her friend from Oakland.''

Jean soon learned that Maggie's beloved apartment consisted of two rooms in the basement of a Greenwich Village apartment building. ''There was a bedroom, a living room-kitchen where I slept and a bathroom down the hall shared with people who seemed to wander in off the street,'' she recalled. ''The passage to the bath was a cockroach promenade. Maggie had a cleaning woman, Matilda, who came in once a week. The dishes rose in pyramids in the sink waiting for her.

''Many times Maggie would come home at midnight with her newspaper friends. There I'd be, asleep on the couch with my hair in curlers. 'We're so tired, won't you fix coffee?' she'd ask. Saying no never occurred to me. People rarely said no to Maggie.''

Sometimes Jean accompanied Marguerite to parties. ''I remember one given by the New York Newspaper Women's Club in some fancy hotel ballroom. Maggie stood leaning against a pillar—posing really—inviting men to approach her, which they certainly did. She had a very interesting figure, seductive as hell.''

Once when Jean was rummaging through the bathroom cabinet in search of an extra toothpaste tube she came across a strange caplike thing. ''What's this?'' she asked, curiously examining the rubber object.

''Maggie looked at me in amazement. 'How old are you, Jean? Twenty-five? It's time you saw a diaphragm.' She then proceeded to explain its use.''

After that Jean observed that the diaphragm came and went. ''I didn't ask questions. I didn't need to. But certainly Maggie was not the only married woman—or man—to behave as a single individual during that crazy, tumultuous time. No one knew what tomorrow would bring, and she had far too much energy and impatience to sit and wait.''

Marguerite moved into a larger apartment, which she shared with the *New Yorker* cartoonist Roberta MacDonald. Writing home enthusiastically, she described the antique furniture and the placement of her parents' pictures on the mantle along with a photo of the family cat, Mr. Tuck. The letter ended with a request that they forward her violin and favorite books: *Leaves of Grass*, *For Whom the Bell Tolls*, *Masterpieces of Modern Art*, *War and Peace*, *In Dubious Battle*, and *U.S.A.*

She was getting by-lines, a rarity on the *Tribune*. Some of her stories were featured on Page One. One assignment involved spending the day with the Duchess of Windsor. In a letter to her mother she described the duchess in more personal terms, as ''extremely thin,'' wistfully adding, ''with diminutive buttocks.'' Accompanying the celebrity to a department store, she noted that the duchess, like Mrs. Higgins, was a canny shopper who contrived to get things wholesale.

Marguerite wrote home of innocent pleasures, outings to Jones Beach with Roberta, theater parties, and a birthday celebration. She carefully omitted John Watson's name from the guest list. She had always been aware of the attraction of her appearance and her intellect, but now she also realized that her emotions were deeply involved. She loved Stanley, wrote to him daily, and fumed when the vagaries of overseas mail delayed his answers; yet the space his absence made underscored her doubts. Could she ever accept the confines of traditional marriage? An added consideration was John Watson. John was amusing, talented when sober, and always devoted to her. Could she love two men at once?

The pressures of work and of her own ambitions allowed her to forestall decision making. One of her most harrowing assignments occurred during this period. On July 6, 1944, a circus tent caught fire in Hartford, Connecticut. More than one hundred people were rumored dead. Ted Laymon, the *Tribune* assistant city editor, was dispatched alone. All other reporters were out on assignment. "Get going; I'll try to send you help somehow," Engelking told him.

"I rushed over to Grand Central, jumped on a train—and waited," Laymon recalled. "It turned out that Engelking had persuaded them to hold the train. As I stared anxiously out the window I caught sight of Maggie Higgins—unwashed, uncombed, blonde hair flying, running the length of the depot. She leaped on just as the train began to move.

"What awaited us was so horrible that it makes me sick to think of it even now. A cigarette carelessly dropped in the men's room caught fire and spread to the main tent, then the largest in the world. A main exit was blocked by animal cages. The matinee audience, many of them unaccompanied children, became hopelessly confused. Within ten minutes nineteen tons of flaming canvas dropped on the screaming spectators, many trapped in their seats, unable to fight their way out of the inferno.

"By the time Maggie and I got there the rescue work had begun. Circus performers in their tights and spangles were assisting the police, some of whom were weeping openly as they carried out hideously burned children. Many families had become separated. The horror and confusion was indescribable. Private cars, trucks, and even horse-drawn wagons were mobilized to transport the victims.

"The Hartford State Armory had been converted to a morgue where the difficult and heartrending task of identification took place. Outside long lines of people gathered, many of them sobbing hysterically. They were admitted in groups of twelve. Maggie and I watched as the grief-stricken relatives walked up and down the aisles. Many of the bodies were unrecognizable. The final death toll was one hundred sixty-eight, so many of them kids.

"Later, when Maggie filed her stories from the concentration camps, I felt that this ghastly baptism of fire had helped to prepare her. The two of us had to compete against six *Times* men. Maggie worked so hard. We finally got to bed at 4:00 A.M. She was up early the next day down at city hall, pressing for answers. 'How could such a thing have happened?'

" 'Where did you get that girl?' one city official asked. 'She's so aggressive.' That was Maggie all right, not afraid of anything or anybody. She could be pushy as hell, but there was never anything small or spiteful about her. She was quick to congratulate others on good work and was ready with compliments or commiseration for the ups and downs of other writers.''

While perfecting her skills as a city room reporter, Marguerite was busily campaigning to get sent overseas. Besides studying Russian and Spanish, she could speak fluent French and had taken German in college. These were facts she emphasized and reemphasized for the benefit of any of her bosses who would listen.

''Do you think I'd make a good war correspondent?'' she winsomely queried Morton Glatzer, assistant night editor.

''She was everybody's little girl,'' he remembered. ''Any man who wasn't openly on the make for her at least felt fatherly. She was so pretty and so sloppy. God, was she sloppy! Carbon all over her. She had a fast, quick walk showing off that fanny of hers that was quite captivating. I remember the first time that John Watson saw her. 'There's one beautiful ass!' he said. Next thing I knew they were an item. It may or may not have been his downfall. One might see it as a lovely interlude in a brilliant but erratic career or the turning point that ultimately led to uncontrollable drinking and the termination of his association with the *Tribune*.''

Glatzer tried to guide Marguerite. ''She was always eager to listen, those big blue eyes of hers hanging on every word. Of course that didn't mean she would follow my advice or anyone else's. She had a mind of her own. She didn't need my encouragement, though I certainly gave it to her. 'Yes, Maggie,' I assured her, 'you'd be a fine correspondent.' The next thing I knew the staff had one more Maggie Higgins story to mull over. She'd gone over everyone's head to take her case to Helen Rogers Reid, the owner's wife. Mrs. Reid took an active part in the management and was known to be a feminist.''

Marguerite buttonholed anyone and everyone at the *Tribune*, stating her case coolly and factually, and when that failed, passionately. In speaking of the ultimate decision of Helen Reid to send Marguerite overseas, Ogden Reid said, "Mother simply recognized Marguerite's skills as a reporter. She had the courage of a lion. There was no story that she wasn't prepared to go after. In the long run one has to respect that kind of initiative. Sure, Marguerite stepped on some toes, but that was all part of the package and had to be accepted. Mother believed that a woman could do any job a man could do—and sometimes better. She had no doubts about Maggie's ability to cover the war."

Subsequent events would confirm Helen Reid's judgment; but initially there were some very angry male staff members on the *Tribune*. One of them was L. L. Engelking, the man who had hired Marguerite in the first place. The city editor made no effort to conceal the fact that he resented her receiving the assignment over his head.

"Miss Higgins, I understand you're going abroad," he greeted her one morning.

"Yes, I am," she answered, smiling demurely.

"I'd like to take you to dinner at Bleeck's," he surprised her by saying.

She accepted with delight. The following evening, as they entered the popular meeting spot, Marguerite looked about the cartoon-covered walls nostalgically. She had spent countless happy evenings there with John Watson. Smiling, she recalled her excitement the first time she had spotted Bogie and his Baby in a corner holding hands and her shock the first time she had watched Tallulah Bankhead dancing on the tabletops wearing no underwear.

Engelking watched as Marguerite tossed a penny into the visor of a prominently placed suit of armor for luck, a Bleeck's tradition. The two sat down and ordered drinks. Engelking looked at her in silence, with the appraising scrutiny that had disconcerted her three years before.

"Miss Higgins," he said at last, "before you exchange the humdrum existence of a mere reporter for the glamour of a war correspondent, I'd like to ask you something. You're the dirtiest woman I've ever met. Why don't you wash your neck?"

Marguerite's response went unrecorded.

What mattered most was the announcement, made by George Cornish, *Tribune* managing editor, that she was to join seven other war correspondents on the *Queen Mary*.

Converted to a troopship, the former luxury liner made a twice-monthly, highly nerve-racking, five-day crossing to Southampton. The *Queen* was known to be fast, but she had to be lucky as well. It was a spooky trip, with fate occupying the seat of honor at the captain's table.

The ship sailed at midnight, in virtual darkness, in an effort to avoid the German U-boats that lay in wait. When the correspondents assembled on deck it was soon apparent that one of their party was absent. An unknown reporter had literally missed the boat.

As the vessel reached Ambrose Light, the pilot was lowered over the side. A few minutes later the ladder was raised. Clinging tenaciously to the side was a slim young woman. She wore full army uniform, including a canteen strapped to one shoulder. Her helmet had slipped back, revealing an unruly mane of blonde hair.

The correspondents, the crew members, and an entire division of soldiers watched in amazement as she clambered aboard. Janet Flanner, a correspondent for the *New Yorker* and one of the veteran journalists standing on deck, recounted the story to a group of intimates six years later. "It was my first encounter with Marguerite Higgins. She looked so sweet and innocent. I immediately thought of Goldilocks and wanted to protect her. If I'd known then what I know now I'd have thrown her overboard."

PART III

WAR
CORRESPONDENT

Six

Marguerite stepped off the boat into the arms of Stanley Moore. He had been transferred from Russia to Headquarters Air Forces in Europe, located at that time near Hampton Court. The couple, separated for more than a year, attempted to pick up the tattered threads of a frayed marriage.

Their first and only home was a room in the Savoy Hotel, the elegant haunt of the rich and famous made affordable by special military rates. This bastion of Victorian elegance had been the scene of many dramas. Pavlova had danced there; Irving Berlin had played; George Gershwin had introduced "Rhapsody in Blue" to its first London audience. Noel Coward and Maurice Chevalier currently performed in the cabaret.

Marguerite and Stanley, playing their own parts in the wartime drama, delighted in the mellowed opulence and the sense of continuing history. They sipped tea and drank cocktails. They danced and sat by a window overlooking the Thames, holding hands. They talked, planned, and argued. For a time it was easy to escape their mounting personal problems by exploring the devastated but still dynamic city.

Bombings and blackouts had instilled a kind of camaraderie that cut through class and privilege. Rationing had insured that rich and poor shared as equally in the shortages as they did in the dangers. For once, civilian and soldier experienced a grim commonality. The colossal struggle was a lottery: Peer might as easily be killed or maimed as private.

More than five years of war had rendered Londoners both plucky and practical. One result was an innovative variation on the double date. "Meet me at the—or the—" was the standard social agreement; an alternative was always necessary because one could never be sure that a certain restaurant or theater would be standing at the appointed time. Shortages virtually guaranteed that inside the restaurant the food would be dreadful, yet the queue outside was invariably patient and good-humored.

Lines formed before theaters where enthusiastic audiences could see a young Laurence Olivier or Ralph Richardson perform for sixpence. The ravaged theater might look like a warehouse, but inside one could expect a performance made all the more brilliant by the knowledge that it might be the last for actor and audience alike. There was an exhilaratingly conspiratorial hands-across-the-footlights atmosphere about theater-going. If the air raid sirens sounded during a performance no one knew for certain if he or she would leave the theater alive. Still, what better way to go, most agreed, than watching *Blithe Spirit*?

London had been under fire from the V-1, or buzz bomb, since June. The engine-powered artillery shells had just enough fuel to wing their way across the channel. Once over London their motors would fail and they would swoop down, warhead first. People who were outside could observe and sometimes avoid the terrifying approach. Inside, you could only listen and hope. If the snarling motor passed overhead you waited for the inevitable crash, knowing that if you heard it you hadn't "had it."

By the time of Marguerite's arrival an even more horrifying bomb had been introduced, the V-2. Looking like a luminous pencil drawing a line of fire across the blank sky, these projectiles came plummeting down with no warning. You'll never know what hit you, people joked, then went on to relate macabre tales of the resulting carnage. A man's trousers were blown off but he was uninjured. At a dinner party the host and hostess were blown to bits but the guests were left untouched.

The Germans boasted that there would soon be nothing left of London. Marguerite's dispatches reported that recent explosions had destroyed blocks of flats, an urban bungalow development, a hospital, a library, and a vicarage. Although government censorship prevented her from disclosing the locations of the disasters, she did reveal that women comprised the large majority of the many thousands killed.

The result was an almost feverish fatalism. Restaurants and theaters were packed, but music halls and art galleries were also jammed. Though pubs were forced to close at 9:00 P.M. because of nightly air raids, they did a brisk business beginning at 5:00.

Possibly the constant threat of death underscored Marguerite and

Stanley's need to put their lives in order. Living together for the first time on a day-to-day basis, both became aware of differences that had been hidden or avoided on brief, blissful weekends. Stanley had imagined himself as a Pygmalion with a compliant Marguerite who could be molded into a ladylike helpmate. His chipping did bring the statue to life but not in the manner he envisioned. Confronted at last with the demands of a full-time marriage, Marguerite realized that she was unwilling to pay the price. Overseas reporting had only whetted her appetite for more adventure. There was too much out there to do, to see, to experience. She would not be confined.

Initially bitter, Stanley spoke harshly of his wife to Anne Waybur, a friend from Berkeley then serving with the United Nations Relief Administration. Recalling Moore's disappointment, Anne said, "He had perceived her as innocent, malleable. When he realized that she was in fact a single-minded woman of steel, he felt betrayed—conned. 'It was a mistake in judgment,' he said to me, cool contempt masking his pain and disappointment. The idea conveyed by this socialite turned liberal was that she was beneath him."

Marguerite also discussed the break with a friend, Jim O'Donnell, then a *Newsweek* correspondent. "There was just too much against us," she explained, "our youth and inexperience, the demands of our jobs, the fortunes of war. By the time we finally got together we realized that we didn't have as much in common as we'd once thought."

Later in her autobiography Marguerite was to write, "I don't think I ever needed my first husband at all because there never was a time or an occasion for the need to develop."

By November, when Stanley was moved with headquarters to Saint-Germain on the outskirts of Paris, the break was almost complete. "We realized that if we were to find happiness it would not be with each other," Stanley said in retrospect years later. The two spent Christmas together in an unsuccessful effort at a reconciliation.

"Bundles for Britain" was a national passion in the United States. During the holiday season Marguerite received a bundle. Sent by Larry and Marguerite Senior, it contained a pair of red velvet mittens and a small leather case containing favorite recordings, including Peggy Lee's rendition of "Get Out of Here and Get Me Some Money, Too" and Tchaikovsky's "Swan Lake."

Maggie's mittens came in handy in the bleak, bombed-out city, which suffered cruelly from fuel shortages. Her enthusiasm generated a glow of its own. She wrote about British women who had done everything from manning antiaircraft guns to holding down key parliamentary positions. One story described how female members of the House of Commons carried the day in a controversial bill allowing the Auxiliary Territorial Service (the British equivalent of the WACs) to participate in the war overseas. In opposition to the bill, F. W. Pethick-Lawrence argued that "in civilized countries women, whose job is primarily that of raising a family, should not be sent overseas to risk death and injury." Other male members of the House added that in view of "the laxity in some places there were moral reasons for keeping the ATS at home."

Such reasoning was clearly absurd to Lady Astor, who stoutly defended the measure, calling the dissenting men a "bunch of nervous Nellies." The accusation so provoked Aneurin Bevan that he cried out, "Oh shut up, you cheapjack! The woman gabbles and gabbles all the time. We really ought to have some protection against her. I see no reason why we should have minds of that sort inflicted on the House."

In those days of objective news reporting, Marguerite's sentiments went unrecorded in her stories.

Marguerite covered addresses by Winston Churchill and King George VI and interviewed British politicians—left, right, and center. All this was heady for a reporter only days past her twenty-fourth birthday, but she felt a sense of urgency that amounted almost to panic.

Standing amid the jostling celebrants thronging Trafalgar Square on New Year's Eve, Marguerite was oblivious to the snowflakes falling about her. The last seconds of December 31,1944 were being chanted into eternity. Despite the ever-constant threat of bombings, the crowd was happy, hopeful, and festive. World War II was drawing to a close. Would it end before Marguerite could reach the front?

Anxiously Marguerite studied the daily headlines:

U.S. FLYERS BLAST NAZI ARMOR FLEEING BULGE
REDS SMASH TO WITHIN 165 MILES OF BERLIN
BRITISH IN GERMANY, 29 MILES FROM DUSSELDORF
TWIN DRIVES IN HOLLAND BREAK NAZI LINE
BRITISH LAND IN GREECE, NAZIS WITHDRAWING
3RD ARMY SMASHES THROUGH SIEGFRIED LINE
ALLIES GAIN IN BELGIUM, HALT FOE IN ALSACE

Marguerite continued to be obsessed with the idea of war reporting and feared nothing but the possibility that the conflict would be over before she could get to the thick of it. This was the girl who had grown up surrounded by pictures of her father as a World War I aviator and had watched his eyes shine with excitement as he talked of his wartime experiences. Even as a child she had wondered what was shared in the turbulence of battle that caused one to actually long for those emotional peaks many years later. The highs experienced by Larry Higgins and his craving for them must have been in her blood. She had always known that if there was to be a war she would have to experience it for herself, learning firsthand what the force was that cut so deeply and permanently into the hearts of men.

Then a personal disaster struck. Weakened by overwork and the emotional strain of her separation from Stanley, Marguerite contracted jaundice and was hospitalized. The illness, coming at a time when she had been frantically campaigning for a European assignment, was a severe setback. The acute shortages of food and fuel and the bitter cold did not help her battered spirit.

Years later the columnist Ralph McGill recalled visiting Marguerite in the hospital. "I went with Wilbur Forrest, associate editor of the *Herald Tribune*. It was my first introduction to the woman who was already becoming a legend in newspaper circles. Lying there in the hospital bed, wearing a candy-striped flannel nightgown against the cold of the room, she looked like a tiny young girl."

The tiny young girl willed her body to heal. She was weak but ready in February when clearance came for her to join the other correspondents quartered in Paris.

The time could not have been more opportune.

Seven

"1 Rue Scribe," Marguerite wrote with a flourish, marveling at the address and what it meant.

She was quartered at the Hotel Scribe. Built in 1863 on a street dedicated to Augustin-Eugene Scribe, a popular writer of comedies and operas, the grand old hotel had been commandeered by the Germans for their press center. Following the liberation of Paris, it had been assigned to American journalists to serve as their headquarters.

Marguerite looked out the frosty window at the intersection of the Rue Scribe and the Boulevard des Capucines below her. Bare-branched trees lined the once-fashionable streets darkened now by severe fuel shortages. The night was dark, crisp, and incredibly cold. Snow blanketed the mansard roofs opposite her. Downstairs the lobby was as clamorous and bustling as a railway station, its floor littered with mud-caked typewriters, bedrolls, and helmets waiting to be claimed by correspondents going to or coming from the front.

"I, war correspondent Higgins, am a colleague of war correspondent Ernest Hemingway. How about that?" Marguerite looked at the words just inscribed in her journal, her emotions a mixture of disbelief, awe, and anxiety.

Earlier in the evening she had met and spoken to her idol in the correspondents' mess. "How was London?" he had asked.

"Lousy," she replied, scarcely able to believe that she was conversing with the author of so many of her favorite novels. "I got jaundice."

"Bad case?"

Marguerite sighed with feigned exasperation. "I'm on a no drinking routine." Although unable to tell the difference between scotch and bourbon she hoped to convey the proper degree of sophistication. Hemingway nodded sympathetically before drifting off to another conversation.

Checking into the Hotel Scribe as a fully accredited war correspondent, Marguerite had barely had time to savor the scene—big-name journalists who were crowding the lobby, swapping stories and more importantly accepting her as a colleague—before she was taken aside by Russell Hill, another *Herald* reporter.

Hill was also a hero of hers. Only two years older than she, he was considered a prodigy among war correspondents. Hill's narrow escapes had become legendary. During the German invasion of the Balkans, he somehow obtained a small boat and fled to Greece only moments before the final takeover. From there he covered the fall of Greece, the North African campaign, and the cross-Channel invasion. Shortly after reaching the German front the jeep he had been sharing with the *New Yorker* correspondent David Lardner hit a land mine. It was the twenty-three-year-old Lardner's first day in the combat zone and his last. He had been killed instantly. Russell Hill had only recently been released from the hospital.

This handsome young man with his blond hair, fine manners, and sensitive face was watching Marguerite with a mixture of eagerness and concern. "You don't know how lucky it is for the paper that the weather finally cleared and they got you over here," he surprised her by saying.

Dazed, Marguerite listened as he chronicled the misfortunes that had depleted the Paris bureau. "And that means," Hill concluded at last, "that I'll have to take over the lead military stories while you do everything else."

Everything else turned out to be all other international stories, with an emphasis on French politics. It was, she later acknowledged, an example of the sink-or-swim school of journalism. Marguerite was totally on her own for the first time, with no one to assign stories or catch errors. Hard work under the tutelage of John Watson and the others who made the *Herald Tribune* one of the most respected papers in the world paid off. The instinct and drive that distinguished Marguerite as a superb city-room reporter surfaced. This time her arena was the central area of an entire continent at war.

The French, she found, were angry and grumbling. The casualty list mounted as the war dragged on while two-and-a-half million French men and women remained in German prisons.

During the occupation Parisians had lost an average of forty pounds of weight. The tuberculosis rate had risen twenty percent. A continuing scarcity of soap brought on a frightful crop of skin diseases that still persisted. Hospitals abounded with cases of influenza and pneumonia.

One of the coldest winters in history had coincided with acute food and fuel shortages. Huge blocks of ice had choked the canals, preventing the flow of supplies, and a shortage of spare parts and tires had halted trucks. When Marguerite arrived the city was without electricity until 5:00 P.M. each day. Factories were unable to run during daylight hours, which caused the unemployment rate to soar.

Hungry Frenchmen complained that fresh fruit and vegetables did not exist. Eggs, when obtainable, went for about twenty-four dollars a dozen. Milk was very scarce. Butter, if it could be found, sold for about eight dollars a pound. The fine French wines, which were great favorites of the Germans, had disappeared. A riot broke out in a motion picture theater when a segment of the film, *Andy Hardy Goes to Town*, showed a huge platter of caviar and cold salmon on the screen. The police were called in to restore order and the upcoming film, *The Private Life of King Henry VIII*—showing great roasts of beef and other food—was quickly canceled. Weary, ill, and discouraged, many of the French declared that they had been better off during the German occupation.

Marguerite quickly discovered that the near-famine conditions had expanded the black market to outrageous proportions involving thousands of those in the service. The rationale, she found, was not unlike that of Prohibition. Selling readily available American goods to the hungry French at a comfortable profit was technically wrong; yet the degree of immorality involved was open to question. Black market dealing was also insidious: Many young soldiers sold a package of cigarettes, then went on to a carton and finally cases. Eventually the situation was so rampant that a massive sweep by the military authorities uncovered two hundred scapegoats, who were sentenced to forty or fifty years of hard labor in a dramatic effort to discourage others.

The stunning severity of the action provoked a storm of protest from the French. One elderly woman wrote to *Combat*, a leading Paris daily: "We owe them our freedom. We shall never forget that the Americans are our friends. Can we not start a campaign for leniency for these men?" Another letter stated, "I have been distressed by the harsh punishment inflicted upon these young soldiers who have come so far to lose perhaps their lives at the age of only twenty years."

Marguerite covered this controversial story and countless others. General Charles de Gaulle had assumed the reins of the provisional government and was already making waves. Stung by his exclusion from the "Big Three" conference attended by Roosevelt, Churchill, and Stalin, he refused a special invitation to meet with President Roosevelt. For the most part Marguerite found the French people critical of his action. "France cannot afford to play the role of grand coquette on the stage of international diplomacy," one political strategist frankly told her.

Marguerite attended General Eisenhower's daily press conferences held at the Scribe. She covered the trials of collaborators and was present when Admiral Jean Pierre Esteva was found guilty of high treason and sentenced to life imprisonment, national degradation, loss of military rank, and confiscation of property. Her fingers numb from cold in the unheated courtroom, she wrote of how many had cried at the plight of the deaf old man who claimed that he had complied with the enemy merely to prevent deadly reprisals against French men, women, and children.

Covering these events Marguerite was thrown into direct competition with reporters who had had months to build contacts. Where they had a network established to keep them apprised of significant developments, she had to work from scratch. To compete she read twice as much background material and asked three times as many questions. During those early days in Paris, Marguerite sought out every major official from foreign minister on down (finding them working in their overcoats to fend off the cold). She cultivated embassy sources and interviewed top military officers. She worked every night, filing as many as three thousand words daily with at least one dispatch headed for each day's front page.

While in Paris Marguerite and Stanley met a last time to discuss their failed marriage. They considered a French divorce, but the idea was discarded for being too complicated. They decided that whoever returned first to the United States would get an uncontested divorce.

A happier meeting for Marguerite was a reunion with her father, who was now a major serving with the Office of Strategic Services. Arriving unexpectedly in Paris, Larry brought news of members of the French side of their family whom he had encountered en route. Marguerite's young cousin Jacques had been a leader of the Maquis, the French underground guerrilla forces, and was now fighting at the front. All her relatives had survived the occupation with the exception of Jacques's mother, her Aunt Genevieve, who had died on her farm after the Germans had refused to give her medical aid.

In addition to her *Herald* work, Marguerite was also writing a series of articles for *Mademoiselle*. Reporting on the fashion scene, Marguerite observed that a handkerchief cost from three to five dollars and a black silk slip one hundred dollars.

The only industry currently flourishing was that of haute couture. The government, recognizing the important place that fashion played in the nation's economy, had seen to it that the houses had been allotted all necessary materials, thus keeping alive France's reputation as a world fashion leader while providing employment to vast numbers.

Discussing the rash of fashion shows, Marguerite wrote for *Mademoiselle* readers, "Most of the fashion writers agreed that the openings showed Paris dressmakers in the full flowering of their great art. It was displayed in the handwork on a skirt, in unusual drapery, in amazing puffed sleeves turning an average coat into a masterpiece and in the craftsman's eye for the right color and texture."

Rushing to and from the fashion houses of Lucien Lelong, Paquin, Molyneaux, and Jean Patou, Marguerite became acquainted with Judy Barden, a correspondent for the *New York Sun*. Much to her chagrin, Judy had been ordered back from the front to cover the fashion shows, which were considered to have international significance.

Judy recalled Marguerite as being very pink and white and pretty. "She had a squeaky little girl voice and was very feminine. When I thought of what was going on at the front, I thought, 'Oh, dear, she won't last a day!' Well, she maintained the little girl voice but outlasted everyone."

Marguerite was charmed by the slightly older woman's wry good humor, savvy, and sophistication and listened enviously to her stories of war reporting. A warm friendship developed that left Marguerite all the more frustrated when the fashion showings were finally over and Judy was allowed to return to Germany.

As the weeks passed and Marguerite's network of contacts became established, her hard work paid off in exclusive stories with international reverberations. The attention was gratifying but fell far short of the front-line action she desired. While Allied troops massed along the

Rhine, Marguerite felt herself trapped in Paris. She would never see the fighting or have an opportunity to report on it.

Then, just as the great river was crossed, the Eighth Army Air Force announced that it was going to fly two jeeps and a half-dozen journalists to look at the areas inside Germany that had been heavily bombed. New reinforcements for the *Herald*'s Paris bureau had arrived. It was now or never if Marguerite was to cover the war.

The official word was no. Geoffrey Parsons, editor of the reestablished Paris edition of the *Herald Tribune* and Marguerite's boss, had assigned himself to the story. A correspondent since 1940, Parsons had been stuck with diplomatic stories or handling releases from military headquarters far from the battle lines. "I've never yet heard the sound of a bullet fired in anger," he explained ruefully. Parsons was determined to seize for himself this last opportunity to see the war firsthand. Marguerite could not dissuade him.

The night before the press junket was to begin was a sad one for Marguerite. After a drink or two of the sickly pale vin rosé—all that remained from the German invasion—she and Russell Hill left the Scribe bar and returned to their office to finish some late news releases. At 11:00 P.M. the call came. It was Geoffrey Parsons. A crisis had developed on the Paris edition of the *Herald*.

"Do you still want to go?" he asked her wearily.

Early the next morning Marguerite was aboard the plane. It was March 1945 and she was on her way to war.

Eight

Dodging bomb craters the two-motored C-47 carrying Marguerite and the other correspondents landed at Darmstadt. Jeeps and journalists were unloaded and headed toward the battle zone. Marguerite, like the other writers, traveled light, with only a typewriter, a sleeping bag, and a few extra clothes.

Her stories bore the datelines WITH THE 7TH ARMY or ON THE ROAD TO MUNICH. It appeared that the ambition of a lifetime had been realized. She smiled happily to herself, remembering those who had sought to bar her way, or worse yet, laughed at her dreams. If they could see her now!

Those early sensations of triumph, though, were fleeting. The havoc, the desolation, and the despair she saw around her were overwhelming —a shocking contrast to the World War I adventures described by her father. Larry's tales of glory had done nothing to prepare her for the mosaic of misery waiting as she advanced toward the battle zone and saw the first crumpled bodies of dead soldiers, both Allied and Nazi.

More shocking were the wounded, many her own age or younger. Some were blinded, others cruelly disfigured. Not all the injuries had been inflicted by gunfire. The winter, unusually severe, had taken its toll as well, and the spring thaw revealed still more motionless forms. Many people had lost hands or feet to frostbite.

Searching the weary, bitter faces of the men marching beside her, Marguerite wondered if anything could restore the youth and idealism that had been the birthright of these young victims. She recognized one reason why her father's war had been so different: When not flying, he had been quartered in the comparative luxury of barracks, not in muddy foxholes. Memory was a selective thing, distilling out the exhaustion, the pain, and the boredom. She realized too, that airfields are much closer than trenches to where the women are; so much for the glamour of war.

The reality of war brought fresh horror. The Nazi high command, in a frantic attempt to stabilize the western front, was throwing in every available male who could fight. Many German soldiers had destroyed their artillery prior to surrender. Replacements without weapons were ordered to the front with instructions to find implements on the battlefield. Thus the weary, plodding GIs were now matched against the Hitler Youth, boys in their midteens with no combat training and frequently no guns. Marguerite saw their corpses, faces frozen in expressions of surprise and terror.

Reaching Frankfurt, she viewed the rubble and the grotesquely twisted steel girders that were all that remained of the vast airplane propeller and component parts factories, the armored vehicle plants, and the marshaling yards that had once made the ruined city a priority target for the Allied air forces.

Appalled at the awesome destruction, Marguerite toured the former cultural and industrial center by jeep, struggling to recall the Old World city as it had once been. Marble columns and bronze statues had been pulverized. The carcasses of proud planes were twisted into weird shapes.

Among the obscene contortions of the devastated city former slave laborers walked dazedly, many unable to believe that—for them at least—the war was over. The sudden sweep of the American army had liberated more than forty thousand Polish, Russian, and French workers. A majority of these had taken to the woods following the original instructions dropped in leaflets from Allied planes and were now streaming back into the city. Many returned to the factories where they had once been slaves simply because they had no idea of what else to do.

Wading through the rubble, Marguerite approached a scarecrowlike figure huddled against a wall that had been formed by piles of cleared debris. Venturing a few words in French, she was delighted to see his expression of weary bewilderment change to one of hope. It developed that the man had been a prisoner in a Frankfurt munitions plant since 1940. "What shall we do? Where shall we go?" he asked her. Then haltingly he asked, "Do they still remember us at home?"

This man and others were aided by Marguerite's ability to provide practical information and encouragement in a language they could understand. Many others were not so fortunate. The occupying army—with not a single liaison officer from the French, Russian, or other governments to assist in handling their various nationals—and a staff of only twenty to deal with the administration of a city of 150,000 nonetheless had managed to set up a displaced persons center. Informing the foreign laborers of its existence proved a greater obstacle. Many were desperately hungry and had begun to loot the food supplies and wine cellars of the Germans.

Maintaining order posed unexpected problems. Marguerite overheard an officer being instructed to send a detachment to guard a German food store. "Wouldn't you rather see the ex-slaves get the food than their German masters?" she asked him privately.

"Hell, yes!" he replied.

Somehow the order was "lost."

The docility and often embarrassing eagerness to cooperate that characterized the defeated Germans proved a far cry from the twilight of the gods envisioned by Hitler. The mandate that the German people fight gloriously to the death in the grand Wagnerian tradition had met with little if any local enthusiasm. The people of Frankfurt assumed a surprisingly pragmatic stance. For them, the war was over. It was business as usual.

On one occasion Marguerite was sitting in the newly established military headquarters when a German policeman appeared, insisting vehemently that he had never been a Nazi. The man reported that nine explosive charges had been left in buildings along the river. He offered to lead a party of other Germans to the area to defuse the charges if permission for the mission was granted. It was and he did.

With Frankfurt settling into some semblance of order, Marguerite was eager to move eastward where the final battle was still being waged. Hitchhiking on a cargo plane carrying barrels of gasoline to General George Patton's rapidly advancing tank division, she landed at the Weimar air strip. There Marguerite was able to persuade a Third Army jeep driver to take her to nearby Buchenwald.

She reached the concentration camp only hours after it had been liberated by Patton's Third Army. It was a crisp April morning. The promise of a verdant, blooming spring contrasted with the monotony of naked walls protruding awkwardly against a bright blue sky. Approaching the camp with an air of skepticism, she was determined not to be influenced by the macabre rumors currently making the rounds. Atrocity stories were part of every country's propaganda machine. Equally gruesome tales had been circulated during World War I when the Huns had been accused of cutting off the hands of Belgian babies. That frightfully graphic story had been deliberately planted to incite soldiers and civilians alike, only to be exposed after the war as fabrication.

Thinking that the camps' reputations were part of a propaganda campaign, Marguerite interrogated the wretched inmates relentlessly. As she meticulously collected names of victims and guards and dates and details of mass executions, it became apparent that the horror tales she had heard previously had not begun to approximate the magnitude of the actual crimes committed at Buchenwald. Sick with shame, she realized how insensitive she had been to the first prisoners she interviewed.

Marguerite was shown the oven room, where she talked with survivors who had seen guards actually force victims to enter. Beyond she saw the rigid bodies of thousands of prisoners who had been murdered in the last days. "Bodies had spilled out of trucks and carts," she wrote. "Others were piled in corners or propped against buildings. They had been left without clothes or other covering to mask the attitudes that told of the agony of their passing. As if to emphasize the horror, the frosty spring nights had frozen into ghastly stalactites the trickles of blood and yellow bubbles of mucus that oozed from the eyes and noses of the many who had been bludgeoned or otherwise tortured to death."

To cope with the situation it was necessary for Marguerite to compartmentalize her mind. Her moral outrage, disgust, and physical revulsion had to be placed on hold. Like a surgeon, she forced herself to perform her job with rapid precision. An early deadline and the tremendous importance of the story required that she gather the most pertinent facts in the shortest possible time. All her energies were concentrated upon the mechanics of that task.

Later she accompanied a group of Germans ordered to Buchenwald by the American military, who hoped to instill in them a belated sense of responsibility for the atrocities committed only a few miles from their homes. Marguerite's account of the grim confrontation ran as an editorial in *Stars and Stripes* on April 20. It read:

> The German citizens of Weimar, weeping and protesting the horror of the sight, were led today by American military government officials through the panorama of sadism and mass torture that had made the giant

Buchenwald concentration camp the most demonic of the various prisons yet liberated by the Allied armies.

The men and women were marched past heaps of stiff and naked bodies of people who through starvation, beatings, and torture had died in such great numbers that the Gestapo had not had the opportunity to dispose of them before the American conquest of the camp. At the crematorium where some 200 prisoners were disposed of daily, several women fainted at the sight of half-burnt humans still in the oven. Others attempted to put their hands over their eyes. But one of the government officials immediately stepped forward and ordered them to look, saying: "You must find the courage to face things for which you are responsible."

The military government put on a graphic demonstration for the 1000-odd townspeople who were the vanguard of others to follow on successive days. They were taken to a separate "small camp" where about 200 men had been starved and beaten to a point where they lay dying. The men were so emaciated and weak that most of them could not raise their voices above a whisper. Under the Nazis they lived in unimaginable filth and were virtually without care. The odor of excrement, vomit, and the smell of death still lay heavy over the camp. Two of the men died this afternoon, quietly and without a second glance from their desperately ill companions.

A demonstration was also given of how the Gestapo forced the prisoners themselves to hang their comrades. A prisoner dressed in a Gestapo uniform told how the thick club he carried had been used to prod on those prisoners reluctant to bring about the death of their compatriots.

The Germans left the camp in a solemn mood and with obvious relief. Throughout the tour, there had been a certain nervousness among them, apparently inspired by the belief that the military government might have had sinister designs in bringing them to the camp.

Marguerite's own emotions were mixed. The shame and anguish she read on the faces of the observers evoked a reluctant sympathy, yet she had only to look again at the rotting corpses about her to feel a wave of rage at those who had stood mutely by in the midst of such torment.

She later returned to Buchenwald to attend a ceremony presented by the inmates in memory of the 55,000 men, women, and children who had been slaughtered by the Nazis. Row after row of newly liberated men and women still wearing their black-and-white striped uniforms stood at attention. Each carried a handmade replica of his or her nation's flag. Among the Polish, French, Rumanian, Hungarian, Yugoslavian, Greek, Italian, and Russian emblems flew the German flag, a reminder that some German citizens had been the first to fight the Nazi system.

Marguerite's attention was caught by a young GI who approached the correspondents excitedly. "If you press people want to see something, follow me," he urged. He led them to a remote cell block where some twenty-five GIs were mercilessly beating six German soliders who had been found hiding in a nearby forest. A young lieutenant appeared and quickly put an end to the sporting event. As it turned out the soldier-victims had been members of the Hitler Youth, drafted just four days before. They ranged in age from fourteen to seventeen.

The incident made a profound impression on Marguerite, contributing to the development of a political philosophy that was rapidly crystallizing. The impact of the scene struck her as if she, too, had been brutalized. The youth of the boys and their lack of guilt was immaterial. What mattered to her was that the GIs had been guilty of the same wanton cruelty and the same inhumanity for which she had so recently condemned the Nazis.

She began to analyze the grim drama that had just taken place. The difference between the impulsive violence of the GIs and the calculated carnage of the Nazis was one of degree. The travesty of justice had been halted because of a system that decreed that no one could be condemned without a hearing. The democracy that spawned such a system recognized the inherent brutality in both nations and individuals. It differed from a totalitarian police state by accepting the need for vigilance and self-criticism and reinforcing them by maintaining a system of checks and balances. A series of such episodes and the resulting insights followed swiftly upon one another for the twenty-four-year-old Marguerite. She humorously dubbed her conclusions "the Higgins theory of human relativity." Their main tenet was the concept that the true marks of progress are the mistakes later corrected, the defeats outweighed by victories.

A correspondent is nothing without mobility. When Sergeant Peter Furst of *Stars and Stripes* offered to share his jeep with her, Marguerite gratefully accepted. It was the beginning of a great working partnership, not only professionally advantageous but personally rewarding.

Although surrounded by men, Marguerite was often lonely; her extraordinary good looks were at times more a liability than an asset. An outrageous flirt at parties, she was at first surprised to find herself barred from the male camaraderie of the other correspondents. A woman with talent and nerve was a challenge to their masculinity as well as to their journalistic skill. Once colleagues discovered that behind the pretty blonde facade lurked a relentless competitor, they did not know how to handle her.

Peter Furst didn't feel this threat. Born in the Rhineland, he had fled with his parents when Hitler began his persecution of Jews. Feelings of highly personal involvement and a strong survivor instinct gave him a cutting edge that transcended the macho fantasies of the other reporters. Marguerite's soft voice and gentle manner belied a dogged determination that matched his own. Peter admired her brain, was amused by her enthusiasm, and respected her courage.

At another time the relationship might have developed into something more. As it was, each was too involved with war to consider romance. Only a few years older than she but vastly more experienced, Peter had a reckless streak that excited as well as challenged Marguerite. It never occurred to her to wonder at his daredevil exploits, much less to attempt to curb them for her own protection. She went everywhere that Peter went.

Once the two took a shortcut through enemy territory and actually found themselves staging a one-jeep liberation of six German villages. Fortunately for them the Germans, who were cut off from communications and any type of assistance, were anxious to end their ordeal of fear and uncertainty. Peter and Marguerite were in obviously American uniforms and spoke fluent German. That was enough for the war-weary citizens.

Heading toward the battle zone, Marguerite and Peter found the roads choked with endless columns moving in both directions. The advancing armies marched relentlessly eastward while spontaneously formed lines consisting mostly of French men and women—former prisoners, many of whom had not seen their homeland in five years—pushed west. Smiling happily and shouting to the jeeps that passed them, the French affected a semimilitary formation, marching proudly four abreast in columns sometimes twenty deep.

In Lichtenfels, Marguerite filed one of the most bizarre stories to come out of World War II. On April 24, 1945, her by-line report appeared on the front page of the *Herald Tribune*. The secret correspondence of Dr. Alfred Rosenberg, the chief political philosopher and formulator of Nazi racial theory, had been discovered in a cellar five stories below the sixteenth-century Lichtenfels Castle.

The highly incriminating documents, some dating back to the early 1920s, had been turned over to the Americans by Rosenberg's right-hand man, Baron Kurt von Behr. The baron had approached the American military with a surprising offer. In exchange for leaving some space in the castle for himself and his wife (the historic residence had been taken over by the Allies), he would reveal the hiding place of Rosenberg's grand plan for world political domination.

The deal was made. The documents were found sealed in a giant vault in a subterranean cellar. The baron and his wife were granted the right to occupy a room in their castle. The bizarre episode closed when the couple was found dead in the luxurious room. They had taken poison, washing it down with an excellent French champagne.

Marguerite's career as a World War II combat correspondent may have been brief (about six weeks) but no one could say that it was without drama. Only the most envious would suggest that it was without great personal heroism.

The first journalistic award in her career came as a result of her unintended participation in the liberation of the concentration camp of Dachau. At the time when American troops were converging on it Marguerite and Peter were separated from the infamous prison by some eleven kilometers, in an area as yet to be secured by Allied forces.

Hoping to be the first reporters to reach the camp, they debated the risk. The Gestapo had fled its headquarters in Aschaffenburg, only a few miles away, but the German commander had ordered the entire village—mostly women, children, old people—to defend their town house by house. "We must offer complete sacrifice to the Fuehrer," the major had ordered. "Not a single inhabitant can be excused from combat. Sitting down is absolutely forbidden. Sleeping more than three hours a night is hereby forbidden. Our mission is to send the largest number of Americans to the devil."

Sixteen hundred twenty people had died in the bitter battle. Marguerite and Peter had little desire to meet the devil in a similar fashion; they had been lucky thus far.

Smiling grimly at one another as they loaded their supplies into the jeep, they headed east. The sight of a village strewn with white flags was encouraging. "Still," Marguerite wrote later, "it seemed mighty lonely as our vehicle drove past group after group of Wehrmacht soldiers bearing rifles, pistols and grenades." Fortunately the bedraggled infantrymen were ready to surrender. Marguerite and Peter took the weapons offered by the Germans until their jeep could hold no more.

Finally they instructed the soldiers to keep marching west until they found someone else to accept their surrender.

"The drive was uncomfortable for me because I thoroughly disliked having loaded weapons around," Marguerite admitted later. "I was especially uneasy about the German grenades clunking about in the back of the jeep."

Reaching the tidy, well-preserved little town of Dachau, they found the shuttered windows hung with white sheets in the now familiar signal of surrender. The citizens were friendly and appeared eager to be informative. Two American divisions were still fighting SS men on the northern outskirts of the concentration camp, they told Marguerite and Pete, who exchanged disappointed glances. They had expected to find the camp newly liberated. Then another German volunteered more information. He had seen white flags flying on the southern edges of the large camp area where the main administration buildings were located. Once again the couple decided to take a chance. Marguerite and Peter would detour around the fighting and head for the administration buildings.

As they drove on they became aware of a strange smell, at first almost sweet and cloying, then heavy with decay. As they approached a string of boxcars, a scene of unbelievable horror confronted them. Looking at the cars parked before a large archway topped with a Nazi eagle, Marguerite felt herself convulse with nausea.

The boxcars were filled with rotting corpses. Forcing herself to look at the hideously emaciated bodies, Marguerite realized that none of them could have weighed more than sixty or seventy pounds. They had been forced on the trains in Buchenwald by captors who had been sure they would die of starvation if not suffocation. The captors had been wrong. Some had survived. Some had actually lived through this hell and reached Dachau alive. Some had walked or crawled out of the cars. Perhaps others had been dragged out and then shot. Compelling herself to look at the grisly spectacle before her, Marguerite realized that it was the lucky ones who had been shot. The remainder had had their brains beaten out. Staring at the mangled corpses, she had to turn away to be sick.

In the meantime Marguerite and Peter had been joined by two jeeps from the Forty-second Infantry, which followed them to the main gate where an SS general stood holding a large white flag. Beside him was a German civilian who claimed to be a member of the Red Cross. Trying to speak calmly, Marguerite explained to them that the American officers in the jeeps behind them would accept their surrender. She and Peter were anxious to get to the barbed wire enclosure where the prisoners were confined.

Peter, suspecting the fence to be electrically charged, asked the general to assign an SS officer to escort them to the enclosure and open its gate. The man hesitated, not sure whether the watchtower guards stationed above the enclosure were ready to surrender. Possibly, they, like the citizens of Aschaffenburg, were proposing to fight to the death.

Marguerite and Peter looked at one another and shrugged. There was only one way to find out. The trembling SS officer had no choice. He was ordered by his commander to accompany them. The three drove on toward the watchtower area where Peter braked the jeep, suggesting they go the rest of the distance on foot. Marguerite agreed. Recalling all the grenades in the back, she hopped out and ran toward the gate. Beyond it she could see a broad courtyard, a pretty affair with trim walkways and beds of roses just coming into bloom.

Peter's voice put an abrupt end to her walk. "Come back!" he shouted.

She turned, glancing in the direction of his pointing arm. Right above her the watchtower was crammed with men, their rifles and machine guns trained on her.

In that awful moment Marguerite could see no point in running. Escape was impossible. Taking a deep breath and hoping her voice wouldn't crack, she called out, "*Kommen Sie her, bitte. Wir sind Amerikaner.*" (Come here, please. We are American.)

Twenty-two guards walked out with their hands in the air. Marguerite and Peter coolly accepted their surrender, ordering one of them to open the gate to the internment camp. With the watchtower seemingly secured, Peter shoved the SS officer onto the hood of the jeep, cocked one of their newly acquired pistols and handed it to Marguerite, and then shoved the jeep into gear.

The three proceeded without incident into the enclosure containing the prisoners, who exploded out of their barracks screaming with joy. The first to reach them flung his arms around Peter in a bear hug that lifted him off the ground. Then he did the same to Marguerite.

Nerin E. Gun, an inmate, described the scene. "A Polish priest who happened to be in the front row threw his arms around the neck of one of the liberating officers, kissing effusively. The object of his intense gratitude submitted without resistance, then stepped back. A helmet was removed freeing golden locks and revealing a pert young face. The officer was a woman—a woman war correspondent. The priest was most uncomfortable, but the newspaper woman seemed used to such mistakes.''

His confusion was not surprising. Marguerite was clad in a fur-lined helmet with ear flaps, fatigue pants and shirt, and a bulky fur-lined German Army jacket that she had ''liberated'' from a warehouse in Weimar.

"Mon Dieu! Mon Dieu! C'est une femme! Pardon Madame!" the priest shouted to Marguerite and to the throngs of prisoners surging about them. The scene was one of joyous pandemonium. In his dispatch to *Stars and Stripes*, Peter told how Marguerite, speaking in French, English, and German, announced to the captives that they were free. The prisoners crowded about her with tears streaming down their worn, bearded faces. They limped, ran, and crawled toward her in a state of hysterical frenzy, their excitement producing unaccustomed strength. Virtual skeletons grabbed Marguerite, joyfully lifting and sometimes tossing her from one to another to parade with her on their shoulders. Each of the thirty thousand inmates seemed determined to personally embrace her.

As the officers and men of the Forty-second and Forty-fifth Divisions began to stream into the encampment some of the attention shifted from Marguerite and she was able to get on to her story. While she stood in the midst of a crush of former prisoners all speaking at once, an American officer reached through the grillwork of the main gate, grabbing her by the collar. ''What the hell are you doing in there?'' he demanded to know. ''Don't you realize the place is raging with typhus? Get out of there!''

Marguerite was at first baffled and then furious. Her body, already battered from the enthusiastic greetings of the prisoners, was now being buffeted against the gate. For a moment she looked back at him in pain and astonishment and then she shouted. All the fear, the anguish, the intense emotions of the past hours erupted into rage. ''Goddammit to hell! I've had my typhus shots! Lay off me! I'm doing my job!''

The officer reluctantly released her and Marguerite continued with her work.

Marguerite as well as Peter was able to assist the occupying forces. When the prisoners were told that they would have to be screened for typhus before being allowed to leave the camp, rioting broke out. In the midst of the melee, Marguerite and Peter remembered the electric current running through the barbed wire. While Marguerite attempted to calm the mob over the loudspeaker, explaining in three languages the danger of electrocution, Peter frantically searched the camp for a technician who could turn off the master switch. Tragically, despite Marguerite's warnings, six prisoners flung themselves against the fence in suicidal protest.

Marguerite Higgins received the army campaign ribbon for outstanding service with the armed forces under difficult conditions for her participation in the liberation of Dachau and the New York Newspaper Women's Club award for the best foreign correspondence in 1945.

"It was one of the most terrible and wonderful days of the war," Marguerite wrote of the Dachau liberation. "It was the first and the worst concentration camp in Germany."

From a professional standpoint it was also a day of total frustration. Long before departing from Dachau, she possessed enough material to write a prime story. Yet, when Peter urged her to wind it up, Marguerite protested, "Let's check just one more fact." Consequently when at last they drove away from the camp, the road was blocked by convoys. At midnight, when the RCA transmitter closed down, they were miles from the press center. It would be sixteen hours before her deadline rolled around again. Marguerite and Peter were left with the exclusive of a lifetime and no place to file it. Pulling off the road, they attempted to sleep despite the flashing lights and shifting gears of trucks roaring by.

The next day neither Marguerite nor Peter could resist taking a slight detour to Munich to cover the liberation of the fabled Bavarian capital, which was also the birthplace of Naziism. Marguerite succeeded in getting back to central communications in Weimar but had little time to polish either story. As she sat with a mug of coffee held in two very weary hands, a blaring German radio broadcast penetrated her numbed senses. "*Hitler ist todt! Hitler ist todt!*" The death of Hitler signaled the end of the war.

The following day the *Herald Tribune* carried two exclusive front-page stories datelined April 29 (delayed) and April 30, both by-lined to Marguerite Higgins. They told of the liberation of Dachau and Munich. That same day Peter Furst was transferred to Italy. Although the two reporters exchanged letters and then Christmas cards for years, they were not fated to meet again.

On May 8, the night of Germany's total surrender, Marguerite had joined General O'Daniel's Third Division, whose headquarters was the former castle of the Nazi foreign minister, Joachim von Ribbentrop. In this mountain retreat where von Ribbentrop had once feted guests and tortured victims, a grand party had been arranged.

At exactly one minute after midnight, officers and correspondents moved out onto the massive balcony that commanded a view of the vast alpine valley. A signal was given and artillery blazed, red and blue flares ripping across the black velvet sky while antiaircraft and tank guns roared and tracer bullets streamed cleanly through the night. The heights and depths of Berchtesgaden roared and shook as wave after wave brilliantly exploded.

Marguerite withdrew slightly from the others, tears stinging her eyes. The war was over and with it a part of herself. The romantic, dreaming girl was gone forever. In her place was a woman who had been to war and back and then sat down and written home about it. What next? Marguerite wondered. She had come to Europe expecting war.

What she did not anticipate was love.

Nine

Marguerite Higgins lost her spiritual virginity in the spring of 1945.

At twenty-four, she had known many men and married one. But never had she given completely of herself; never had she needed anyone so intensely that it was more painful to be without him than it was to be together, regardless of how soul wrenching their nearness might be. Never had she experienced what she called enchantment.

The romance between Marguerite and the talented, heroic war correspondent George Reid Millar began, appropriately enough, in a Bavarian castle. The legendary exploits of "Golden" Millar had not yet reached Marguerite on that warm, sunny May afternoon when the English journalist strode into a press conference held in the former palace of the German foreign minister, Joachim von Ribbentrop. Unaware that his knee-length shorts and open-collared, short-sleeved shirt were regulation summer British army gear, she thought him eccentric. She also considered him the most beautiful man she had ever met, tall, blonde, with an air of delicacy that belied his strength.

Marguerite was not the first to be impressed, puzzled, and dazzled by the Millar mystique. In his book, *Not So Wild a Dream,* the journalist Eric Sevareid found himself subordinating the arrival of the Allied forces at Besançon to his own reunion with Millar.

> After his [Millar's] disappearance from the Western desert into captivity I had almost come to regard him as one who was dead. Here suddenly he was, striding toward me more radiantly alive than ever, his incredibly beautiful face blooming like that of a young girl in love.
>
> He was dressed immaculately in the uniform of a British captain, his square shoulders squarer and more solid than before, and his bearing, his

whole being, conveyed an impression of personal triumph and happy self-mastery. He gave an air of elegance to any type of clothing and when he was dressed as he was now no one would have suspected, nor did I know till later, that just a few hours before he and an American captain had been surrounded in a forest while the Germans searched for them. They had lain for two days in the dripping wood, scarcely daring to stretch a muscle for fear of cracking a twig. In the end they had crept to a road, mounted a motorcycle and driven at top speed through a party of Germans who were preparing a bridge for demolition. By the time the startled enemy was able to bring a machine gun to bear in their direction they were around the bend.

This was one story among many told about Millar. After the fall of France, he had abandoned a highly successful career as a London journalist to enlist in the Rifle Brigade. Captured in North Africa and imprisoned in Germany, he made a daring escape, getting across occupied France. Returning at last to England, Millar was trained as a commando and parachuted back into France to work with the Resistance forces sabotaging German communications. As the war drew to a close, he returned to reporting for the *London Daily Express* and was assigned to Germany.

Besides being a bona fide hero and devastatingly good-looking, Millar was an English aristocrat, the product of privileged schools and exposure to what was then called the international set. Initially Marguerite was intrigued by his knowledge of wines and cheeses, his prowess at fox hunting, and his ability to fly a plane. Soon she was enthralled. Who in Oakland or even New York had ever thought of taking a donkey trip through the mountains of northern Spain, traveling from monastery to monastery—much less done it? Now Millar was talking of sailing south through the canals of France to the Mediterranean. Marguerite longed to accompany him.

The bad parts of Millar's character were not immediately apparent to her. Brave though he may have been, George was also a bigot. Unfortunately for Marguerite, his prejudice centered on Americans. Many of the British must have felt similar resentment toward the rich new nation that had suddenly assumed leadership of a world England had ruled for so long. For most, the animosity remained in the abstract; with Millar, it was personal and direct. "Why are you Americans so instinctively vulgar?" he would demand of Marguerite when an American observed at a bar or a restaurant offended his sensibilities.

Jim O'Donnell, the author and former *Newsweek* correspondent, recalled Millar's open hostility. "For a time during the war I was on detached service to the British and wore their uniform. One evening shortly after the war ended I was having a drink at Harry's Bar in Paris. George approached me and said with that condescending arrogance that only a Brit can affect, 'I suppose it's asking too much of an American to know, but that's actually a regimental tie that you're wearing.'

"I nodded to him. 'I realize that, but we weren't allowed to wear them during the D-Day invasion. That's why this one was sent to me today.'

"It wasn't an unusual experience. Many Americans had similar encounters with Englishmen who were instinctively resentful. What made this one unique was that George didn't have the grace—or the guts—to acknowledge that he was wrong."

Love is notoriously shortsighted. Marguerite's considerable charms outweighed the disadvantage of her nationality. George would attempt to overlook it; she would hope to convert him. In the meantime there was the romance and the adventure of a great love affair that Marguerite innocently assumed would conquer all obstacles.

Quests for stories took Marguerite and George through the pine-scented mountains and quaint valleys of Austria and Germany. One day they interviewed Emil Jannings, who had starred with Marlene Dietrich in *The Blue Angel*. The actor introduced them to "Turk's Blood" (red wine and champagne), and at midnight they were still singing variations of "Lili Marlene."

While swimming nude in a mountain lake the couple was arrested by military police who thought they were spying on King Leopold of Belgium. For once both had been oblivious to the possibilities of a story—neither was even aware the king was in the vicinity.

Later a series of tips led them to a mountain cabin where Arthur Kannenberg, Hitler's majordomo, was hiding. Marguerite and George were welcomed enthusiastically by the portly, smooth-talking butler who assumed mistakenly that they would intercede for him with the American military. Seated beside his wife, Freda, who had been Hitler's housekeeper, Kannenberg painted a bizarre picture of the man who had tried to conquer the world.

Kannenberg first became acquainted with Hitler in 1931 when the future dictator came to one of his Berlin restaurants. "I recognized him instantly, bowed and called him Fuehrer. Then I served him Wiener schnitzel,'' Kannenberg recalled nostalgically. ''After that the Nazis more or less took over the place. Hitler reserved a little red room upstairs. He always insisted on chairs for himself and twelve others. I think he sort of thought it was like in the Bible with Jesus and the Twelve Apostles.''

The drive from Kannenberg's mountain retreat to Kitzbühel, one of the most popular mountain resorts in Europe, proved equally memorable. George and Marguerite's jeep passed convoy after convoy of German vehicles driven by German soldiers proceeding unaccompanied toward Munich. ''It was truly one of the most remarkable moves in history,'' Marguerite wrote in a *Herald* dispatch. ''The undefeated German First Army was following with docility and discipline the orders of absent Americans, taking full charge of transplanting themselves from Lower Austria to Germany where they would be gathered in assembly centers preparatory to either discharge or internment in prisoner-of-war camps.''

Accompanying the soldiers were women known as SS Helfeinnen (helpers to the SS), blonde, buxom, and sensual in a Nordic way. Marguerite thought they had been selected for their faces and figures rather than their brains. One American major summed it up for her when he said, ''These SS women don't bother much to hide the fact that their main duty is just plain camp following.'' The SS women, wearing pearl gray silk shirts and shorts, occupied a conspicuous place in the convoy, generally riding in the front seats of open convertibles. The rest of the women's army—twenty-five hundred captured in the German First Army alone—had to be content to ride jammed together in the backs of trucks. Unlike the average German soldier who readily answered questions, most of the SS women remained sullenly silent or replied, ''I don't care to answer.''

In an article, ''Voices of the Defeated,'' written for *Mademoiselle*, Marguerite rhapsodized about the beauty of the Austrian countryside. It was idyllic and fantastic. Mountain lakes blue as a forget-me-not lay hidden among the Tyrolean mountains. She and George had gone there to interview Franz Lehár, the Hungarian-born composer of many beloved operas. They were the first people from any Allied country to visit the seventy-five-year-old musician since the war began.

Marguerite found the small, gentle-faced man visibly moved at the sight of them. Framed by the outline of the large window behind him, Lehár played, somewhat haltingly at first but then with increasing assurance, his famous "Merry Widow Waltz." It was the first time he had played in more than two years.

As the old man hummed along to indicate the voice parts of his score, his petite, vivacious wife, Sofia, occasionally interrupted: "Ah, there is the aria that brought crowds to their feet" or "Remember the applause, Franz, that followed that scene."

Lehár turned to face Marguerite and George in the fading light of a rainy afternoon and tears came to his eyes when he saw their nods of approving recognition. "Ah," he said, his voice trembling slightly, "the world has not forgotten me after all."

Pursuit of still another story led Marguerite and George to an isolated farmhouse that had been the hideout of the infamous Nazi Julius Streicher. Streicher, famous for his stance with legs apart, bull neck thrust forward, hands on hips, and whip dangling from his wrist, had been captured only a few days before. Now the reporters' jeep driver followed the only road, a narrow goat trail cut out of the mountain with an almost sheer drop on one side and green hills on the other. At the top they found Streicher's young wife, Adele, whose soft, gentle manner and plump prettiness contrasted with her husband's brutal image.

As Adele Streicher talked of their last days together, when her husband had attempted to pose as an artist, she started to weep. Once the flood of tears began it was difficult for George and Marguerite to leave. Adele clearly adored the man that most of the civilized world regarded as the epitome of bestiality. She insisted upon showing them the watercolors her husband had painted during those final days. The poorly done landscapes were further blotched by Mrs. Streicher's tears.

"When they came for him a thing happened that I shall long remember," she confided. "I asked the American major, who was of a race of which my husband thought ill, if he would leave me the watercolors. With great kindness, he agreed to my request."

When they at last left the farmhouse, the jeep driver commented, "It's too bad that that woman's capacity for devotion had to be so misdirected. In America or England she might have been a happy housewife now. Do you suppose these people would be all right if they just lived in the right country with the right kind of leaders?"

No one answered.

The subject of housewifery was much on Marguerite's mind. Her concept, however, differed somewhat from Adele Streicher's.

She had visions of herself and George roaming the world together, sailing down the Nile and up the Amazon, and climbing the pyramids. They would expose the corrupt and champion the true, always adventuring, and always in love.

In the meantime she and George drove to Paris in Marguerite's newly "liberated" car, a smart sports model, the smallest of a fleet of sleek vehicles that had once belonged to von Ribbentrop. Crossing the border into France, they delighted in the vital expanse of vines and trees sprawling into one another and the gleam of bright red poppies dotting sun-burnished wheat fields.

Paris, the city that had lain somnolent only weeks before, was recovering its vitality as well. Stores were now filled with asparagus, artichokes, and lettuce. Street vendors were hawking cherries, peaches, and plums. The flower market was a riot of color. Elegant restaurants were reopening; fine wines were magically reappearing. The time and the place were made for lovers. Why should it not last forever if one truly loved? Marguerite asked herself the question with increasing frequency.

George took her to meet Madame Lore, a Russian princess who had once hidden him during his flight from the Germans. The gallant old woman was eking out a living by making lampshades. Marguerite listened spellbound as the two talked late into the night about the exciting adventures they had shared in the past.

But it was George's future and her own that interested her most. What was to become of them?

Judy Barden, Marguerite's friend and colleague from the fashion salon openings, reentered her life at this time. Judy recalled Marguerite as being madly in love. British herself, Judy thought George a "lovely, delightful man with a rather droll sense of humor." She remembered, "He loved to go about in big, baggy football shorts and gave Maggie a pair as well. They were miles too big for her but she wore them anyway. They went everywhere together and seemed to be crazy about one another."

George was married but estranged from his wife, who had fallen in love with someone else while he was imprisoned in Germany. Marguerite awaited the finality of her divorce from Stanley. Comparing her feelings for the two men, she realized that the first association had been one of admiration but not love. ''With George I had discovered love and the kind of need for another of which I had not imagined I was capable,'' she was to write in her autobiography some ten years later.

At the moment Marguerite was discovering that love was not always enough. In addition to the continuing and increasingly bitter argument about the respective merits of America and England, the couple suffered from the effect of George's growing boredom with newspaper work. At thirty-five, he had spent too many years writing sensational stories about errant heiresses and continental Lotharios. Now he wanted nothing more than to settle down in a quiet English village where he could write fiction. Marguerite tried desperately to reconcile herself to the idea but could not. The excitement, the challenge, and the allure of deadline and by-line were far too strong.

The relationship continued, radiantly sunny or violently explosive. Paris would be a marvelous place to write books, she urged. Sometimes he agreed; yet his yearning remained. As a soldier and a journalist, George had been a long time away from home. He was ready to return.

''Go then! I don't ever want to see you again,'' Marguerite cried out in the midst of a particularly bitter argument.

He went.

Ten

Absence does indeed make the heart grow fonder but not always in the manner one might anticipate.

George's abrupt departure and the violent arguments that had preceded it left Marguerite emotionally drained. At first she felt a sense of release. Here at last was a breather, space for herself, and time to rearrange the scattered threads of her life. She wrote a series on French politics for the *Herald* and an article on Sartre's existentialism for *Mademoiselle*. There were bull sessions with her *Herald* colleague, Russell Hill, and late-night talks with Judy Barden.

But slowly her enthusiasm faded until it was merely a charade. She desperately missed George. Her initial relief was only a temporary respite for an exhausted spirit. With or without him, her love remained an ever-present condition of her life as the weeks passed.

Then the wire came. George would remain in England. Worse yet, absence had caused *his* heart to grow fonder—of someone else.

Certain that she could make George change his mind, Marguerite flew to London. She was confident of charms that had never failed her before and sure that she could get him back. How could he refuse her, Marguerite reasoned, once he realized that she was ready to make any concession?

"Marguerite returned to Paris totally devastated," Judy Barden recalled. "She had not only confronted George but his new wife, Isabel. Marguerite's complete surprise that this usurper wasn't perfectly willing to step aside would have been amusing if she hadn't been in such obvious pain. Dreams of romantic reunion shattered, she was heartbroken but also indignant. Accustomed to getting her own way, she simply couldn't understand how such a thing could have happened to her."

For a time the cruelly disappointed young woman was tormented by ifs—if George hadn't been determined to make a fetish out of resenting Americans; if she had been more patient and less competitive. She made endless rationalizations and speculations. Most agonizing was the inevitable question: Why had she experienced enchantment only to lose it? Naively Marguerite had believed that a spell once cast would last forever. The death of the dream hurt her more deeply than the loss of the man.

Fortunately there was the pragmatic French side to her character. Marguerite worked harder than she had ever worked before and during the year immediately following the war in Europe is credited with more front-page stories than any other foreign correspondent.

Work, however, did not make a dull girl of Marguerite. There was time to play as well. "Women are like streetcars," she reminded Jim O'Donnell, her good friend and colleague, when he had just received a Dear John letter. (She trusted that the same held true for men.) Both were well aware that a great love didn't come along every ten minutes, yet diversions were easy to find. Didn't everyone know that the easiest way to forget one lover was with another? On a short-term basis the formula worked well enough.

The ambience of the Hotel Scribe was not conducive to celibacy even if Marguerite had been inclined to it. "Immediately following the liberation of Paris, the hotel had been requisitioned for war correspondents," Russell Hill recalled. "Most of the male reporters had women living with them on a more or less steady basis. This had been going on for nearly a year when the first wife arrived. The astonished desk clerk had no idea what to do with her. 'I'm sorry, madame,' he said at last, 'wives are not permitted here.'

"The outraged wife clarified her position, but in the ensuing furor of seeking out the assistant manager and finally the manager, the woman sharing her husband's room was able to remove her belongings and move down the hall."

Ann Hunter, correspondent for the *Chicago Times*, remembered Marguerite at this time. "She was the first American I met when I returned to Paris from Germany. They were short on rooms at the Scribe and I was assigned to a double with Marguerite. I dragged my gear down the hall, shoved open the door, and just stood there for a moment catching my breath. The first words I heard were spoken into the phone: 'A blonde just walked in, I'll bring her along.' Marguerite had accepted a party invitation and included me."

It was easy for the two women to find a common bond. Only a few weeks before they had covered the last stages of the war. "We'd both shared sleeping accommodations with as many as six men at a time and been grateful to have a roof over our heads," Ann explained. "People always ask about the bathroom situation. There wasn't any his or hers in the war zone. I've had everyone from a sergeant to a colonel standing guard for me, but many times you just had to take your chances." Ann recounted the story of Helen Kirkpatrick, whose savoir faire had become a legend among correspondents. Kirkpatrick had been reading in the latrine when a man came in and sat down beside her. She just went right on reading.

"Maggie and I found it all terribly exciting. Chow was fun with so many men who were delighted to have a woman with them for a change. Life was fast paced to say the least. Someone was always 'liberating' a bottle and passing it about. Death was going on all around us but always related to someone else. Consciously or otherwise, we were already storing up war stories to impress the folks back home. If we hadn't actually shared in the fighting, we were still part of the live audience— apart from the people who merely read about it in the stories we were privileged to write.

"There were many colorful people about postwar Paris, but Maggie stood out. She had such a confident air, probably a front—she was very young—but it fooled me at the time. I liked the rakish tilt of her army cap and that brisk, self-assured walk. I remember her surrounded by men; she was attractive and very popular. Of course there were people who said she used her femininity to get what she wanted. I suppose she did sometimes. What did it matter? One had to admire her for what she accomplished. Who cares how she lived or who she slept with?"

Russell Hill, Marguerite's senior at the Paris bureau, feels today that she was the victim of a double standard. He said, "Maggie was controversial largely because her newspaper rivals felt she used unfair methods to achieve her ends. Maggie's own view was that since women war correspondents were already discriminated against, she was merely righting the balance.

"Actually Maggie's success as a war correspondent was due largely to her courage. She would take great personal risks in order to get a story. One must judge the quality of her writing for oneself. Personally I never thought her a great writer, but few could beat her reporting skill. She had a talent for getting difficult stories and getting them right.

"The question always comes up about her sleeping with men to get stories. She really didn't need to. It was enough just to roll her eyes. Remember, too, that the years during and just after the war were wild. Nobody was bound by conventional restraints. All the male reporters were sleeping around. Marguerite liked sex but didn't consider herself promiscuous. She had her own curious code. Once she said to me, 'I don't see how—can sleep with two men at the same time.' I said, 'Don't you really, Maggie?' looking at her very hard. She had the grace to blush.

"I shared many intimate moments with Maggie but always had the feeling that love wasn't all that important to her. Maggie's primary drive was ambition. She wanted to get to the top of her profession and eventually did. After Millar, nobody ever got in her way again."

In the early fall of 1945 Hill was named Berlin bureau chief for the *Herald* and Marguerite became his assistant. Describing their arrival in a *Mademoiselle* article, she wrote, "The pattern of destruction in Berlin stood out clearly even from the air. But after the plane had glided in at Tempelhof Airdrome and we began jeeping into town, it became evident that in spite of the pattern—dull and familiar by now—Berlin has an atmosphere that sets it apart from the rest of Germany's ruined cities. This is mainly created by the presence in one city of soldiers of four different powers—Russia, France, the United States and Britain."

Marguerite's first act on reaching the American press camp was to request a jeep to take her to the Russian sector. Her initial interview was with a woman of her own age, a German-speaking Soviet soldier who had fought as part of a tank crew during the war and was now directing traffic in the Russian zone. The young woman talked earnestly to Marguerite while continuing to wave on a stream of passing trucks and jeeps. "We see these German women in their lovely woolens, wearing silk stockings and coats with fur on them." She was clearly envious. The Russian fascination with the trappings of the good life had initially triggered grand-scale looting. Now starving Germans were eagerly bartering any luxury item that had previously been secreted for a bit of butter, a few eggs, or some meat.

In January 1946 Marguerite began to observe and report the first glimmerings of the cold war. Freedom of the press had become a serious source of controversy among the four occupying Allied powers. Western nations had united in opposition to a Russian ban on distribution of

Western-sponsored newspapers in their zone of Germany. Particularly disturbing to Westerners was the appearance of posters warning the German populace in the Russian zone that anyone caught reading one of the banned newspapers would be punished. The posters were signed by the respective chiefs of police.

For a time this was merely a straw in the wind to Marguerite, overshadowed by her assignment to cover the war crimes trials in Nuremberg. In those drama-packed days she sat only a few feet from the former titans of the Third Reich.

Marguerite and the other correspondents in the press box of the International Military Tribunal listened numbly as the horror stories unfolded. Reporters following the trials by means of headphones that translated testimony into English, French, German, and Russian sometimes found the enormity of the crimes obscured by legal maneuverings.

The *Newsweek* correspondent Toni Howard sensed something "crawlingly horrible" about the very familiarity of the war criminals before her. Thousands of words and feet of film had been expended to describe every fleeting expression of the imprisoned Nazis. Once recognized as leaders of a great state with whom America had done business and conducted diplomatic relations, they were now regarded as criminals. They appeared to Howard as "bored old gangsters waiting for the legalistic Extreme Unction to be over so they could get on with the business of dying for their crimes." She wrote of "staring at the much-photographed faces—pale and unreal under the blazing blue-white klieg lights—of the conspirators sitting stiff and impassive in the prisoners' dock like amateurish and uninspired sketches of themselves, each one withdrawn into the closed and private world of his own earphones, docile and inoffensive."

The exception was Hermann Goering, who listened avidly to every word, switching his earphones from language to language. Marguerite's most significant Nuremberg release was her account of Goering's defense. She found the Nazi second-in-command to be a slippery, self-possessed witness who kept the courtroom tense and attentive throughout three days of testimony. "The skill and care with which he had prepared his defense—first of Naziism and second of his personal role in it—made it clear that the former Reich Marshal hoped that he was speaking for history and for the Fatherland," Marguerite wrote.

Goering's dramatic finale came late in the afternoon of the third day. Marguerite wrote, "Glancing at the courtroom clock the confident and unrepentant leader of the Luftwaffe said he wanted to conclude with the words of one of Germany's greatest and toughest opponents—Winston Churchill: 'In the struggle for life and death there is no legality.'

"Goering spoke the words in a low, ringing voice, and the entire courtroom remained hushed and immobile for a few minutes after he concluded. He then jumped briskly to his feet and, returning to the defense dock, was greeted like a hero by his co-defendants. Former Foreign Minister Joachim von Ribbentrop patted him excitedly on the shoulder and Field Marshal Wilhelm Keitel hugged at his arm.''

In the days that followed Marguerite listened in fascination to the cross-examination that seemed to exhilarate Goering even more. Taking every opportunity to praise Adolf Hitler and the Nazi system, Goering employed the technique of turning questions intended as accusations by a slight twist of interpretation into admissions of which he was clearly proud. He remained calm and good-natured while Associate Justice Robert H. Jackson, the chief American prosecutor, seemed irascible and frequently on the verge of losing his temper.

In the course of one of their verbal duels, Jackson asked: "Do you believe then that a strong police state with concentration camps is the only kind of government for Germany under past and present conditions?" Goering replied: "Under the conditions of 1933 the Nazis demonstrated that with a strong state we could raise Germany from the dragging poverty in which she existed to relative prosperity." His co-defendants beamed and nodded approval.

Later in the final stages of the cross-examination, Goering replied to Jackson, "I have already told you that I did not want war. But I have always believed in the proverb, 'He who has a strong sword has peace.' "

"Do you still believe that?" Jackson queried.

Goering answered, "When I see the international complications that exist in the world today I am more sure than ever of that opinion."

The following month found Marguerite in Prague where it was officially assumed that the Russians would allow Czechoslovakia to retain its national identity. On her first morning there, Marguerite was awakened at 5:00 A.M. by Czechoslovakian security police who broke into her room demanding her passport and, more significantly, her notebook and papers.

A few days later, while interviewing Jan Masaryk, the Foreign Minister and son of Thomas Masaryk, the founder of the Czechoslovakian Republic, she brought up the incident.

"These are just isolated mishaps, I can assure you," Masaryk replied.

"I am completely optimistic about this country. Czechoslovakia is destined, I am sure, to serve as a bridge between the East and the West. The Czechoslovakian people have a history crucially different from that of the Russians. Here we know what freedom is. But the Russian people have never really possessed it. The Czechoslovakian people could never be regimented the way the Russians have been regimented. Our foreign policy will continue to be one of friendship with Russia. It is quite reasonable that the Russians should wish their neighbors to be their friends, and we certainly don't wish to give them any excuse to interfere with our national life."

When Marguerite asked if he feared Communist officials within his own government, Masaryk's response was an emphatic no. He explained, "There is a fundamental point that you must understand. Here in our country even the Communists are Czechs first and Communists second."

Within two years the idealistic leader was dead, having jumped (or been pushed) from his apartment window. But in 1946 Marguerite could not anticipate that, nor could she conceive what would be the fate of her next destination: Poland.

Against the advice of her colleagues in Berlin, Marguerite drove her tiny sports car alone through the Soviet zone of occupation in Germany and on into Poland. She had been warned of kidnapping, robbery, and murder, for whole sections of Poland were still in a state of civil war. Many Polish patriots who had risked their lives against the Nazis refused to lay down their arms on the order of a government they felt had been foisted on them by Russia.

It was a long, lonely night, with the roads icy and virtually deserted. As Marguerite drove into Warsaw in the early hours of dawn, she was weary but optimistic. She was about to cover Poland's first political campaign since the war.

Marguerite drove about the war-torn country with a small American flag affixed to her car. Even in the remote villages the sight of the flag was enough to draw throngs of Poles. The story they told was always the same. The police were kidnapping, threatening, or beating those suspected of political opposition. Why does the United States allow this to happen? the despairing people invariably asked.

Their mounting fear and growing disillusionment severely challenged Marguerite's personal system of belief. Struggling to understand the tragic events going on about her, she attempted to evaluate the erupting political chaos. What resulted was a major philosophical crisis as well as a journalistic one. The facts were evident, but how was she to interpret them? Communist theory she knew, but what of tactics? Were the violent police state incidents products of the government's inexperience or were they actually carefully planned?

Theoretically the Communist party in Poland was bound by the Yalta agreement, in which it was pledged that the country would be permitted to choose its own form of government through "free and unfettered elections." In reality, Marguerite learned, the Communists had been handed control of the police by the Russians, whose armed forces occupied the country at the war's end.

In January 1947 Marguerite's political philosophy was further undermined as she watched a "Landslide victory" for the Polish Communist party (actually a small minority in the predominantly Catholic country), achieved through blatant terrorism. Her stories revealed how Warsaw workers were lined up by the police, handed premarked ballots, and marched to the polls. The reaction from the left-wing press was one of rage. She was denounced as being prejudiced, ignorant, and hostile. When the publisher of one liberal paper attacked her in print as an "unreconstructed war correspondent who had declared war in print on the Polish government," Marguerite's anxiety and uncertainty were so extreme that she broke out in a flaming skin rash.

Speaking of her at this time a British diplomat told a journalist friend, "The *Herald Tribune's* star reporter moves so rapidly through life that it makes my fingers itch. I want to run them through her hair to straighten it out for her because she has obviously been so breathless that she hasn't combed it since she got to Warsaw."

The end product of her self-doubt was tragedy. Confused and shaken by personal attacks from veteran newsmen, Marguerite agreed to interview a young but important member of the opposition party. Although he had been cruelly beaten by the police, he courageously insisted on supplying her with the details of his experience, hoping to arouse world opinion. It was a fatal mistake. Following publication of her story, he was rearrested.

"It was a terrible responsibility," Marguerite wrote later. "I blamed myself for having been foolish enough to acquiesce to his demand for publicity. His fate gave me the last emotional shove toward the conclusion to which my mind—and the evidence—had long been pointing. Sadly I turned off the bright hope that Poland would be allowed to fashion its own *modus vivendi* between Western heritage and Eastern power. It was clear that terror was the deliberate weapon of ruthless leaders.''

Marguerite's disenchantment with Soviet imperialism was doubly painful in light of her youthful enthusiasm for Communism. Although much of her early zeal had been dissipated, she, had approached the Polish elections open-mindedly and with high hopes that a middle passage could be found between the ideologies of East and West. She still considered herself a liberal, believing that some kind of socio-economic experiment was necessary to solve the conditions that had resulted in the breadlines she still remembered vividly from the 1930s.

Even as a student she had been aware of the cruelty of the Russian police state, but she had believed the party line that such injustices were the temporary results of governmental immaturity. Now, after having seen firsthand the results of police state terrorism, she could no longer rationalize about it.

Only a few short years before her father had argued that human nature could be controlled but never fundamentally changed, and she had thought him reactionary. Now Marguerite, too, had reached the conclusion that it was improbable that man's nature would ever be perfected in this world. It seemed all the more appalling that the horrors she had witnessed had been committed in the name of a system that promised a utopian society.

This was the death of yet another dream.

Eleven

Nineteen forty-seven was a year of endings and beginnings for Marguerite.

She had been a foreign correspondent for three years. Although still eager for adventure and alert for opportunity, she felt an unexpected yearning for old friends and familiar places. At first she ignored the insidious longing, afraid of missing some momentous front-page story. But when her unaccustomed homesickness began to have an almost numbing effect, Marguerite yielded. She requested and received leave to go home.

En route to California, she took a brief side trip, a sentimental journey to Saint-Tropez, the resort most favored by George Millar. Two years had passed since their parting, but Marguerite could not resist walking in her former lover's footsteps, even going so far as to seek out and find the sandal maker whom George had described as the best on the Mediterranean. Marguerite sat quietly while the artisan took her foot measurements and made sandals to be treasured for many years.

Sipping cassis at a sidewalk cafe, she gazed wistfully out at the yachts and schooners crowding the wharf before her. Recalling George's plans to sail the waterways of France down to the Mediterranean, her heart skipped a beat each time a sailboat flying a British flag came into view, knowing all the while that George had already taken his longed-for voyage with Isabel as his sole crew and companion.

She reflected that possibly the quality she admired most in George was his spirit of adventure. She had felt reassured in his company, certain that despite his avowed longing for a quiet place to write, he would never sink into the rut that had trapped her father. Much aware of Larry's frustrations and their effect upon him and his family, she wondered how many others accepted the humdrum for the sake of security only to pay the price of boredom. Marguerite was certain that George would do the things that others dreamed of doing but never had the courage to try. "I had hoped that George's courage would give me courage," she said later in her autobiography, *News Is a Singular Thing*, "and in a way that did happen but not in the manner I expected."

Marguerite left Saint-Tropez and continued on to California. Larry also was home from the war—in this case for good. The two sat up late at night exchanging stories. Her father had come alive during the war. Since meeting Marguerite in Paris he had, at forty-nine, been placed in a commando unit and flown to China to do secret intelligence work in Chungking and Formosa. He was being trained as a paratrooper when the war ended, but the cease-fire didn't end the excitement. Larry was nearly killed when his ship was caught in a savage typhoon while returning to California. Now he reluctantly removed his major's oak leaves and returned to being a stockbroker. The romance that would fuel the rest of his days would be vicarious, provided only by his daughter's adventures.

Marguerite met with Stanley Moore, who had begun divorce proceedings in January of that year. Henry Wallace was running for president, and Marguerite and Stanley went to hear him speak on the Berkeley campus. Some eggs were thrown, and one splattered on Stanley's coat. When the speech ended he returned Marguerite to her parents' home, kissed her good-bye, and went home to wipe off the egg. They did not meet again.

Marion Devlin, women's editor of the *Vallejo Times-Herald*, remembered the fanfare of the hometown papers that gave Marguerite a heroine's greeting. Only six years before, Devlin had hired Marguerite for her first newspaper job out of Berkeley. The June graduate had worked during the summer months until she had earned enough money to buy a ticket to New York.

"It was difficult to reconcile the much-publicized foreign correspondent with the fragile little thing that I remembered," Devlin admitted. "She was so pretty and such a dreamer, rather helpless-seeming; really unsuited, I thought, to rough-and-tumble newspaper work." Devlin recalled that Marguerite's mind was a million miles away from the women's club notes she had been given to write, yet she was always a willing worker and would even take want ads during slack hours. "Occasionally," Devlin recalled, "she got to cover city hall assignments, which she definitely preferred, but it was clear her heart was not in Vallejo."

Her leave coming to an end, Marguerite stopped in New York on her way back to Berlin, determined to make use of some of the money she had accumulated. Russell Hill, who was now back at the *Herald*'s New York office writing editorials, accompanied her on a shopping spree. "Marguerite was her mother's daughter, a canny shopper," he recalled. "She wanted a good fur but couldn't pay the price, so we went to a secondhand dealer. The coat she coveted had originally been sixty-four hundred dollars. The dealer insisted that it had never been worn and that appeared to be the case. 'You can have it for twenty-eight hundred dollars,' he agreed at last.

"Marguerite paid the money and put on the coat. 'Why was it never worn?' she asked casually while admiring the effect in the mirror. 'Madame, that is one question that is never asked,' the dealer answered. Obviously it had been a gift to a lady who valued money more than the coat or sentiment.

"Maggie merely shrugged. She was thrilled with her acquisition and looked marvelous in it. She was ready now to tackle the Berlin winter or anything else that life had in store."

A day or so later Marguerite had lunch with a former friend from her Columbia days. As the two dallied over coffee in the Rose Room of the Algonquin, the man admitted that he had once been very much attracted to her but had felt that she was too dedicated to her career to be approachable. As they left the restaurant, crossing the street to the Royalton where Marguerite was staying, she turned to him. "It isn't too late, you know."

"I can take the afternoon off, what about you?" he replied.

She hesitated, "I've got some appointments."

He recalled watching her. "I could see the wheels going around in her head. Obviously she was weighing whether it was worth it to take two or three hours off to make love. Eventually she decided with some apparent regret that she'd better keep the appointments. I didn't feel particularly rebuffed because it only reaffirmed my original impression of her. I understood that if I could have helped her with her career or even had she had no other obligations, the remainder of the afternoon would have been delightful—or *could* have been. Who knows until you're there?''

They lingered for a moment or two on the sidewalk. "What are you going to do with the rest of your life, Maggie?" he asked before parting.

She looked thoughtful. "I'm not sure just now," she said at last, "but there'll always be something." He noted the familiar glint in her eye and never doubted that there would be. They never met or even corresponded again.

The something turned out to be a promotion as Berlin bureau chief for the *Herald*. She was then twenty-six years old. It was a stunning triumph that Marguerite equated with an army captain suddenly being promoted to colonel. Once again she had advanced over or around the male competition.

Jim O'Donnell, her close friend who was then *Newsweek* bureau chief in Berlin, compared her at this time to a rookie pitcher who had been sent out to compete in the major leagues. "The amazing thing was that she beat them," he said. "She did it with sheer determination but it cost her in many ways. Marguerite felt that her position as bureau chief existed in a state of grace. She took any major scoop by a competitor as a personal disaster and reacted accordingly. Many evenings we'd be relaxing over a late-night drink at the press club, assuming that the work was over, when all of a sudden she'd spot a *Times* man striding purposefully out the door. Marguerite would gulp her drink, say a quick good-bye, and follow him. The only way that she could be completely certain that he didn't know something crucial was to tail him.

"It made for very busy days and nights. The story possibilities were endless—the displaced persons, the food crisis, the acceleration of the cold war, the de-Nazification of Germany. It was immensely appealing to Marguerite, who preferred to shoot the bird on the wing and go on to new quarry. Covering Germany meant hard work and great headlines, and Maggie adored it."

The nature of her job and the upcoming world-shaking events would lead to one of the most dramatic phases of Marguerite's professional life and an even more important personal development, but for the moment the most significant change was the opportunity to move out of a suitcase and into a house.

At first correspondents had been quartered at the press club, but now they were rapidly being assigned to villas which had been requisitioned for them by the military. As many romantic liasons were formed during this freewheeling period, a frequent topic of conversation was who was currently "villaed up" with whom. The press corps, whose social and professional life centered about the club, was a close-knit family. As in any family, there were rows and rivalries, pets, patriarchs and "pills."

Marguerite's home, originally built for the Japanese mistress of a German chemical cartel executive, was a romantic hideaway screened from view by a grove of pines. The house at 5 Lima Strasse was like an exquisite jewel box. The rooms had a slightly oriental feel to them; most had floor-to-ceiling windows facing onto a lawn that sloped down to a small lake framed by silver firs and weeping willows. The rent, paid by the *Herald* to the American military government, was 125 dollars a month and included the services of Anna, a cook-housekeeper. It seemed that Marguerite had come a long way from Chabot Court.

"Life in the American occupation zone of Germany has a dreamlike quality," she wrote in *Mademoiselle*. "And it is not a nightmare, but rather a fantasia with Arabian Nights characters. It is an unquestionable fact that the move from America to Germany has meant a sharp rise in standards of living for nearly every soldier's family from private to general, for the Army believes in doing well by its victorious soldiers." (She did not add "for its correspondents as well." Most had never nor would they ever again live so affluently.)

"There is no trouble in Berlin in obtaining servants. The hungry Germans long for a chance to work in an American household because it means a square meal. The contrast between the defeated, despairing Germans scooping up cigarette butts from the street and foraging in garbage cans and the confident Americans with their pink-cheeked children has created a warped psychology on both sides. In the Germans it has fostered a cringing obeisance, a frantic desire to please. And in too many Americans it tends to create a rajah complex."

In her own household Marguerite soon discovered that she was feeding not only Anna, but Anna's large family as well. She would serve a very large roast for a dinner party and anticipate dining on leftovers the following night only to be told there were no leftovers. What was there to say? All around her Germans were literally starving.

There were other surprises. Once Anna mistook the canned fruit cocktail for some kind of drink and served it in a large crystal pitcher at an elaborate reception. Another culture shock occurred when Marguerite, away on a story, offered her home to a *Herald* colleague, Don Cook, and his wife, Cherry, who were vacationing. The Cooks and their three-year-old son had taken the night train from Paris, arriving at Marguerite's home at 8:30 A.M. Anna greeted them effusively, ushering them into the living room. A few moments later she reentered carrying two "absolutely perfect martinis" on a silver tray. "So this is how Maggie gets all those exclusive interviews," the Cooks speculated, half in earnest.

Unlike the inner city of Berlin, which was a mishmash of broken stones and gaping holes, the area designated for the press was a golden ghetto centered around the posh press club, which had formerly belonged to Hitler's finance minister. Marguerite's friend Jim O'Donnell and Toni Howard, number two person on the *Newsweek* bureau, lived next door, with the rest of the press corps all within walking distance. The atmosphere in the elegant suburb, which had suffered no bomb damage, was lively and very social.

It was inevitable that Marguerite would learn that her greatest rival, Drew Middleton, the *New York Times* bureau chief, had let it be known that he was amused that the *Herald* hadn't provided him with stiffer competition. Middleton had far greater newspaper experience than she as well as a crew of nine. Marguerite's staff included her and one secretary. To meet the challenge, she worked twelve, fourteen, and sometimes eighteen hours at a stretch, often falling asleep at her typewriter from sheer exhaustion.

As though that wasn't enough, Marguerite also had to fight the social establishment. On one occasion she had accepted an invitation to a party from Ambassador Robert Murphy, knowing that there would be high-level news sources present. Back at the office a story had to be written and filed before the night was over. Placed at the far end of the dining table, she was unable to question the guests who were her reason for attending. Then to her dismay Marguerite and the other women were abandoned while Middleton and the officials adjourned to another room for brandy and cigars. Straining to hear, she occasionally caught snatches of conversation. Middleton was asking pertinent questions, but try as she would Marguerite could not make out the answers. The tête-à-tête lasted so long that she was forced to return to her office before the men rejoined the ladies.

Fortunately there was a flip side to the coin, with which Marguerite had always been familiar. The score was evened somewhat when she became romantically involved with Middleton's assistant, Edward A. Morrow (not to be confused with Edward R. Murrow). Of the many benefits to her in the relationship, not the least of them was the sense of unease that it must have brought to Middleton. Yet it would have been unfair to both Marguerite and Morrow to assume that it was merely an affair of convenience. Morrow was considered very handsome and, like so many of the men that Marguerite was drawn to, he was an adventurer. Tough and courageous, he had fought with the Abraham Lincoln Brigade in the Spanish civil war. She admired his nerve—a decided asset in a Berlin characterized by riots, shootings, and abductions—and regarded him as one of the best investigative reporters in the business.

On one occasion the two of them were very nearly killed while covering a riot that had erupted in the British sector near Brandenburger Tor. The Tor, a giant stone gate, marked the dividing point between the British occupied sector of the city and the Russian sector. The melee had begun with a peaceful demonstration by West Berliners. Just as they were beginning to disperse, several trucks of armed, Communist-controlled German police roared in from the Russian sector.

There were angry catcalls. Rocks were thrown at the police. Three German boys climbed onto the Tor, grabbed the Russian flag, and threw it into the street below, where the crowd quickly burned it.

A jeepload of Red Army tommy gunners pulled to a screeching stop before the Tor. The crowd grew silent as one of the Russians leaped from the jeep and began to wave his gun at the crowd. Unaccountably he opened fire, splattering bullets in all directions. Marguerite heard screams and saw several people crumple to the ground. She, Morrow, and everyone else who could began to run. "I've never seen so many thousands of people run so fast," she recalled to Judy Barden that evening at the press club. One more time Marguerite had escaped unscathed.

An affair with a competitor involves ego, ambition, and a degree of callousness. Such an association is easy to begin, more difficult to maintain, and generally very hard to end. Almost always someone is hurt either personally or professionally. In this case the relationship was ended abruptly when Drew Middleton transferred Morrow to Warsaw.

Marguerite Higgins, like many ambitious individuals, may have found pillow talk a great advantage. Her appearance and charm were distinct assets. The spoonful-of-sugar approach manifested most frequently in the "purpose party," for which Marguerite's chic house was an ideal setting. Guests ran the gamut from political, military, diplomatic, and journalistic dignitaries to officials from the occupying powers.

Richard Lake recalled one of Marguerite's intimate soirees. Lake was then a captain and held a position that was later used as a prototype for a character portrayed by Gregory Peck in the movie *Night People*. His intelligence assignment was packed with danger and intrigue.

According to the four-power regulations, the Soviet part of Berlin was open to the Western allies just as West Berlin was open to the Russians. As the cold war accelerated there were kidnappings by Russians, Russian-provoked arrests of German or even American citizens, and blatant cases of Russian espionage occurring on a daily basis.

As chief liaison officer for the American Police Battalion, Lake had to keep tabs on Americans in the Soviet zone and Soviets in the American zone. The story potential was obvious. When the young intelligence officer took over the position he was alerted to yet another hazard. "You'll be getting an invitation from Marguerite Higgins," his predecessor warned.

"Who's that?" he asked.

"You'll find out," he was assured.

A few days later when Lake held his first press briefing, a willowy blonde remained as the other correspondents filed out. "I think we should get better acquainted," she suggested. "What about dinner at my place?"

Lake was tempted but wary. He was also very busy settling into a highly demanding job. But a few days later the second invitation came.

"The house was pretty, sort of exotic-looking," he recalled, "but I remember the woman and the atmosphere she created far better. The table gleamed with polished silver. The tapers in the elaborate candelabra were sixteen inches high. The excellent dinner included a fresh mushroom soup I'll never forget. Marguerite wore a low-cut, black dress that set off her considerable charms to perfection. I was impressed. Well, isn't that why boys leave home? No, I was not one of her lovers. Whether that might have changed had I gone back another night for another helping of mushroom soup, I'll never know. Marguerite was a most attractive woman, but there was an air of directness, of toughness, that I found a bit off putting.

"Marguerite was a woman who knew damn well what she wanted. She was dedicated to getting the big story, and that story was invariably built on people. The nuances, rumors, feelings, and facts surrounding the people who generated news were essential to her. To get all that, she needed a network of loyal informants. Maggie played on a broader stage than most. I admired her style and her determination to the extent that I helped her when possible by calling her first when something news-worthy came up.''

Lake also recalled another equally revealing meeting. This time Marguerite was his guest. ''I was hosting a party in honor of Robert Hinkley, then president of the American Broadcasting Company. All of a sudden in walked Maggie, dressed in a very demure manner and acting like the sweetest girl in town. As it turned out, Hinkley was a friend of her father's, but I didn't know that then and must have looked very surprised at her sudden transformation. Before long she was at my side giving me a sharp dig in the ribs. 'Don't you dare tell Bob Hinkley anything about me!' she whispered.

'' 'What makes you think I would?' I asked.

'' 'I'm not taking any chances.' ''

Marguerite liked to think of herself as a very private person but at this time was beginning to wonder if such a thing was possible in postwar Berlin. ''Am I getting a reputation for sleeping around?'' she asked Judy Barden one night as the two were finishing dinner at the press club.

''I'm afraid so,'' Judy admitted.

Marguerite sighed. ''Is that really so terrible?''

''I don't think so.'' Judy's words were underscored by a crisp British accent. ''It's such a nice ending to a pleasant evening and a lovely compliment to the gentleman you're with.''

Marguerite smiled, pleased by the reassurance of a slightly older friend whom she liked and admired. Not too long afterward Marguerite was able to reciprocate with her own kind of reassurance.

''It was in winter,'' Judy remembered. ''I had left the press club about 1:00 A.M. feeling pretty low, as I'd received some beastly news from England. I walked home but couldn't bring myself to go in. Where could I go at that time of morning? I wondered. Marguerite lived a few yards up the road and I found myself wandering in that direction. Her house was dark but I rang the bell anyway. In a few moments Marguerite came to the door in a glorious filmy nightgown, something few of us had in those days.

''Without registering any surprise or asking a single question, she said, 'How nice to see you, come in.' She settled me into a comfortable chair, got out some ice, and quickly made a drink. 'Do you like Tchaikovsky?' she asked, handing me the glass. When I said yes she left the room and came back a moment or two later wearing ballet slippers.'' Marguerite had put on a record.

''Then suddenly—unexpectedly—Marguerite began to dance. She danced as if there were a tremendous audience. She did it well and without a word.

''When the record was over, she made me another drink, showed me to the guest room, handed me some night clothes. 'Good night, see you in the morning,' she said before closing the door and returning to her own room. It was a manifestation of a rare and valuable friendship that I can never forget.''

Looking back across the years at her friend's matter-of-fact approach to life, Judy was candid. ''If you mention any man who had anything going for him at all, you can be certain that Marguerite had some kind of association with him. But why not? I've never understood why people got so annoyed about it. God knows there were enough disadvantages to being a woman in a so-called man's world. The generals who were the main news sources certainly didn't want you—oh well, they wanted you on *their* terms, in bed when it was convenient for *them*—but they couldn't be bothered other times. They didn't want you 'interfering with the men.' People accused Marguerite of taking advantage of men, but I could never understand that. Her relationships, sexual or otherwise, were mutually pleasurable associations. Whose was the advantage?''

Jim O'Donnell was also a partisan. His *Newsweek* associate and soon-to-be-wife, Toni Howard, was not. During their Berlin days Toni secretly was writing a novel said by some to be loosely based on Marguerite's amatory and professional adventures. The setting was postwar Berlin, and the protagonist was a woman correspondent with an unconventional approach to news gathering. The title of the book would be *Shriek with Pleasure*.

At least one outrageous anecdote is known to be drawn from fact. Marguerite and Jim frequently worked together to outwit their respective competition. ''We had an understanding,'' Jim explained. ''Maggie worked for a daily paper, I for a weekly magazine. As such, we weren't in direct competition. Our real struggles were with the *Times* and *Time Magazine* respectively and the payoff came on the streets of New York. Sometimes we worked together to beat them both. Many times I'd give

Maggie stories with the understanding that they wouldn't appear in the *Herald* until *Newsweek*'s publication date. We went along this way for a while, both hitting the competition pretty hard.''

Then a priest who had become a friend of O'Donnell's came to him with a very special story. The cleric was Cardinal von Preysing, a former member of the German Resistance. ''I'm dreadfully afraid of sensationalism but feel that I must speak out against the Russians as I once did against the Nazis,'' he explained. ''Rapes and kidnappings are rampant. People are disappearing all over the city. Someone has to take a stand against this brutality.'' Von Preysing offered O'Donnell the text of his forthcoming sermon, the first public outcry against this tragic but politically incendiary situation, knowing that he would treat it carefully.

''Some instinct told me to hold the story back from Maggie,'' O'Donnell recalled. ''I still planned to give it to her, but closer to Wednesday, *Newsweek*'s publication day. Saturday afternoon I filed the story. That evening Toni and I had a dinner party and invited Maggie. My secretary came rushing in just as I was fixing drinks for the first guests. I could see she was frantic, and so I left the drinks to Toni and followed her into the hallway. 'Mr. O'Donnell, I've done a terrible thing,' she apologized. 'I left the sermon out on your desk. Miss Higgins came in through the office and saw it. She's reading it now.'

''I reassured her that everything would be all right and went back to my guests. By that time Maggie had joined the others. 'What are you going to beat *Time* with this week, Jim?' she asked innocently. 'Anything special?'

'' 'No, nothing special,' I assured her just as innocently. 'There was a little something, but well, I'll tell you the story over dessert.'

''We sat down to dinner and Maggie began to fidget. Finally at quarter to eight, she jumped up. 'I have to leave. There's something in my story I have to check. I'll be back within an hour,' she promised, racing out.

''Pretty soon she was back, looking very pleased with herself. That's when I let her have it. 'Maggie, I *did* have a great story about this cardinal who was going to speak out on Russian brutality. I'd planned to give it to you but it fizzled. He changed his mind.'

''Maggie turned dead white. I knew exactly what was going on in her mind. She was right on deadline. 'Excuse me, I've got to go,' she gasped. 'I forgot something important.' This time she ran out even faster. I called the press center and asked a friend, 'Did Miss Higgins file a story a few minutes ago?' The answer was *ja*. 'Was it the same story I filed this afternoon?' *Ja* again. Then I called Drew Middleton at the *New York Times* bureau and gave him the whole story.

"Naturally Maggie's scheme backfired completely. She'd run out the second time to get the story pulled, but by the time the *Herald* got the message the first edition was already rolling. She got it pulled, an expensive, difficult procedure. When virtually the same story appeared in the *Times,* the *Herald* was furious. 'WHAT'S GOING ON THERE? ARE YOU DRINKING?' the cable read. Maggie very nearly lost her job, which is a little more than I bargained for when I decided to teach her a lesson."

Marguerite's comeuppance was greeted with much chortling in the press community. Toni Howard, who had never liked Marguerite and resented her working relationship with Jim, gleefully added the episode as one more dirty trick employed by Carla MacMurphy, the protagonist in her novel.

Jim was far more forgiving. His attitude was one of a big brother, protective, tolerant, and sometimes proud.

A few months later he announced a trip to the Ruhr. "Can't I come along?" Marguerite pleaded. "The *Herald* has cut way back on my expense account. It would help to split some of the costs. I promise I won't get in your way."

O'Donnell reluctantly agreed. "We stayed at the British press camp and Maggie went off and did her thing and I did mine," he recalled. "Then she discovered that I was seeing Carl Arnold, mayor of Düsseldorf. It had been difficult to obtain the interview, for Arnold wasn't well. 'Can't I just go along for my own education?' she urged." Once again O'Donnell agreed.

"Mayor Arnold took us to a hospital where the very young and the very old were dying like flies," Jim remembered. "It was incredible; in the past forty-eight hours two hundred twenty had died of malnutrition. When Maggie and I returned to the camp, I warned her, 'Don't you dare pull a Cardinal von Preysing on me. You can have this story, but we'll both file on Wednesday.' She nodded innocently enough and then left, affirming that we'd meet for dinner.

"As cocktail time approached and then dinner—with no Maggie in evidence—I was pretty certain what she was up to. Finally at nine, she appeared, looking very meek. 'What have you done? Did you file that story?' I demanded.

"'I cannot tell a lie,'" she replied, looking contrite. But then her expression changed. 'I couldn't live with my conscience if I'd sat on that story. Can you imagine how many people might die between now and Wednesday?' "

O'Donnell was both annoyed and chagrined. "Cynics like Toni Howard might have laughed at her rationale, but I realized Maggie was absolutely right. I was ashamed for having gotten so caught up in my own ego that I'd lost sight of what really mattered."

The story had a sequel. Some years later O'Donnell was reminiscing with General Lucius D. Clay, who had been the American military governor of Germany during those tumultuous times. "As far as I'm concerned that was the most important story that Maggie ever filed," Clay surprised O'Donnell by saying.

Clay had been in Washington at the time, testifying before the Senate Foreign Relations Committee. "I was pleading with them that food had to be diverted to the British occupied zone before starvation reached the Buchenwald level," he explained. "I'd already figured out that they were eleven to one against what they called 'feeding Germans.' I went home that evening feeling sick. I knew that I'd lost and that thousands would die for it.

"The next morning I returned to the hearing and could tell immediately from the men's faces that something had changed. Looking down I saw the *New York Herald* on the table. There on the front page was Marguerite Higgins's starvation story. Somehow it brought the impending disaster into focus for them in a way that I could not. The food was sent. Who knows how many lives were saved?"

Jim O'Donnell was to recall Marguerite in his best-selling book, *The Bunker,* a chronicle of the last days of Hitler. The germ of the narrative, which would not be written until 1978, was sown in the early postwar days. O'Donnell had visited the underground hideout where Hitler, Eva Braun, and the Goebbels family had committed suicide a few weeks after the war ended. Already the refuge was rat infested, looted, and totally controlled by the Russians.

This grim setting was recalled more than a year later when he received a call from an East Berlin tipster. In guarded language, the caller told O'Donnell that the old Hitler bunker site was bustling with camera activity.

"By the time I arrived it was *Daemmerung,* the slowly fading light of a long midsummer evening," he wrote. "Moving about in the shadows, I spotted my friend and enterprising colleague, Marguerite Higgins. As we discovered later that evening, to our chagrin, we both had the same alert German tipster on the payroll. When competing for something, Maggie, the blonde bombshell, seemed to have three elbows, but that had not helped her to gain access to the bunker. She had already been twice turned away. Both of us were now learning Russian the hard way. We quickly joined forces and approached the bunker entrance."

This time they were chased out into the street by four sullen sentries brandishing submachine guns and then joined by a Russian officer who told them to leave, emphasizing his point with a drawn pistol. They retreated about one hundred yards to the rooftop of the New Reich Chancellery. Dusk had fallen. Owls glided by. Voices drifted upward and they became aware of people milling outside.

"Suddenly," O'Donnell recalled, "Klieg lights illuminated the bunker and the Old Chancellery garden. Now we could see cameramen and hear the whirr of their cameras in what looked like a movie stage set. Some four or five Russian officers were giving directions to a group of about twelve actors, silent performers who were clad in what seemed to be deep purple fatigue uniforms." The scene was shot, the lights were turned out, and the group vanished back into the bunker.

"But twenty minutes later, the same group emerged again to shoot a second scene. We guessed—correctly as it turned out—that these two scenes must be the burial of the Hitlers and the suicide and burial of Joseph and Magda Goebbels. These, as we already knew, were the only two events that had taken place outside the bunker. Marguerite and I came to the conclusion that a Russian movie company was making a film documentary with Red Army help. Soon the whole mysterious troupe departed in trucks. A spooky feature, we thought; another Berlin midnight rendezvous and nothing more."

For once Marguerite and Jim had missed a big story. The actors were from the original cast. They were the same dozen missing major witnesses from the Reich Chancellery Group who had vanished from Berlin in the first week of May 1945. Now they had been reassembled in Russia, flown back to Berlin, and made to reconstruct the bunker melodrama, step by step, on the original location. In Berlin for less than twenty-four hours, they were flown back to Moscow where they would be held in Soviet prison camps for another decade.

It would be more than thirty years before O'Donnell was able to accomplish the task at which the Russians had failed: the reconstruction of what really happened to Hitler and his entourage. When this brilliant

piece of research was published it bore the dedication: TO MAR-
GUERITE HIGGINS, a salute to a spirited colleague who by then had
been dead for twelve years and a passing wave at the shadowy shapes of
two very young journalists who'd come together that warm summer
night believing that the whole world was theirs to discover and write
about.

"Maggie's untimely death was doubly tragic," O'Donnell said, "because—unlike so many of the people who criticized her, who *still*
criticize her—success made her a kinder, more generous, and compas-
sionate person. For all her shenanigans she was a good and loyal friend,
the sort of person who went through life doing good deeds concealed.
Maggie combined the realism of a French peasant with the idealism of an
Irish drunk. There was a whimsical irony about her that I think many
people missed. I caught it one afternoon when we were on a holiday in
Paris. A beggar approached her on the street and asked for ten francs.
Maggie studied him a minute and then asked, 'If I give the money to you,
will you spend it on bread or booze?'

"The beggar must have been a marvelous judge of character. 'Madame,' he replied, 'I'm sorry to admit, but I'd spend it for booze.'

"Maggie smiled. 'Why be sorry?' she said, handing him twenty."

Marguerite had barely adjusted to her job as bureau chief when the
biggest story in the world broke. The Berlin blockade and the monumen-
tal effort of the United States to feed 2,250,000 people by airlift were on.
The Berlin siege was an inevitable result of the mounting incompatibility
of the Western powers and the Soviets and the refusal of the West
Berliners to submit to oppressive Communism. Soviet policy, having
impoverished East Berlin, could not permit the adjacent and competitive
presence of a resuscitated West Berlin.

On June 15, 1948, Marguerite wrote: "The Russians have held up 140
carloads of coal headed for Berlin from the British zone in the last 48
hours, and today they closed down the Elbe River bridge on the Auto-
bahn through the Soviet zone which links this city with the west. No
formal advance notice was given on either action."

At about the same time Marguerite was filing this story General
Lucius D. Clay had called in his director of army intelligence, Major
General William Hall. "Tell me exactly what it would take to supply
Berlin by air." He asked the impossible with the calm understatement of
one who knew his man.

Five hours later Hall returned with a package that included the quantity and kind of aircraft needed, the amount of steel matting for runways, and the number of personnel required. The plan submitted by Hall contained exactly the numbers and procedures used during the next eleven months to ferry food, fuel, and medical supplies over Soviet Germany to besieged Berlin. Hall was placed in charge of the action.

The relationship between the two men went back many years to the time when Clay had been an instructor (and football fan) at West Point and Hall was an outstanding cadet as well as one of the top centers ever produced by the academy's football program.

At forty-one, Bill Hall was a tall, lean man with a ruggedly handsome appearance. Richard Lake, who worked with Hall during the Berlin days, described him as a "grown-up Alan Ladd, possessing the same bright, heroic character that Ladd portrayed, but with more depth and openness. Bill was a man's man without being macho. He was intelligent, alert, extremely courteous, a good guy, and a great match for his officers."

It seems inevitable that Bill and Marguerite would meet, although the general said that he tried very hard to avoid it. "After all, it was her business to find out what it was often my job to conceal. I'd heard how persistent and attractive she was and attempted to keep my distance, but we finally met one night at a party given by mutual friends. I think we both knew then that it was a big deal."

It was also quite complicated. Bill was married and had a wife and four children living in the United States. Marguerite was married to her work. Somehow the romance flourished despite the handicaps.

The two were well matched in their craving for excitement. One of Bill Hall's most vivid memories of those days was of the two of them dressing in ragged clothes to attend Communist rallies in the Russian sector. "We used my motorcycle. It was so cold; I can still feel Marguerite's arms holding me tightly after all these years."

The romance flourished as one administered and the other reported the most elaborate and thorough rescue mission in history. Starvation, pestilence, blackout—all were inevitable. In normal times West Berlin's population required at least 13,000 tons of food and fuel each day to subsist. The regular supply was now completely blocked. At least one-third of West Berlin's electricity had come from Soviet-controlled power plants. West sector plants couldn't operate without a steady supply of coal.

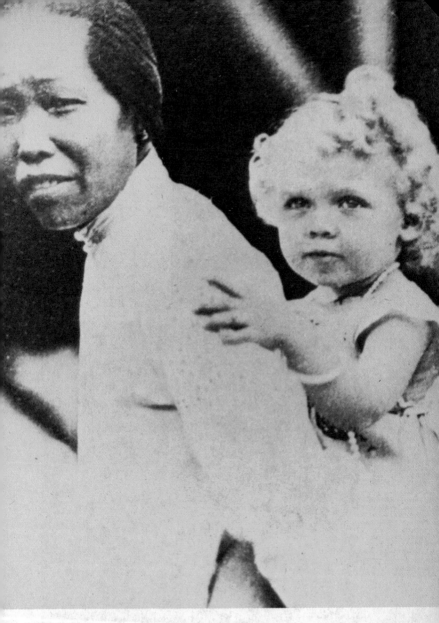

Marguerite with her Chinese nurse, about 1922

Graduation from
Anna Head School, 1937

Marguerite at a sorority
party, 1938

Chosun Hotel, Seoul, Korea

Mid-way across the Atlantic, Marguerite Higgins interviews Bernard Baruch. *Marguerite Higgins Collections, George Arents Research Library for Special Collections at Syracuse University*

Marguerite and General William Hall, 1951

Marguerite on her first book signing tour, 1951

Marguerite with Linda Marguerite, 1961

Marguerite's photo for her column, 1960

Marguerite with President Lyndon Johnson
Marguerite Higgins Collections, George Arents Research Library for
Special Collections at Syracuse University

The question of evacuating American military dependents and civilian employees became an immediate concern. General Clay was adamant. The only way to ensure German morale was to maintain the American community in Berlin. He called for full support to deny the Soviets victory in their efforts to subjugate the city. The Berlin teletype message flashed onto the screen in the Pentagon, four thousand miles away in Washington. "If we mean to hold Europe against Communism, we must not budge. If we withdraw, our position in Europe is threatened. If America does not understand this now, does not know that the issue is cast, then it never will—and Communism will run rampant."

By June 28, an American C-47 was landing every eight minutes to discharge two-and-a-half tons of cargo at Tempelhof air base. On that day planes carried nearly four hundred tons of food, fuel, and medicine to Berlin through the air corridors of the West.

The Communist-sponsored East Berlin press and radio ridiculed what they called "the futile attempts of the Americans to maintain their untenable position in Berlin. Never could airplanes carry enough supplies to feed and heat the city." When mockery failed the Soviets began intensive antiaircraft artillery exercises within earshot of the city. Fighter planes began to buzz the incoming transports. One actually collided with a British passenger plane, causing the loss of thirty-five lives.

Anti-Soviet sentiment ran high. There were riots—one of which put Marguerite on the sidelines and very nearly removed her from the Berlin bureau entirely. The scene was again the Brandenburger Tor. The crowd was so closely packed that Marguerite, in the center as always, was caught up and dragged. As the East German police began to fire, panic broke out and she was knocked down onto jagged rubble and loose rocks containing fragments of glass. When at last she got free, her arms and legs were badly lacerated. This aggravated a skin rash she had at the time, which spread and developed ugly, oozing sores. Finally hospitalization was necessary.

Almost happily, Marguerite settled into a Swiss hospital with a collection of mysteries and Stalin's *Treatise on Leninism*. Then a phone call jolted her back to reality.

A friend was calling from Berlin. "Are you planning to come back?"

Indignantly Marguerite demanded an explanation. It seemed that her caller had been talking with Steve White, the *Herald* troubleshooter who was currently spelling her in Berlin. White had recommended that she be transferred to the Paris bureau.

"The *Herald* was a team enterprise and Maggie was not a team player," White says today. "She was alienating everyone and running herself ragged with that dogged sense of competition. It wasn't necessary. I worked very well with Drew Middleton. She could have made it much easier for herself and everybody else if she'd done the same, but that just wasn't Maggie's style. She'd always gotten on well with Russ Hill, who was now the Paris bureau chief. We'd all have been better off if she'd been there covering fashions."

Marguerite thought differently. She was discharged from the hospital and back in Berlin the next day.

There were many at the main *Herald* office in New York who shared White's viewpoint, but Marguerite's determination was not easy to withstand. For the time being the matter was tabled as the blockade continued to be front-page news. On April 16, 1949 Marguerite recorded that 1,383 loaded airplanes flew into three Berlin airfields in an unceasing stream carrying 12,849 tons of supplies to the city. A plane landed in Berlin every sixty-three seconds.

After eleven months the futility of the blockade became obvious to the Soviets. Rather than terrorizing West Berlin into the Communist bloc, they had actually brought the West Berliners closer to the Allies. No longer was West Berlin a city of occupiers and occupied. Shared hardships had brought both closer. The standing joke among the Berliners was, "No blockade is good, but if there has to be one, the best is to be blockaded by the Soviets and fed by the Americans. Imagine what the opposite would be like?"

Finally the pronouncement came: The blockade was to be lifted. On the night of May 11/12, thousands of Berliners milled about the railroad stations waiting for the first trains to arrive. Hundreds of journalists who had come to Berlin to write the obligatory "I flew in on a sack of coal" story were now on hand to record the end of the siege. Flags and banners fluttered along the streets where the first trucks would travel.

An uproarious, full-throated cheer went up at one minute past midnight when a Russian sergeant grasped the road barrier across the highway and flung it into the air. The first great truck, bearing tons of fresh fruit and vegetables, began to roll. At the same moment the long, low hoot of a train whistle was heard and the first locomotive in eleven months steamed into Berlin.

It was a night of jubilation for Marguerite as much as for the others, but the end of the siege presaged the termination of her Berlin assignment as well. With the blockade over, the German news focus shifted. The emergent news centers were now West German Chancellor Konrad Adenauer's struggling recovery program in Bonn and the military government in Frankfurt.

Don Cook, who had been dispatched to Germany to cover both these centers, generously offered Marguerite the military story. "I wasn't totally naive," he explains today. "I knew that nothing or no one would transform Marguerite Higgins into a team player, but I felt that there was plenty to keep both of us busy. We were satisfied with the arrangement, but the big brass back in New York was not. Very soon we each received telegrams. I was to cover Bonn and Frankfurt; Maggie was to remain in Berlin until further notice. This really rocked her. They were saying in effect that she was to stay out of the mainstream. The Berlin blockade had been a kind of cops-and-robbers, cowboys-and-Indians story and she'd handled it well. Now the picture had grown far more complex; diplomacy was essential. Maggie had never learned intramural politics and that's what cost her the assignment she wanted."

Marguerite was still reeling when a second bombshell dropped. Again it came in the form of an office communiqué and could not have been more devastating. She was to be transferred to Tokyo. A new perspective was needed there, Marguerite was told, *her* perspective. There was no gypsy on hand to foretell that the high point of her career and her greatest recognition were waiting across the world. All she knew was that her predecessor there was lucky to get one story published in a week.

PART FOUR

ALONE
AT THE FRONT

Twelve

Marguerite had lost the battle but very soon she would win her own private war with destiny. The foreign editor of the *Herald* had listened to her arguments and then informed her that no one was indispensable. The assignment was to cover the Far East. What she chose to do about it was up to her.

Marguerite arrived in Tokyo in April 1950. She was twenty-nine years old. She missed her elegant home in Berlin, her cook, and her secretary, not to mention the exhilaration of the big story and its attendant by-line. Far Eastern correspondents were quartered in small, humid rooms at the Tokyo press club.

Reluctantly Marguerite came to acknowledge that she also missed Bill Hall. Although he and his wife had grown apart, there were four children to consider, plus the effect of a divorce on a brilliant military career. It was best, she had told him, that they be halfway across the world from each other. Now Marguerite was beginning to have second thoughts.

The resident press viewed the coolly confident newcomer cautiously at best. "Our beat may not have been much of a story, but it was the only story we had and we didn't like outsiders knocking it," Keyes Beech of the *Chicago Daily News* explained. "Maggie didn't do much to disguise the fact that she found the Far East assignment about as exciting as a duck pond."

The *Life* photographer Carl Mydans remembered Marguerite as "pretty, alluring, and very determined. How could she fail to set the other correspondents on edge? Everybody was talking about her, speculating."

Allen Raymond, Marguerite's predecessor, was well liked, a non-boat rocker whose departure was much lamented. As a newcomer and a woman, Marguerite must have anticipated a certain initial reserve. What she received was suspicion, resentment, and often open hostility. The reason was at first puzzling. She had no idea why conversations abruptly terminated as she entered a room or why trivial remarks on her part would cause the other correspondents to exchange knowing glances.

The mystery eventually was solved when Marguerite discovered one of her colleagues reading *Shriek with Pleasure*. Toni Howard's novel of fun and games played against the Berlin rubble might not have made the national best-seller list, but it was a hot item among journalistic circles. The racy exploits of the glamorous correspondent who slipped casually from bed to bed always managing to take her lovers' prime stories with her were discussed in infinite detail. A final bit of evidence, many readers believed, was the conclusion in which the feckless heroine departed Germany in search of fresh adventures—where else but To-kyo? Who else but Maggie Higgins? Men worried about their stories. Women worried about their husbands.

An exception was Helen Lambert, wife of the Associated Press correspondent Tom Lambert. "Marguerite's arrival was like the drop-ping of a small bomb," she recalled. "Possibly I felt differently from the others because I'd been a prosecutor at the Tokyo war crimes trials, and learned firsthand what it meant to be a woman in a so-called man's world." Helen made a point of inviting Marguerite to lunch and getting to know her. It was to become a lifelong friendship. For the moment it was Marguerite's only friendship.

Within her first week, Marguerite learned that Korea would be hold-ing its national elections on May 30. It was to be the first general election in the country's four-thousand-year history. She was intrigued by the little-known country, which, like her longed-for Berlin, was next door to a Communist power. Here was a substantial news story only a four-hour flight away. She arranged to arrive in Korea a few days ahead of the voting to get some feel for the country.

Marguerite immediately saw story potential in the "Land of the Morning Calm," which like Germany had been arbitrarily divided. Since the end of the nineteenth century, Korea had been a pawn in a power struggle between the emergent empires of Russia, China, and Japan. The conclusion of the Russo-Japanese War in 1905 had left Korea firmly within the grasp of Japan. The pretense of a protectorate was maintained for five years until Japanese annexation forced the last Korean king to abdicate and the country to become a part of the Japanese Empire.

Korea was forgotten and didn't reenter the world view until 1945 when the interests of Russia and the United States collided in a vacuum created by the collapse of Japan. As Marguerite explained later in a *Herald* dispatch, "The 38th parallel of latitude, which ultimately became the demarcation line between Red Korea and Free Korea, has no basis in international law. This parallel was selected arbitrarily by the United States and Russia to solve the problem of splitting up the Japanese war prisoners. According to agreement, all Japanese who surrendered above the parallel would be prisoners of the Soviet Union and those who surrendered below the parallel would go into American POW camps. When it proved impossible to establish a coalition government acceptable to both Russia and the United States, the parallel turned into a permanent barrier bristling with guns and barbed wire."

The geographic split, totally ignoring Korean politics, resulted entirely from enmities between the United States and the Soviet Union. If these powers had remained out of Korea, it is highly unlikely that a division would have occurred. Various factions within the country possibly would have fought among themselves, but the whole of the country would have been the prize. The cold war removed that option from Korea.

As a result of the division, the Korean North, with most of the country's wood, iron, tungsten, gold, copper, and graphite, as well as much of its hydroelectric power, was a Russian satellite ruled by Kim Il Sung. The South, containing two-thirds of the 30 million Korean people and the majority of its agricultural production, was struggling toward democracy under United Nations sponsorship. Its ruler was President Syngman Rhee, a seventy-five-year-old Methodist minister educated at Harvard and Princeton, who had been for many years the head of a group of Korean patriots in exile agitating for Korean independence.

It was prophetic that the first story of Marguerite's Far Eastern assignment was filed from Korea. The story's placement on Page One was more indicative of Marguerite's growing following than of the current national interest in the little-known country. The date was May 29, 1950; the headline:

REPORTER GOES TO BORDER DIVIDES KOREA
FINDS REDS FIGHT WITH WORDS AND SHELLS

Marguerite wrote of how the remote mountain town of Kaesong, located just below the thirty-eighth parallel, had been the target of continual attack from the Communist North. The activity had accelerated in recent days as the election approached. The previous night Communists had lobbed eleven artillery shells into the town and followed with a menacing harangue from a mountaintop loudspeaker. The people of Kaesong had been warned that the election would be the signal for a North Korean attack all along the parallel and that the Communist air force would bomb all polling places.

Marguerite interviewed Colonel Sung Ho Chan, the South Korean regimental commander of the area, who seemed more concerned by the terms of the demarcation than the threats of the guerrillas. The majority of the strategic peaks overlooking his city had been ceded to North Korea, leaving Kaesong with only one vantage point below the parallel. Marguerite accompanied him to this craggy stronghold located just seventy-five yards from the nearest Communist pillbox, from which hand grenades recently had been thrown. Carefully protected by sandbags, the South Koreans were calling to their Communist cousins: "Guards of the thirty-eighth parallel, come across and see us and let us talk. We will convince you that it is best to join the winning side."

The next day Marguerite found Seoul in the last throes of a spirited political campaign. The key issue was President Rhee, whom Marguerite described as "democratic in conviction but autocratic by temperament." Rhee's term of office had two years to run. Opponents sought to limit his powers during that time and establish presidential accountability to the legislature.

Marguerite was impressed by the orderliness of the election, although by western standards the arrests of 30 of the 2,156 candidates would be deplored. Upon investigation she found that nine of them were Communists (outlawed in the South) and the rest were accused of committing assault and battery on the other candidates.

President Rhee emphasized his determination to uphold individual liberty and offered correspondents the opportunity to examine any cases they cared to question. He also suggested that in a country where Communist guerrillas were continually terrorizing the populace, the police might be understandably a little overzealous.

According to United Nations observers, cases of political injustice were the exception and democratic electoral procedure was generally followed. In Seoul Marguerite found both wealthy and poor voters taking scrupulous pride in observing election rules. She could not help but contrast this with the travesty she had witnessed in Poland four years before.

The results of the elections caused South Korean optimism to soar. President Rhee had always been recognized and applauded for his almost phenomenal ability to curb inflation under the most adverse circumstances. Now with a free election resulting in 121 of the 210 National Assembly seats going to nonaligned candidates, most people were enthusiastic about what they perceived as a liberalizing, stabilizing influence. The economy and the spirits of the South Koreans were riding high.

Marguerite wrote her observations to Bill. Things looked good in the South. Were they too good to last?

Returning to Japan and the office she shared with Keyes Beech, Marguerite found her colleague's greeting anything but enthusiastic. Beech had previously shared the office with her predecessor, the easygoing Allen Raymond.

"The arrangement had worked beautifully," Beech recalled. "Raymond and I complemented each other. Maggie was something else. Every time I picked up the phone she was right there hanging on every word, wanting to know exactly who I was talking to, what it was all about, and whether she could go along. I had decided to abandon the office to her and was looking for another space for myself when we were thrown together by unexpected circumstances. Our relationship may have been a combative one, but we did have something very important in common, the passionate, ruthless desire to cover war. That kind of reporting assignment doesn't come every day."

Their big chance came on June 25, 1950 when civil war erupted in Korea. The two sides, North and South, were polarized by conflicting social and economic principles and by the ambitions and the fears of their leaders. The significance of their struggle was not immediately apparent.

As Marguerite would write later, "The Red invasion of South Korea exploded like a delayed-action bomb." John Muccio, United States Ambassador to Korea, had been playing strip poker with the embassy secretaries the night before the invasion. Returning home in the early hours of the morning, he was informed by the military attaché's chief deputy, Everett Drumwright, that the North Koreans were crossing the thirty-eighth parallel. This had been such a common occurrence of late that Muccio wasn't unduly alarmed. "If it begins to look important, call me back," he instructed. At 6:00 A.M. Muccio was summoned. "This *is* important," Drumwright informed him. "They're crossing all along the border."

In Tokyo Muccio's reports were received by a duty officer who didn't even bother to awaken General MacArthur. But within hours the swift advance of the attackers revealed their strength. South Korea, the last non-Communist outpost in northern Asia, was crumbling.

Marguerite placed an early-morning call to Bill. "Well, they've finally done it," she said. Neither felt the surprise that rocked Far Eastern headquarters. Bill shuddered inwardly, knowing that soon the woman he loved would be in the thick of the action.

The United States was under little obligation to enter the conflict. It had no formal alliance with the South Korean republic. The decision of whether or not to commit troops was still pending two days later when Marguerite managed to wangle a ride to the war zone on a plane that was being sent to evacuate the last of the American civilians. Traveling with her were Keyes Beech, Frank Gibney of *Time*, and Burton Crane of the *New York Times*. It was their second attempt to reach Seoul. Two days before their plane had been mysteriously turned back shortly after takeoff. Later they learned it was because Kimpo Airfield was being strafed by Russian planes. Undeterred, the four had driven south to Itazuke Air Force Base to await the next flight.

At the last moment before boarding, Frank Gibney attempted to dissuade Marguerite from going. "Korea is no place for a woman," he warned her.

Keyes Beech, who by this time knew Marguerite well, agreed with Gibney but added, "It's okay for *her*."

Thirteen

"My instructions are to swoop down over the field and try to sight Americans," the pilot explained to Marguerite and the other three correspondents.

"If we don't see any, it means we get the hell out but fast. The field will be in enemy hands. A green flag means we land." Two flaming planes were visible as they circled the rubble-strewn field that apparently had been strafed only minutes before their arrival; standing by were a group of some thirty Americans signaling frantically.

Once on the ground they were briefed by an American officer who looked up from his job of burning documents long enough to inform them that Seoul was still in friendly hands. Sixty officers of the KMAG (Korean Military Advisory Group) had been ordered back into the city that afternoon on direct orders from General MacArthur, who belatedly had been given responsibility for American personnel in Korea; at least two days passed after the invasion before he was placed in charge.

American refugees crowded onto the plane. The pilot looked doubtfully at Marguerite and the other correspondents. "Are you sure you want to stay here?"

The answer was unanimous. Each of the four was aware that they shared a world scoop. They were the first correspondents to reach South Korea and wanted nothing more than to head for the capital. For once transportation was no problem. Departing Americans had abandoned all types of vehicles. Some had locked their cars, but most left the keys behind. Beech and Marguerite selected a shiny red Studebaker. Gibney and Crane followed in a jeep.

It was dusk and a light rain had begun to fall as they drove toward

Seoul. In the distance machine guns stuttered. The road was clogged with refugees heading in the opposite direction. Suddenly recognizing approaching Americans, they began to cheer, believing that they were about to be rescued.

"Poor souls, cheering us dumb correspondents—in those days they had faith in anything American," Keyes recalled. "It's an exhilarating experience to be cheered by a beleaguered people. I remember yelling to Maggie, 'Vote for Beech, he's a peach!' as we crossed the Han River."

Arriving at last at the KMAG building, they were briefed by Colonel Sterling Wright. "The situation is fluid," he explained. Keyes interpreted: "That means they don't know what the hell is happening."

The three men were quartered with a friend of Beech's, and Marguerite was given a room in the colonel's headquarters. She didn't like being separated from the others, but by this time it was late and an argument seemed a waste of energy.

Despite her fatigue, Marguerite followed some inner warning and lay down fully clothed. It seemed that she had barely closed her eyes before Colonel Wright's aide was shaking her violently. "Get up!" he shouted. "They're in the city. We've got to run for it!"

Mortar shells were bursting all about them as Marguerite ran after the aide to a waiting jeep. Colonel Wright and his executive officer were parked in a vehicle next to it. Keyes and the other correspondents were nowhere in sight. The muffled thunder of guns was audible as the two jeeps slowly navigated their way through the black night. The rainy streets were filled with thousands of refugees as well as the South Korean army and its equipment, all trying to escape across the Han River just below the city.

The bridge ahead was clogged. Some people plodded along pushing carts or carrying their possessions in bundles, while others crowded into every kind of vehicle moving at bumper-to-bumper speed. As Marguerite's jeep at last reached the northerly approach to the three-lane span a sheet of flame lighted up the sky before her. "My God! There goes the bridge!" someone cried. "We're trapped." Thousands were killed instantly by the explosion; others were plunged into the river and drowned. A large truck was blown high into the air right before Marguerite's eyes.

Later she was to learn that incredibly the bridge had been blown up by the South Korean army, even though Seoul was still in their hands. The explosion occurred at 2:30 A.M., thirty minutes after President Truman had announced that American air and sea forces had been ordered to the area and military equipment was committed.

After the bridge's destruction Colonel Wright frantically tried to collect the members of the American Advisory Group and their equipment, hoping to find an alternate route south. His task wasn't eased by the whine of nearby artillery shells or the clatter of enemy machine guns all around them. After hours of confused searching they found that the three railway bridges had also been dynamited. Finally, as dawn broke, it became apparent that the only possible hope of escape meant leaving all vehicles and personal belongings behind and crossing the river by boat or raft.

From time to time Marguerite would ask the drivers of trucks, jeeps, and weapons carriers who were joining the stalled convoy if they had seen the other correspondents. Finally one of them told her, "Oh, they got out in plenty of time. The three of them came by the office late last night. I told them to head fast across the bridge for Suwon."

Marguerite was furious. Not only had Keyes and the others abandoned her, but they were also undoubtedly sitting safe and snug in Suwon with their stories long since filed.

While waiting for a scouting party to locate a place to ferry their group across the river, Colonel Wright noted Marguerite's dejection. "What's the matter, kid, afraid you won't get your story out?" She nodded glumly and he offered her his best: "Stick by the radio truck and we'll try to send a message for you if you can keep it short."

Marguerite quickly grabbed her typewriter and set it on the hood of a jeep. Streams of retreating South Koreans gaped curiously at the blonde woman dressed in navy blue skirt, flowered blouse, and bright blue sweater typing briskly, oblivious to the cries and confusion about her. She completed her story, but communications were never established long enough to send it.

By this time the artillery fire was picking up and the situation had grown critical. A few small boats that had been located were defended at gunpoint. Captain Harry Taylor managed to get Marguerite and a few others in their party on one of these. He and the rest swam the entire width of the river, holding their weapons aloft. "The bullets pelted the water around us like rain," Taylor remembered, "but miraculously no one was hit."

Marguerite and her boat companions didn't fare much better. Halfway across the Han the overcrowded raft sank and she and the others had to swim the rest of the way. Lieutenant Colonel George Kelley, who was on the boat, too, recalled pulling himself out of the river, dashing across the sandy beach, and then diving into a rice paddy to escape the mortar fire that was coming from Seoul. "Finally I stopped panting long enough to look around and see who was with me. There lay Maggie with a grin on her face! I said, 'You scared, Maggie?' She shook her head. 'No. But how the hell are we going to get out of here?' "

The dismal answer was to walk the long mountain trail to Suwon twenty miles to the south. Soon their single file of soldiers was joined by refugees. Marguerite recognized the Korean minister of the interior, who had once been a Buddhist monk, trudging along with a pack on his back. "Before long," Marguerite was to write, "the Americans were leading a ragamuffin army of tattered soldiers, old men, diplomats, children, and a woman war correspondent. I was very conscious of being the only woman in the group and determined not to give any trouble in any way, shape, or form. Luckily I'm a good walker and by enormous good fortune was wearing flat-heeled shoes. For much of the march I was close to the head of the column."

Marguerite walked fourteen miles through very rough terrain before a jeep appeared on the dirt trail. Somehow the occupants made room for her and Colonel Wright.

Once in Suwon Marguerite almost immediately encountered Keyes Beech, who had his own tale to tell. Beech had also been awakened in the middle of the night and told to get to the bridge.

"I didn't worry about Maggie since I knew she was with Colonel Wright and if anyone could get out, he would," Beech recalls today. "Just as we were crossing the southerly section of the bridge it exploded. Our portion didn't collapse—at least not then—but the section just behind it did. Gibney and Crane both received head wounds when the jeep windows blew out. I grabbed my typewriter; the others left theirs behind. We also left Maggie's suitcase—which she later told me contained a Paris gown—in the middle of the Han River Bridge, or whatever was left of it. We were a sorry sight slogging through the rice paddies. My loafers kept slipping off; then my belt buckle broke. Pretty soon I was trying to hold up my pants, hang on to my typewriter, and lead Burton Crane, who was bleeding pretty badly from a head wound.

"Maggie was mad about losing the dress, mad because we'd left her, mad because we'd finally found a jeep and driven to Suwon while she walked most of the way. She only calmed down when she discovered that we hadn't been able to file our stories either. The only way to score the scoop of a lifetime was to catch a 'commuter' back to Japan and file it there, which is exactly what we did. And that's how the war began for Maggie and me.''

Back in South Korea the following afternoon, Marguerite set her typewriter on one barracks bag and sat on another, typing a quick story. She was working intently, trying to ignore the distractions around her; the windy airstrip, the dirt, the confused activity, and the artillery fire in the distance.

Slowly she became aware of someone standing beside her. Frowning slightly, Marguerite raised her eyes. There next to her, wearing his gold-braid hat and summer khakis with the shirt open at the collar and smoking his corncob pipe, was General MacArthur. Behind him was a retinue of assorted military officers who had just returned with him from an inspection trip to the banks of the Han.

Marguerite and MacArthur exchanged polite smiles that masked curiosity and appraisal. There was a kind of ''Dr. Livingstone, I presume?'' quality about the meeting that both found slightly amusing. MacArthur's offer of a flight back to Tokyo was all the more precious because it meant return to a communications center with her new story.

Aboard the *Bataan* a few minutes later, Marguerite learned that MacArthur had held a press briefing that morning. ''I'm sure he would talk with you now,'' Major General Whitney, the General's aide, said. ''Why don't you go up to his cabin and see him?'' Marguerite needed no urging. Picking up her notebook and pen, she hurried forward.

MacArthur had long been an enigma to her. For nearly one hundred years Japan had been ruled by a succession of shoguns, military leaders who ran the country in the name of the emperor. In a sense MacArthur was the last shogun. Since 1945 he had served as a benevolent military despot, arbitrarily deciding who would own land and who would not, and more importantly dictating and enforcing an all-new constitution. One of his most drastic reforms—Marguerite's favorite—was his insistence that Japanese women be allowed to vote.

One day, Marguerite had been told, an old Japanese woman had thrown herself face down on the sidewalk in front of the general to demonstrate her respect. MacArthur had gently raised her to her feet, explaining, ''Now, now, we don't do that sort of thing anymore.''

Marguerite had loved that story, but there were many others told of the general that were far less appealing. This was her first opportunity to form her own opinion of the controversial man. Of their initial meeting she later wrote, "In personal conversation I found General MacArthur to be a man of graciousness and great lucidity. So far as I'm concerned he is without the poseur traits of which I have heard him accused." As for the story, there was little to report. General MacArthur would submit his impressions to President Truman as he had been asked to do. He would recommend, he said, sending American divisions to fight in Korea. The rest was up to the president.

On June 30 Marguerite returned to Suwon. Her original landing near Seoul, now one retreat away, had been only three days before. It seemed an eternity. American troops had been committed. The war had begun in earnest.

Although eager to reach the scene of the action, she shared the anxiety of the others aboard the heavy, unarmed ammunition plane. Russian fighters had been spurting bullets at the Suwon airstrip for days. Yesterday a transport had exploded in flames over the field. As they approached Pusan Bay, the pilot ordered them to get into parachutes and helmets. Then glancing back at the 155-millimeter shells they were carrying, he conceded the futility of it all. "I don't know what the Christ good a chute would do if we do get hit."

Marguerite felt the rush of fear that would become so familiar in the weeks ahead. She later said, "It seemed to turn into a trapped ball of breath that was pressing against my heart. I could see from the faces of the crew that I was definitely not worrying alone."

An unidentified plane was sighted but apparently did not see them. Their mood didn't lighten even as the plane bumped its way to a stop on the Suwon airstrip where the pilot had to brake suddenly to avoid the wreckage of bullet-splattered planes that had not been cleared from the runway.

Shakily Marguerite climbed out from the plane, vowing never to ride in another ammunition ship. Her first greeting was from a dour-faced colonel. "You'll have to go right back, young lady," he informed her. "You can't stay here. There may be trouble."

"I wouldn't be here if there was no trouble, sir," she patiently explained. "Trouble is news and gathering the news is my job."

As the colonel hesitated, a knight in a dusty jeep drove up and saved the day. It was Lieutenant May, Wright's aide, Marguerite's comrade from the long march across the mountains out of Seoul. "How about a ride?" she shouted. He nodded, smiling, and she jumped in. They roared off in a cloud of dust before the colonel could recover.

The message was clear: The best means of getting her stories was to stay as far from the brass and as close to the front lines as possible. Covering the war had become a personal crusade. It was as though she represented every woman who had ever striven to do a so-called man's job. As the representative of one of the world's most noted newspapers, she was responsible for that paper's coverage of the war. The bottom line was her right to be judged as an individual, a reporter doing a job. From her earliest days at the *Herald* she had argued that she was as capable as any man. Failure to reach the front would prove to the main office and to the entire world that her sex was a handicap.

An atmosphere of panic, rumor, and counterrumor swept Suwon. "The Reds are down the road!" "No! They're everywhere!" "Tanks have been spotted in the north!" "We're surrounded!"

Finally Major Walt Greenwood decided on a course of action. "We're going to defend the airfield. We'll stand and fight." Marguerite watched Keyes Beech and Tom Lambert grimly arm themselves with carbines. There were sixty men and Marguerite. "All I had with me was my typewriter and toothbrush," she recalled later. "In my retreat from Seoul, I'd learned they were all I really needed."

Major Greenwood did his best to organize a perimeter defense of the bomb-pocked airstrip, believing it to be their last chance. Mines were laid, machine guns entrenched, and small-arms ammunition distributed. It began to look to Marguerite like a Korean Corregidor. She wondered if the outcome would be as futile.

Then just as suddenly plans changed. They were not *yet* surrounded. Everyone was to head for Taejon some eighty miles to the south. Marguerite began the trip at 11:00 P.M., just as torrential Korean rains started. The open jeep driven by Keyes Beech reached its destination at 6:00 A.M. The deserted city of Suwon fell three days later.

In Taejon Marguerite ran into her friend from the Han River shipwreck, Lieutenant Colonel George Kelley, who had now been designated rations and gasoline officer. "Seems like it was July 4 when Maggie came to me and asked for two 'C' rations and a five-gallon can of gas," he recalled. "It seemed that she had run across a *Stars and Stripes* reporter who had somehow purloined a jeep but had no gas. She'd struck up a bargain with him. If he'd take her to the front, she'd get the gas.

"Her clothes were filthy, she was wearing an army shirt and a pair of Korean pants held up by a grass rope. Her smile was winsome. Of course I gave her what she needed. Later that day she returned alone and very depressed. The *Stars and Stripes* reporter had been killed; Maggie had driven the jeep back without a scratch. She went off by herself, refusing to talk about it." The colonel reflected for a moment. "Maggie was a friend to all for the time we were in Taejon. She talked to everyone from privates to generals and the men adored her. She was a lovely lady and the bravest woman I ever knew."

Unfortunately her front-line popularity didn't extend to the big guns within her own profession. The next challenge she faced was far more formidable and difficult to circumnavigate than the doubtful colonel who had attempted to stop her in Suwon. The *Herald* had been delighted by Marguerite's eyewitness account of the fall of Seoul, which they had splashed across Page One in a four-column box complete with a photo of the author and a headline proclaiming: SEOUL'S FALL BY A RE-PORTER WHO ESCAPED.

Although proud of Marguerite, they now sent, without any advance notice, a far more seasoned reporter, presumably to relieve her. Homer Bigart, a senior foreign correspondent on the *Herald Tribune* staff, arrived at the battle zone expecting to take over. Marguerite was to return to Tokyo and resume her originally assigned duties as bureau chief. "This is a small area; there's no room for both of us. What there is to cover, I can handle alone," he informed her with patient firmness.

Marguerite was angry but uncertain, intimidated by Bigart's reputation and seniority and the weight they carried with the home office. At the same time, she considered Korea *her* story. She had been among the very first to arrive and had dug in and made it her own. To be ordered out now seemed totally unfair.

"I won't go," she told him, but her soft voice quavered.

"You *will* go or you can expect to be fired."

Bigart's parting line that she hadn't a single friend in Tokyo and that the entire press contingent there was down on her added to her pain and confusion. Now what? Surely they still weren't holding *Shriek with Pleasure* against her. Marguerite's trips to Tokyo since the fighting began had only been long enough for her to file a story, shower, change clothes, and hop on a plane back to Korea. There had been little opportunity to talk to anyone. Who had she offended this time, and how?

The past week had left Marguerite physically and emotionally drained. How could she cope with this new obstacle? Fortunately, whatever the attitudes of her colleagues covering the war from the Tokyo press club, unexpected moral support existed in Korea, where she needed it most.

Carl Mydans was told of the firing threat directly by Bigart. "What's more important to you, Maggie, the experience of covering the Korean War or the possibility of losing your job?" Marguerite nodded gratefully. The *Life* photographer had put the issue into perspective for her. She would return to the front regardless of the consequences at the *Herald*.

When Keyes Beech added, "We've got the jeep all set and there's a place in it for you," it was hard to keep the tears from her weary eyes.

The Korean monsoon was continuing to beat down early the next morning when Marguerite climbed into the jeep beside Beech. Riding with them were Carl Mydans and Tom Lambert. Within hours they would see the first American troops dig in and die in their first Korean battle.

Marguerite's instructions were to watch the skies and give warning if she saw a plane. Only the day before American ground forces at the front lines had been subjected to a twenty-five-minute machine gun and rocket attack by their own planes. Fortunately none of the troops had been killed, but as the correspondents neared the village of Pyontek they drove around blackened, still smoldering ammunition trucks. Far more tragic, however, were the mutilated bodies of refugees caught in the strafing. The smell of death rose from the ditches and rice paddies on either side of them.

Command headquarters turned out to be a tiny thatched hut surrounded by a sea of mud. They were greeted by Colonel Harold "Red" Ayers, commander of the first battalion of the Thirty-fourth Infantry Regiment, who shared his post with a noisy, filthy assortment of pigs, ducks, and chickens. They had barely arrived when the order came: Bazooka teams were needed immediately to stop enemy tanks headed their way.

It was a moment Marguerite would remember all her life. America's raw young troops, boys who had reached the Korean front only a few hours before, were going into battle for the first time. Marguerite believed that she had been cut in on a critical slice of history. She did not know that it was the beginning of what she would later recall as the long retreat.

The correspondents' jeep followed the bazooka teams to the crest of a hill, where the convoy halted. Soldiers jumped from their trucks and spread out on a ridge paralleling the road now jammed with South Korean soldiers retreating southward.

Watching from a foxhole dug into a Korean graveyard, Marguerite heard the order to attack given. The boys in the bazooka team remained motionless, looking at the advancing tanks as though they were watching a newsreel. It took much prodding from their officers before the first small groups left their foxholes and crept slowly forward.

A few days later Marguerite's account appeared on Page One of the *Herald*. It began:

"This is how America lost her first infantryman in the mounting battle against the Northern Korean Communist invaders of South Korea.

"As this correspondent watched from a nearby hill the young soldier fired his bazooka against a tank astraddle a railroad hard by. After firing, the American looked up to check his aim and was caught by machine gun fire."

She then went on to describe the engagement.

"Heavily laden with bazookas, ammunition and rifles, the soldiers moved cautiously down the road that led over the crest of a hill to a small village where the tank tracks showed they were headed. 'Dig in on this hill,' ordered First Lieutenant Charles Payne, pointing to ridges flanking the village. 'Stay down and keep guns trained on the road. We can get them easily if they come this way.'

"But the tanks fooled us. As we lay behind grave mounds on the hill overlooking the village tanks clattered machine gun fire into the village. Then suddenly after an hour there was silence. Soon excited shouts from South Korean scouts told us why.

"The tanks had moved to the railroad line and were proceeding along it. Then something went wrong. It looked as if the tank treads had been damaged. Out from our hill went a couple of bazooka teams. From the foxhole where I crouched, I could see Americans crawling through a rice paddy in the direction of the tanks. Unfortunately the terrain was such that the troops were at a disadvantage in aiming. They had to aim up and they tried shooting at too long a range. As the bazooka hammered away at the tanks the first big one swung its turret and the fire flashed as it let loose two blasts at the Americans dug in on the hill. Then the machine guns chattered, the gunners also shooting at the bazooka team.

"After a full hour the tanks still held the bazookas in check. Then the young American 'got it.' Enemy infantry joined in the fire directed at the bazooka team and the latter withdrew.

"Despite driving rain, mortars were brought up, but as of this evening the tanks still had not been destroyed. The bazooka patrol is stationed along the road leading to this command post. Everyone is waiting for dawn and a showdown with the menacing weapons."

Marguerite had returned to the command post shortly after the young man's death. She did not have to be a military expert to realize that the Americans had been defeated soundly in the first skirmish and that a major retreat would soon be under way. Bazookas were not enough to halt tanks, and there were too few of them to prevent the North Korean infantry from breaking through.

There was also a minor but immediate personal problem to cope with: Alighting from the jeep Marguerite slipped and fell flat on her face into a muddy rice paddy. Soaked and caked with mud, she wanted to get dry.

Lieutenant Payne helped Marguerite to her feet, found her some dry fatigues, and gallantly escorted her to an empty thatched hut where she could change. "There's one other thing," she ventured, stepping out of the hut, "the fleas. . . ." A thick network of bites pocked her waist, thighs, and ankles. She had been in agony the past few days but was reluctant to complain.

"Yeah," Payne nodded sympathetically. "We all get them, but the medic has insecticide powder that works." That little gray box of powder would be her most precious possession throughout the Korean War.

Payne walked her down to the medic's hut. Knowing that he was a veteran of World War II, Marguerite asked him how he felt about being back at war. Payne's answer was matter of fact. "When I learned I was coming here I was plain scared to death. I figured that I'd run through my share of good luck in Italy. A man's only got a certain number of close calls coming to him. But as soon as I heard the guns I got over it."

They were still talking when the body of the first casualty, Private Kenneth Shadrick, was brought in. He was fair, frail, and too young-looking for the Army. Marguerite noted that his face bore an expression of slight surprise. "The prospect of death had probably seemed as unreal to Private Shadrick as the entire war seemed to me," Marguerite wrote later.

Handing Marguerite the box of flea powder, the medic glanced down at the lifeless boy. "What a place to die," he said.

"Why don't you tell them back home just how useless it really is?" Marguerite was asked again and again in those first terrible days by soldiers. It wasn't an easy task.

The troops were almost totally green, young, inexperienced men from an occupation army. Some were literally snatched from the beds of their Japanese girlfriends and flown into combat. Most had volunteered for peacetime service to get away from home, to see a little of the world, and qualify for the GI bill.

They were undertrained and unprepared for war. Many had been assigned jobs as bartenders in the officers clubs, clerks in the post exchange, laundrymen, barbers, and storekeepers. Helen Lambert recalled watching as an army truck roared up to a "gypsy wagon" where three soldiers were making and selling hotdogs and hamburgers beside the military swimming pool. The cooks were ordered into the truck, the food still sizzling unattended on the stove as they drove off. Soon the men were aboard a plane bound for Korea, their spatulas replaced by rifles.

Many officers were as inexperienced as their men. Others, who had fought bravely and been decorated in World War II, had returned to civilian jobs only to be called back into uniform within hours and sent to the front. Five years had passed since that war. Hard lessons had been forgotten. Many of these men who had once triumphed so gallantly were among the first casualties.

Ill-equipped officers and men were without preparation plunged into a situation where military intelligence was virtually nonexistent. In the early days of the war the troops at the front lines were strafed six times in as many days by their own planes. "Why don't those bastards stay at thirty thousand feet or go back to the officers club?" a sergeant griped to Marguerite as the two cowered together in a roadside ditch.

Fortunately the Communists were even more poorly informed. Had they fully grasped the situation, they could have pushed the Americans into the sea. As it was, the fledgling troops held out against thirty-to-one odds until they finally ran out of ammunition.

Ironically, while the Communists overestimated the United States, the Americans grossly underestimated North Korean capability. Only that can begin to explain the one question asked most frequently of

Marguerite by the soldiers all around her: "*How can the United States throw us into such a useless, hopeless battle with so little to back us up?*"

The orders were to hold at any cost, and the cost was terrible. Marguerite would remember all her life the fourth day of the war when Colonel "Red" Ayers, weary and tired, asked her and the other arriving correspondents if they had heard of any reinforcements, adding, "I was just kind of wondering whether we would still be around to see them when they get here."

Again and again Marguerite heard the story. "We fired our last round and then just got out. I don't know how many wounded we left behind. One man after fourteen hours of active combat remained at his position to cover the withdrawal of his outfit. What more could we do? One machine gun and fifty rifles against a regiment? They just kept coming out of the hills, shooting at us with automatic weapons."

One sergeant told Marguerite of a boy whose leg was hanging by a shred. "I dragged him into a thicket. There was no way I could have carried him out and no one to help me. I started to explain that to him, but he just shook his head. 'It's okay, Sarge. I don't expect to get out of here, but maybe I can take some of them with me.' I handed him a grenade and crawled out, machine guns firing all around."

As Marguerite and Keyes were returning to the command post one time, an eighty-eight-millimeter shell exploded a short distance from their jeep. Foot soldiers on retreat jumped into the vehicle, their captain shouting to Beech, "Get going fast, I've had enough incoming mail!"

Later they stopped to look back at the flaming city of Chonan where so many had been trapped trying to smash the oncoming Communist tanks. "Our fire got plenty of the enemy," the captain explained, "but you can't get a tank with a bazooka. They [bazooka rockets] just seemed to bounce right off. We fought on until they were within two hundred yards, then took off. Why don't you write it like it really is?" he challenged Marguerite. "It wasn't a battle, it was a slaughter."

Even as he spoke an enemy tank began to aim in their direction. Moving quickly southward, they glanced nervously at the high green hills flanking them, fearful that the Communists might have already begun to move in.

When not spearheaded by tanks, the enemy infantry could take advantage of the Americans' numerical weakness to infiltrate and encircle. In those early days the United States troops were attacked from the rear, sides, and head-on. The war had officially begun for the United States with just three understrength battalions. The odds improved but never approached equality. Both the North Koreans and later the Chinese keyed their tactics to their one big advantage: vast quantities of manpower.

Marguerite and the other correspondents faced a different source of frustration. Hal Boyle, an Associated Press columnist and the most senior correspondent in the battle area, said later that never since the Civil War had correspondents had so few facilities vital to their trade. Transportation and communication were essential but elusive. Marguerite and Keyes were the envy of the group because of the jeep that Keyes had rescued from Seoul. The others hitchhiked whenever they could. When a telephone was finally installed it was ordered that the phone could only be used by correspondents from midnight until 4:00 A.M, later shortened to 2:00 to 4:00 A.M. It made no difference if the lines were free at other times; they were still unavailable to correspondents. Frequently the phones were denied them entirely, meaning that the only effective method of filing a story was to fly to Japan, which meant precious time away from the battle zone.

Marguerite believed that Colonel Pat Echols, General MacArthur's press chief in Taejon, regarded the press as natural enemies. Unable to actually get rid of them, he could and did make their lives a constant hell. They bitterly resented the drain on their energies; the first priority should have been the coverage of the war, not lining up for the phone between 2:00 and 4:00.

Marguerite had now been with the troops three weeks. Realizing that as a woman she was an obvious target for comment, she was determined to ask for nothing that could possibly be construed as a personal favor. Like the rest of the correspondents, when not actually sleeping on the ground at the front with an individual unit, she generally occupied a tabletop in the room where the telephone was located. The custom was to come back from the front, bang out the story, and then stretch out on the table in an attempt to sleep despite the noise of the other stories being shouted into the phone. Once her turn had come to phone in her story, no matter what the hour, Marguerite returned to the front lines, which were now changing so fast that the story might already be obsolete.

"Never once during the Korean War was I satisfied with the writing and organization of a single story," Marguerite said later. "I know all of us in the beginning kept thinking, maybe next time there will be more time to think it through or next time I won't be so tired, but in those early days it was commonplace for Keyes, Tom, and myself to find each other slumped over our typewriters, collapsed in the middle of a story.''

Marguerite attempted to put her own professional concern aside as she continued to do her hazardous and demanding job, but the nagging fear continued. She had heard nothing from the head office since Homer Bigart's warning that she would be fired if she remained in Korea. Carl, Keyes, and Tom were reassuring, but along with the danger of mortars and machine guns, Marguerite continued to feel a personal threat. The insecurities of a depression kid never left her; she went about her duties with the dread of joblessness poised like a sword above her head.

What finally did happen was more like a bomb. Its source was totally unexpected. In the midst of the battle for Taejon, Marguerite received orders that she was to leave Korea immediately.

No one, including the officer who had relayed the message, knew why.

Fourteen

Marguerite watched from the window of the hospital train as ambulance after ambulance disgorged its load of wounded. Silent and sullen-faced, the casualties walked or were carried aboard. Soon the gangrenous odor of untended wounds mingled with the car's own latrinelike smell.

Patients in stretchers were placed across the backs of wooden benches. Other patients tried to lie down on the seats or the floor, but soon the car was so crowded that it was impossible for anyone to stretch out. As the train finally began to move, the wounded soldiers, most of them still in their teens, stared at the reporter with weary curiosity. Often their stares had a kind of angry bewilderment. A sense of guilt that she, too, was not wounded swept over Marguerite, adding to her misery at banishment.

Finally a boy sitting across from her broke the silence, asking the question she had heard so often, ''How come you're here if you don't have to be?''

''I'm a war correspondent,'' she explained. ''People back home want to know what's going on here.''

''I hope you tell it like it really is,'' someone said.

Most of the men sank back into their pain; but one, Captain Lincoln J. Buttery, a medical corpsman, told her his story. Sitting in the stench and darkness of the train, he described the hillside massacre of a band of helpless wounded north of Taejon. A dozen walking wounded and an equal number of litter patients had become trapped. He and two chaplains, Father Hermann Feldhoelter and Captain Kenneth Hyslop, were the only officers with them. Those who could walk were ordered to take to the hills and make out as best they could. Some in better condition stayed behind to help the three officers carry the litter patients.

"The terrain grew increasingly rough, and after midnight we ran into real trouble. We put the litters down and tried to take cover. The two chaplains paid no attention to the fire. Pretty soon Captain Hyslop got hit. Men were dying and Father Feldhoelter went from litter to litter, administering last rites.

"We could hear the Koreans yelling and carrying on the way they do. It was beginning to get light, and we knew they would be on top of us soon. Father Feldhoelter said to me and the Protestant chaplain—the rest of the litter bearers had run away—'You two must leave. You have families and responsibilities. Mine is the duty to stay.' "

Captain Buttery had crawled away from the scene on his belly, dragging a wounded leg. Before clambering down over a bluff, he paused to look back. "The Reds—young kids sixteen to eighteen, they looked—were closing in. The litter patients were screaming while the Reds slaughtered them. Father Feldhoelter, kneeling by one of the stretchers, made no sound as he fell."

Marguerite listened to this horror story and others as the stinking train rattled on into the night. Two of the wounded died. She learned about it only on reaching Taegu the next morning when their bodies were removed from the car.

By now Marguerite knew who had ordered her out of Korea and why. She had not been fired by the *Herald Tribune* as she had originally feared. Instead the order had come from Lieutenant General Walton W. Walker, Eighth Army Commander and head of the American forces in Korea. "This is just not the type of war where women ought to be running around the front lines," he had announced by way of explanation. A spokesman for General MacArthur's public information office had reinforced the edict by stating that General Walker was in direct control of all war correspondents in Korea. "He has the final say on which correspondents will be allowed to stay."

Marguerite had called the *Herald Tribune* and explained, "I'm going to General Walker's headquarters in Taegu to remind him that I'm a duly accredited correspondent and to convince him that I'm here in that capacity and not as a woman." Her words were issued by the paper as a statement and carried over international wire services.

When a Russian publication, *New Times*, ran a cartoon depicting Marguerite being marched out of Korea at bayonet point with a headline that read "MACARTHUR'S FIRST VICTORY," she became a cause célèbre. Suddenly the honor of the paper was at stake. Whitelaw Reid, editor and part owner of the *Herald*, issued a statement of his own: "The *Herald Tribune* is shocked that Marguerite Higgins has been ordered out of Korea. She has been responsible for some of the best coverage of the war since the third day of the invasion. We believe the decision to force her to return to Tokyo is wrong and unfair in view of the outstanding job of reporting she has done. Newspaper women today are willing to assume the risk and in our opinion should not be discriminated against. We hope she will be allowed to continue her work."

The statement, had she known it, would have raised Marguerite's spirits. At least one war had been won.

After the physically and emotionally exhausting night on the hospital train, she went directly to General Walker's office. The general wasn't there, but his public relations man was. "You're getting on a plane right now if I have to call an MP," he greeted her. "Just write that in your little notebook." Making good his threat, the officer summoned two armed soldiers and the three men escorted her to a plane that took off immediately.

The flight back to Tokyo was a crushing, humiliating defeat very different from the farewell she had received in Taejon, where soldiers from regimental commander to private first class had taken time to come to her and say, "We hope you can talk the general out of this and come back to the front." Colonel Richard Stephens, who would emerge as one of the great heroes of the war and who had already distinguished himself by being the last man out of one of the fiercest, most devastating early battles, gave a final word of encouragement. "I tell you what, Maggie, if they try to throw you out as a correspondent, I'll hire you back for my rifle platoon."

Unfortunately, front-line encouragement meant nothing to the top brass in Tokyo. The official word was that war was man's work; a woman just didn't belong. For possibly the first time in history, the press (all male) was in accord with the military establishment. Marguerite's courage and enterprise were making some of them look bad.

Realizing that no one but the commander in chief could countermand Walker's orders, Marguerite took her case directly to General MacArthur.

"There are no facilities for you in Korea," he informed her.

Marguerite scoffed at the euphemism for latrines. "Nobody worries about powder rooms in Korea," she replied.

"The language is bad—unfit for a lady."

"I've already been at the front in Germany. I didn't need another war to teach me to fill in the dots and dashes in Hemingway's novels. The niceties of language just aren't very important on a battlefield," she reminded him.

Recalling MacArthur's historic World War II vow, "I shall return," Marguerite leveled her big gun. "I walked out of Seoul. I want to walk back in," she told him earnestly. That did it. "BAN ON WOMEN IN KOREA BEING LIFTED," MacArthur cabled the *Herald*. "MARGUERITE HIGGINS HELD IN HIGHEST ESTEEM BY EVERYONE."

In Japan Marguerite soon found out what was behind Homer Bigart's statement that she hadn't a friend in Tokyo. She had provoked the ire of the "palace guard," the heads of four major news services assigned to MacArthur's headquarters, by writing early on in the conflict that the bombing of enemy airfields was being considered. The men had known of the possibility but had agreed among themselves not to print it, as a security measure. It was assumed that Marguerite had violated the agreement.

The story of her breach was widely discussed in journalistic circles and had been printed in *Newsweek* along with an account of how she had "wangled her way" aboard MacArthur's private plane and obtained the information then.

Marguerite sat down immediately to set the matter straight. On August 7, *Newsweek* printed the following letter under the headline MISS HIGGINS SPEAKS.

> Having been almost continuously at the front and having been completely shut out from news of the rest of the world. I've only just learned of untrue statements printed in *Newsweek* in the July 10 issue and must now correct them.
>
> It is untrue that General MacArthur told me anything of plans to bomb north of the 38th parallel during the plane ride back to Tokyo as alleged by *Newsweek*. Knowledge of the bombing plans was received from quite a different source at the front. But since I had been continuously at the front when this story was breaking I had no knowledge whatsoever of any agreement between headquarters' correspondents concerning a security blackout on it. I thought it was of such general knowledge that I didn't even lead on it though I believe my editor may have pulled it out of the body of my story.
>
> I wish to make the point that my so-called "scoop trouble" did not involve any break of agreement to which I was a party.

Point Two, I was invited by General MacArthur on the plane through no request of my own.

Point Three, I am twenty-nine, not thirty.

She then wrote a brief note to General MacArthur apologizing for any embarrassment caused him by the brief airlift. The general promptly replied in a note: "Pay no attention to what your jealous male colleagues say about you. I know them better than you do and they have been harassing me for more than four-and-a-half years."

Following the personal triumph of her return to Korea, Marguerite discovered that her friend and benefactor, Lieutenant Charles Payne, (the man who had given her his clothes and introduced her to flea powder) had been badly wounded. Payne was one of six survivors—all wounded—of the original Charlie Company, which had once numbered 135 men.

He had been in continuous combat since the first day of American participation in the war, when Marguerite had watched him lead the first bazooka team into action against enemy tanks. Most recently he had been one of nine soldiers who had shielded forty wounded men in an abandoned mill in an attack that lasted ten hours.

"The main reason we stood them off was because we'd given up all hope of getting out alive," Payne told her. "Two guys had made a break for it across a rice paddy and gotten killed. The rest of us decided to go down fighting. Once we'd accepted death as inevitable everybody calmed down. It became kind of exciting instead of just plain terrifying. We rationed the ammunition, taking it from the dead, the dying, and the wounded. Then we'd stand at the window waiting to fire until each man was sure he could hit someone. The room was so small that the wounded were stacked in the middle two and three deep. It was awful as the day wore on and we ran out of water and medical supplies. Some died. One man kept begging me to shoot him."

What must have seemed the longest day in any of their lives ended when a lone American tank broke through the no-man's-land and temporarily chased off the attackers. Payne, who had begun the war speculating to Marguerite that he might have used up his luck fighting in World War II, gave her a gold pen-and-pencil set that had been given to him by his wife. He later said, "It was a beautiful set and I knew that I hadn't a chance of hanging onto it in the life I was leading—or not leading. Months later when I saw a wire service photo of Maggie at her typewriter, I was really pleased to spot my pen and pencil tucked into her pocket.

"I guess she raised my consciousness and a lot of other men's as well. We wouldn't be seeing women do the kinds of things they're doing today and taking for granted if it hadn't been for Maggie's courage. I think it was that same courage that kind of put off the men at first. Some of them weren't all that sure of themselves. They were afraid of looking foolish or frightened in front of a woman. Seeing her there being so cheerful and confident forced them to reexamine that macho snow job they'd been giving women all their lives. It was a real breakthrough and a good one.

"In the beginning just her presence was a shocker, but I came to have nothing but the deepest respect and admiration for that very likable, very attractive, very professional girl. We face death in many ways, but the intensity of this feeling is awesome beyond belief in front-line infantry fighting. Maggie found this out and it increased her sensitivity and depth and compassion, as it did to all of us who lived. Though we were thrown together only a relatively short time, I'd say we were friends in the honor of it all. Later, when I read that she passed away it saddened me, for she was so young and gifted and precious. Older vets live in retrospect a lot and I would be something less without her. She is one of my better memories and I really feel that thinking about her is good for me—kind of keeps my soul out of the dust."

Marguerite won her battles with the top military brass and the main office of the *Herald Tribune*, but her private battle with Homer Bigart was never resolved. "After a time it became the stuff of myths and legends," Keyes Beech recalled. "In the press club bar in Tokyo, in the press billet at Taegu—wherever correspondents gathered—Maggie threatened to replace the war as the chief topic of conversation. Songs were composed celebrating the Higgins-Bigart feud. Bill Lawrence of the *Times* scored an entertainment hit when he coached a chorus of Korean kids to stand outside the Taegu billet and chant, 'Homer loves Maggie, Homer loves Maggie.' "

Homer and Maggie were not even on speaking terms. Marguerite tried to avoid being in the same battle zone with him, but much of the time the war was contained in such a relatively small area that this was impossible. Most correspondents representing the same newspaper attempt to maintain communication if only to avoid duplication of effort.

"Higgins and Homer were the exception," Keyes recalled. "To my knowledge after their original confrontation when Homer told Maggie in the presence of other correspondents and army officers that she'd better get out of Korea or he'd 'bring the house down on her,' they spoke to one another only once during the entire war. That occurred with almost as much formality as that later observed between the Communist and the UN delegations at the armistice."

The event occurred close to the front lines when Marguerite observed a *Times* correspondent turning back, presumably to file his story. "I don't know what to do," she complained to Keyes. "Either Homer or I should go back and file right now."

"Why don't you ask him?" Keyes suggested reasonably, nodding in the direction of Bigart, who was observing the action from a vantage point about thirty yards away.

"You know he won't talk to me!" Marguerite was growing frantic as she watched the *Times* man fade from view.

"Okay," Keyes recalled agreeing, "I'll go talk to him." He walked across the road and addressed Homer, "Maggie wants to talk to you. Will you talk to her?"

Homer paused, considered the matter, and said, "I think that's possible."

Keyes Beech remembered that the two met in the center of the road and conversed briefly—very briefly. "I always felt that a plaque should have been erected to commemorate the occasion, something simple but eloquent like 'Homer and Maggie spoke here.'

"Homer may have been a great correspondent and a fine writer but he was not a very good judge of character, at least where Maggie was concerned. A sweet approach could work wonders, but attempted intimidation merely set off that fierce competitive instinct. Homer's prestige added to the challenge. She wasn't about to let him get ahead of her."

An example of her refusing to accept any form of limitation is the time Marguerite was injured in a jeep accident. Keyes and Marguerite were driving away from a dinner party hosted by Ambassador John Muccio when the brakes gave out. "I had to make a quick decision whether to plunge over a fifty-foot embankment or stop the jeep by running into a concrete gatepost," Beech remembered. "I chose the gatepost and Maggie hit the windshield. She was bleeding from the nose and mouth and there was a lump on her head the size of a doorknob when the ambassador and an aide helped her into the house.

"Maggie immediately wanted to survey the damage. She looked like hell and I told her so but she wasn't satisfied by that description and insisted on getting up to look in the bathroom mirror. She took a few steps and we caught her before she hit the floor.

"An ambulance came very quickly—this was the ambassador's house. There were a couple of corpsmen and a nice young doctor. They were all set to put her on a stretcher, but Maggie wouldn't hear of it. She insisted on riding in the front of the ambulance. The doctor ended up riding in back. When we reached the hospital she was determined to walk in. She started up the steps and collapsed again. This time I caught her alone. The doctor was so mad; she could have dropped dead for all he cared."

Beech returned to the hospital the following morning. Marguerite was sitting up in bed, wearing a hospital gown. "Those sons of bitches have stolen my clothes!" she exploded.

Noting that the bump on her head hadn't receded, he suggested that she might have a concussion. "You'd better stay in bed and rest."

Marguerite wasn't having any of that. "She was so insistent about getting her clothes and getting out that I finally gave in and went to the press billet and got some things together and brought them back to her," Keyes recalled. "That afternoon she sneaked out of the hospital, got transportation somehow, and headed out to Michaelis's outfit. She reached their headquarters just in time for it to get hit. It was a hell of a good story—assuming she survived to tell it."

General Walker had issued recently his famous "stand or die" order, and Marguerite was about to see it carried out. Homer Bigart and the other correspondents planned to cover the landing of the United States Marines at Pusan Harbor. Marguerite had decided to forgo that and hitchhike her way east.

By late afternoon she had reached Chingdongni, the temporary headquarters of the Twenty-seventh Infantry (Wolfhound) Regiment, excited at the prospect of seeing the Wolfhounds in action and meeting their commander, Lieutenant Colonel John Michaelis. The fighting spirit of this regiment had impressed everyone in the early "bowling alley" days when the Twenty-seventh had held off platoon after platoon of Communist tanks bowled at them in the valley north of Taegu. Marguerite had heard a midnight message bleated over a walkie-talkie radio: "Five tanks within our position. Situation vague. No sweat. We are holding."

Colonel Michaelis, an ex-paratrooper and former aide to General Eisenhower, was a man to inspire troops.

She saw a lean, wiry officer with an infectious grin, icy blue eyes and blond hair that was just beginning to gray. She thought he looked younger than his thirty-eight years and noted that "his ambition and drive have not yet been broken by the army system." On that first night in Chingdongni Marguerite found the colonel in a state of high tension and remorse. Sadly he told his officers, "I gambled and lost."

On a hunch, Michaelis had turned his troops around, hurriedly moving them from their assigned position to the little mud-walled town. Here the regiment was repositioned flanking the road on which he anticipated the North Koreans would soon be coming—except there were no North Koreans. Patrols found no enemy forces on the move, only a band of refugees trudging in their direction with the inevitable carts and bundles. To make it worse, enemy pressure was now reported where Michaelis was supposed to have been in the first place.

Then Michaelis gambled again. If the road was really empty, why not use it to attack? They would recapture a critical road junction some twenty miles to the east. The following morning he dispatched Colonel Gilbert Check with a combat battalion up the road toward Chinju.

Unfortunately not all the refugees observed earlier in their broad white hats and torn white coats and trousers had been fleeing farmers. Hundreds were soldiers carrying machine guns, ammunition, and mortars in their huge bundles. In small groups they had left the others and headed for prearranged assembly points in the hills. From there they watched Colonel Check's battalion pass, and when it was gone they had swarmed down onto the road and set up their machine guns and mortars. Now the worst had happened: The regiment had been neatly split in two, with the supply line cut.

Hindsight made it painfully clear. Michaelis's original decision, to move his forces to block the pathway to the seaport of Pusan, had been right. The one that followed it—to commit his battalion deep into enemy territory—had been wrong.

Realizing that Colonel Check and his men were cut off from gas for tanks, ammunition, guns, plasma, morphine, and food, Colonel Michaelis hurled all his men against the intervening enemy. On the other side Check's men fought valiantly. When the drivers of their three last tanks were wounded, two ex-bulldozer operators and an ex-mason took over. Although totally inexperienced they somehow made it back. Thirty in the battalion were lost; three hundred of the enemy were killed. The advance had turned into the first counterattack of the Korean War.

"Well, is that a story?" Colonel Michaelis asked Marguerite and Harold H. Martin of the *Saturday Evening Post*, the two correspondents present. "You know how it works now, how a man has to make decisions not knowing whether he's right or wrong. You've seen how something that looks wrong at first proves to be right and a plan that looks right turns out to be dead wrong. Then you've seen how a bunch of men with skill, brains, and guts like Check and the kids who drove the tanks can turn a wrong decision into a right one. But is that a story?"

Marguerite thought it was a honey of a story and could hardly wait until morning to head back to Pusan to file it.

She awakened early and sat down to breakfast with Harold Martin and a half-dozen regimental officers. The fare was relatively deluxe: powdered eggs and hot coffee. Someone had placed flowers on the table in her honor. Marguerite was listening halfheartedly to the conversation while mentally composing her story when suddenly bullets exploded in all directions. A machine gun bullet knocked the coffeepot off the table. A grenade blasted the wooden grill on which she had recently been sleeping. Taken totally by surprise, no one knew what to do. Bullets rained down on the rickety schoolhouse that was being used as command headquarters, splintering the flimsy walls.

An officer dove through the window, and Marguerite and the others followed. Outside they found a stone wall that afforded some protection, but it was clear the attack was coming from all directions. They were surrounded.

The courtyard was a wild melee of officers and noncoms attempting to dodge bullets and find their troops. Colonel Michaelis was dragging frightened soldiers from under jeeps and trucks and ordering them to their units. One machine gunner, overcome by terror, was shooting at his own men. One shot from a senior officer disabled him. Just then a reconnaissance man rushed in to report a new group of the enemy massing in the north and another reported that several hundred North Koreans had landed on a nearby beach.

"Suddenly for the first time in the war," Marguerite was to write later in *War in Korea*, "I experienced the cold awful certainty there was no escape. My reactions were trite. As with most people who suddenly accept death as inevitable and imminent, I was simply filled with surprise that this was finally going to happen to me. Then, as the conviction grew, I became hard inside and comparatively calm. I ceased worrying. Physically the result was that my teeth stopped chattering and my hands ceased shaking. This was a relief as by the time Colonel Michaelis came around a corner and said, 'How are you doin', kid?' I was able to answer in a respectably self-contained tone of voice, 'just fine, sir.' ''

Gradually Marguerite saw the confused scramble begin to mold itself into a pattern of resistance. Two heavy machine gun squads crept up the hill under cover of protective rifle fire and trained their guns on the enemy trying to swarm down. Platoons and then companies followed. Light mortars were dragged up. Huge artillery pieces lowered and fired point-blank at targets only a few hundred yards away. Fortuitously it turned out that the enemy soldiers reported landing on the coast were actually South Korean allies.

After a time Marguerite saw soldiers begin to bring in the wounded from the hills, carrying them on their backs to the first-aid station. Crawling to avoid the small arms fire, she made her way to the area to offer help. Mortars were set up next to the building, producing a nerveracking accompaniment for those attempting to administer to the wounded. Both doctors and wounded had to keep low to avoid an almost constant hail of bullets. In her dispatch, Marguerite described the scene: ''Medical corpsmen began bringing in the wounded, who were rather numerous. One correspondent learned how to administer blood plasma.''

Later Colonel Michaelis read the story and wrote a tribute to Marguerite that was printed in the *Herald*. He called her throwaway sentence the height of understatement and added: ''During the attack which lasted over four hours and which reached within seventy-five yards of the command post Miss Higgins, completely disregarding her own personal safety, voluntarily assisted by administering blood plasma to the many wounded as they were carried into the temporary first-aid station. This aid station was subjected to small arms fire throughout the attack. The Regimental Combat Team considers Miss Higgins' actions on that day as heroic, but even more important is the gratitude felt by members of this command towards the selfless devotion of Miss Higgins in saving the lives of many grievously wounded men.''

While assisting the medics Marguerite saw the tide of the battle slowly turn. Amazingly, when the fighting ended only five Americans had been killed although six hundred dead North Koreans were found in the hills behind the schoolhouse. The self-doubts that tormented John Michaelis were not echoed by his superiors. The following day he received, ''for his constant display of initiative, gallantry and qualities of leadership which have distinguished him as a combat commander,'' a battlefield promotion to full colonel. Gilbert Check was awarded the silver star ''for conspicuous gallantry.''

The experience at the schoolhouse, possibly more than anything else, brought Marguerite to her full maturity as a correspondent and forged her scattered experiences into a philosophy of war reporting.

''There is very little that is not wasteful and dismal about war,'' she wrote in *War in Korea*. ''The only clear, deep good is the special kind of bond welded between people who, having mutually shared a crisis, whether it be a shelling or a machine gun attack, emerge knowing that those involved behaved well. There is much pretense in our everyday life, and, with a skillful manner, much can be concealed. But with a shell whistling at you there is not much time to pretend and a person's qualities are starkly revealed. You believe that you can trust what you have seen. It is a feeling that makes old soldiers, old sailors, old airmen, and even old war correspondents humanly close in a way shut off to people who have not shared the same thing. I think that correspondents, because they are rarely in a spot where their personal strength or cowardice can affect the life of another, probably feel only an approximation of this bond. So far as I am concerned, even this approximation is one of the few emotions about which I can say, 'It's as close to being absolutely good as anything I know.' ''

Fifteen

Clad in tennis shoes, baggy pants, and a shirt, an oversize fatigue cap covering her blonde hair, Marguerite endured mud, lice, athlete's foot, and all the other hardships of battlefield life. When she joined the marines for the Masan offensive, Brigadier General Edward Craig ordered a cot set up for her. Marguerite sent a message to the general saying she preferred to sleep on the floor.

Her insistence on sharing Korea's burdens on equal terms with the troops prompted one man to remark, "Maggie's the only gal you can brag about sleeping with and not be a cad."

There were others who took a very different stance. In general, midcentury America cherished its double standards. More than thirty years later Carl Mydans of *Life* recalled the attitudes of his colleagues. "Male journalists were always criticizing each other. They'd say a man was dishonest in his reporting or lazy or possibly an alcoholic, but they never damned a correspondent by accusing him of sleeping around. This charge was constantly leveled against Maggie. It wasn't important enough to even consider in discussing a man and the worst thing they could think of in describing a woman.

"The men regarded reporting as their privileged territory. That a woman would invade the war area—their most sacred domain—and then turn out to be equally talented and sometimes more courageous was something that couldn't be accepted gracefully. Back in Tokyo at cocktail parties, Maggie was alluring, feminine, invariably surrounded by men. At the front, she was all business. She could be tough as nails in a professional setting where she had to combat the system—the man's world of the military. The competitive spirit and determination that would have been admired in a man were the very qualities that caused men to resent Maggie. They expressed that resentment by attacking her morals.

"Maggie had a sensible, realistic attitude about sex but was certainly not promiscuous. Besides by this time she was very much in love with Bill Hall. She talked a lot about him, speculating about the fact that he was married to someone else when he'd met her and worrying that he was too attractive to women. Maggie knew what was being said about her and held her head high—when she wasn't ducking bullets—while continuing to do her job."

Once Marguerite complained about the correspondents' attitudes to Jimmy Cannon of the *New York Post*, who in response philosophized, "If the *Racing Form* sent a race horse to cover the war, he wouldn't be any more of an oddity than you are. That horse's activities would be the subject of all sorts of stories and nobody would care how true they were so long as they were good stories. You're in the same fix and you'd better quit worrying about what you hear."

In retrospect it would appear that Marguerite was accused of sleeping with every man she interviewed. It's unlikely that General MacArthur in his rarefied world even knew that he was considered the top contender. Possibly at seventy he might have been flattered.

John Michaelis, who was reputed to have received his promotion to brigadier general as a result of an affair with Marguerite and her subsequent complimentary articles about him, was not flattered. The accusation was as ridiculous as it was cruel. Michaelis's bravery was a matter of record. In World War II he had jumped with the Five-hundred-second Parachute Infantry of the One-hundred-first Division on the Normandy beachhead and taken command when his superior was killed, which won him a battlefield promotion to full colonel. He had been wounded twice but managed to leave the hospital in time for the Battle of the Bulge where he became chief of staff of the One hundred first at age thirty-two. Following World War II he was considered too young for his rank and had been reduced to lieutenant colonel.

A second battlefield promotion after Chingdongni returned his eagle. "Michaelis will either be a general or a dead colonel," a GI predicted after that. A third battlefield promotion to brigadier general was to prove him correct.

"The very idea of anything sexual going on at the front is—or should be—absurd to anyone who knows what it's like," Michaelis later said.

"It was a terrible war. Centuries of lack of sanitation had taken their toll. The country was filthy. Everybody had diarrhea. Conditions couldn't have been worse. We got our rations in cans but never the right cans or balanced cans. The men on one hill got cans of carrots, the men on another got beef, somewhere else they got beets. The weight loss was unbelievable.

"The first time I saw Marguerite she was covered with dirt. The so-called road she'd just jeeped in on was two inches of dust. A man's a man; you think about sex. I thought Marguerite might look pretty good if I could get her into a tub, but the opportunities just didn't exist in a battle zone. There's no privacy for one thing. I rarely saw her when she wasn't surrounded by about fifty guys who just wanted to look at her because she was a woman.

"People charged her with sleeping around to get her stories but it sure as hell didn't happen in Korea. For one thing, she wasn't a fool. General Walker was just looking for an excuse to get rid of her. One slip and she would have been out. In my own case I didn't have my clothes off in a hundred days. I'd have frozen to death if I had. It was hardly a time for romance.

"The speculation about Marguerite and MacArthur was equally silly. The general lived in the American embassy with his wife. He was highly visible. Guards accompanied him everywhere. The man would have been crazy to consider jeapordizing his reputation in that way and MacArthur wasn't crazy. He wasn't a fool either. He was very adept at picking other people's brains. Marguerite's viewpoint was invaluable. She had a perspective that most of the other correspondents didn't, she knew what was going on at the front. She knew what the GIs were thinking and saying. She could speak firsthand about conditions and morale. Of course he found it worthwhile to talk with her.

"Why was Marguerite the target for so much viciousness? I'd have to say initially it was fear. Her driving ambition forced competitors into positions they didn't particularly enjoy. Later it was jealousy. She became successful; she stood out. Some people never forgave her for that."

Marguerite lived in her dirty slacks and shirt for weeks on end, ate out of cans, and swallowed the brown dust of Korea without a murmur. Occasionally she would fly to Tokyo, soak in a tub, get a manicure and a shampoo, and put on a dress. When she wasn't thinking of war, her mind drifted to Bill Hall. A penciled entry in her notebook is revealing.

Thrilled and so excited about Bill's arrival that I can't settle down to work. Feel enveloped with longing and desire for the affection and passion that I've sometimes found with him. The pull between wanting to live with Bill and wanting to finish out this war is terrible. But it won't be acute until he finally gets his divorce. The prospect of a third world war makes me feel that all this worry about houses and finances is ridiculous. I wonder how much longer any of us have. Disgusted with my lack of concentration. I've had a day of happy daydreaming and that's about it.

Thus far the closest Bill Hall had gotten to Marguerite was to follow her by-line in the *Herald Tribune*. "The first thing I did every morning was to go buy a paper. At least I knew she was alive the day she wrote the story," he recalled. Then in September Hall was sent to the Far East as an official observer for the air force. There was an all too brief reunion in Tokyo before he began his ten-day tour of the Philippines, Cambodia, Formosa, and Vietnam. When he returned to Tokyo Marguerite was gone.

She had left behind a note that read, "I am going on a great adventure which, if successful, should bring this situation to a conclusion." It was a secret even to him that she was on her way to take part in the Inchon invasion.

Marguerite's request to go aboard an assault transport was greeted with the same degree of horror as might have met a leper's request to share a bunk with an admiral.

Captain Duffy listened absently to her request, mentally screened out her arguments about fairness, and relegated her to a hospital ship that would remain achored far outside the assault area. Fortunately for her, his absentmindedness extended further. When Marguerite returned for her orders she suspected they had been written by the hand of fate, not that of Captain Duffy.

The orders mistakenly read: "Miss Higgins may board any Navy ship." Marguerite grasped the sheet of paper and hurried out before the harried officer could realize his incredible error.

Flying immediately from Tokyo to Pusan Harbor in South Korea where the assault team was temporarily based, she hitchhiked to the dock. As she approached the first transport ship she looked up to see the familiar faces of a few male correspondents. When Marguerite attempted to join them she was turned down by the captain. "This ship is already overcrowded," he said. "I could sleep on the deck," she offered. The answer was still no.

On the *Henrico*, the command ship of the transport group, Marguerite presented her orders to the captain, hoping that her apprehension didn't show. When he paused she suggested, "I could put my sleeping bag in the hall, a closet, anywhere."

After a careful study of the orders, he looked up at her. "That won't be necessary. We have a spare room, a sort of emergency cabin."

Trying to control her relief and pleasure, Marguerite nodded a quick thanks and hurried to get her gear. Twin typhoons, Jane and Kezia, were swirling in their direction. Marguerite considered the typhoons kindred spirits, for the transport's eagerness to escape their battering forces would soon have her steaming out of officialdom's reach.

Once back on the ship, Marguerite raced straight to her cabin and locked herself in. She listened eagerly for the hopeful sound of the ship's engines getting under way but heard instead the approach of ominous footsteps. When the dreaded rap on the door came she was certain that someone had caught up with her and was about to have her thrown off the ship. Instead it turned out to be an invitation to join the other correspondents for lunch.

The four-day cruise to Inchon Harbor seemed the height of luxury to Marguerite, who was used to sleeping on the ground, or in a filthy, flea-infested hut. The food, warm and filling, was sometimes even fresh, a vast improvement over the "C" rations that were her normal fare at the front.

During the trip the technical difficulties of the landing were discussed at length. MacArthur had selected Inchon Harbor because the landing was considered impossible. The area was well known for its unusual tides, which rushing into narrow channels cause the water depth to vary more than thirty feet. At low tide, the harbor is a mud flat. The commanding general assumed that if his own advisers considered the landing impossible, the enemy would as well, and leave the area lightly defended. Looking at aerial photographs revealing deep trenches dug on the inland side of the seawall, Marguerite speculated on his judgment.

It was planned that assaults would be made against "Red Beach," near the heart of Inchon, and at "Blue Beach," an area of seawall south of the city. In between was the essential tidal basin, the only portion of the harbor that didn't turn to mud at low tide. The area was of key importance for bringing in cargo from the transports.

On September 15 there was a final briefing. Split-second timing was emphasized. The tide would be at the right height for only four hours.

They were to strike at 5:30 P.M., just one half hour before high tide. Assault waves, each consisting of six landing craft lined up abreast, would hit the beach at spaced intervals. This part of the operation had to be completed within an hour to permit the approach of larger LSTs (landing ship tanks) that would supply the necessary heavy equipment. These ships would land at high tide and then as the water receded be mired helplessly in mud until the next high tide. Sea approaches to supply or reinforce the assaulting marines would then be cut off until the tides changed again. It was a risky gamble but the only one possible.

The rectangular, flat-bottomed craft were lowered into the sea by means of winches. Marguerite and the others made the descent in a cargo net. She held tightly to the huge, rough ropes while her feet groped for the swaying rungs. When she dropped at last into the boat she saw that some of the marines had already broken out cards and were busily dealing gin rummy hands. On board was a mortar outfit, some riflemen, John Davies of the *Newark Daily News*, Lionel Crane of the *London Daily Express*, and a photographer.

The correspondents watched tensely as the first wave pulled out of their circle of hovering boats and headed toward the beach. There were only a few minutes left to wait. Slowly the marines on their ship gathered up their cards. A control ship signaled that it was their turn. They braced themselves as the craft hit a dip in the seawall.

"Come on you big, brave marines, let's get the hell out of here!" an officer yelled. The first men began to clamber over the bow. The photographer announced that he had had enough "color" and would return to the transport with the landing boat. Marguerite hesitated, for an instant tempted to join him. Then she moved forward, maneuvering her typewriter into a position where she could reach up for it once she was over the side. In a second she had pushed herself over the edge and landed in about three feet of water in the dip of the seawall.

Marguerite moved forward, snaking her way over and around boulders to a curve below the top of the dip in the seawall that afforded some cover from the tracer bullets flashing all around her. As she and the others waited there, wave after wave of marines hit the beach. One man ventured over the ridge but jumped back so hurriedly from the barrage of bullets and grenades that his foot came down hard on Marguerite's bottom. "I was glad," she remarked later, to Keyes Beech, "that it was my most padded part."

Marguerite's story of the landing ran on Page One of the *Herald*, It read in part:

"WITH THE UNITED STATES MARINES AT INCHON, KOREA —Heavily laden United States Marines, in one of the most technically difficult amphibious landings in history, stormed at sunset today over a ten foot-seawall in the heart of the port of Inchon and within an hour had taken three commanding hills in the city.

"I was in the fifth wave that hit 'Red Beach,' which in reality was a rough vertical pile of stones over which the first assault troops had to scramble with the aid of improvised landing ladders topped with steel hooks.

"Despite a deadly and steady pounding from naval guns and airplanes enough North Koreans remained alive close to the beach to harass us with small arms and mortar fire. They even hurled hand grenades down at us as we crouched in trenches which unfortunately ran behind the seawall in the inland side.

"It was far from the 'virtually unopposed' landing for which the troops had hoped after hearing of the quick capture of Wolmi Island in the morning by an earlier marine assault. Wolmi is inside Inchon Harbor and just off Red Beach. At H-hour minus seventy, confident, joking marines started climbing down the transport ship on cargo nets and dropping into small assault boats.

"The channel reverberated with the ear-splitting boom of warship guns and rockets. Blue and orange flames spurted from the Red Beach area and a huge oil tank on fire sent great black rings of smoke over the shore. Then the fire from the big guns lifted and the planes that had been circling overhead swooped low to rake their fire deep into the seawall.

"In the sky there was good news. A bright white star shell from the high ground to our left and an amber cluster told us that the first wave had taken their initial objective, Observatory Hill. But whatever the luck of the first four waves, we were relentlessly pinned down by rifle and automatic weapon fire coming down on us from another rise on the right. There were some thirty marines and three correspondents crouched in the gouged-out seawall. Then another assault boat swept up, disgorging about thirty more marines. This went on for two more waves until our hole was filled and marines were lying on their stomachs strung out all across the top of the seawall.

"An eerie-color light flooded the area as the sun went down with a glow that a newsreel audience would have thought a fake. As the dusk settled the glare of the burning buildings all around lit up the sky. Suddenly as we lay there intent on the firing ahead, a rush of water came up into the dip in the wall and we saw a huge LST rushing at us with the great plank door half down. Six more yards and the ship would have crushed twenty men. Warning shouts sent everyone speeding from the seawall searching for escape from the LST and cover from the gunfire. The LST's huge bulk sent a rush of water pouring over the seawall as it crunched in, soaking most of us. The marines ducked and zigzagged as they raced across the open area but enemy bullets caught a good many in the semidarkness. The wounded were piled aboard the LSTs, six of which appeared within sixty-five minutes after H-Hour.

"As nightfall closed in, the marine commanders ordered their troops forward with increasing urgency for they wanted to assure a defensible perimeter for the night. In this remarkable amphibious operation, where tides played such an important part, the marines were completely isolated from outside supply lines from exactly four hours after H-Hour. At this time the out-rushing tides—they fluctuate thirty-one feet in twelve-hour periods—made mud flats of the approaches to Red Beach. The LSTs bringing supplies simply settled on the flats, helpless until the morning tides would float them again.

"At the battalion command post the news that the three high ground objectives, the British Consulate, Cemetery Hill, and Observation Hill, had been taken, arrived at about H-Hour plus sixty-one minutes. Now the important items of business became debarking tanks, guns, and ammunition from the LSTs. Every cook, clerk, driver, and administrative officer in the vicinity was rounded up to help in the unloading. It was exciting to see the huge M-26 tanks rumble across the big planks onto the beach which only a few minutes before had been protected only by riflemen and machine gunners. Then came the bulldozers, trucks, and jeeps. It was dark and in the shadow of the ships the unloaders had a hazardous time dodging bullets, mortar fire, and their own vehicles."

By 7:00 the beach was nearly secured and Marguerite and the other two correspondents decided to head back to file their stories. Once again they threaded their way across the beach, this time through a heavy traffic of tanks, artillery guns, and trucks as well as occasional mortar fire and bullets until they reached the seawall. There they waited until a boat came close enough for them to climb down the shaky ladder to board.

The tide had turned, and by the time they reached the flagship *McKinley* it was difficult for the little ship to hold steady against the current long enough for them to clamber up yet another ladder. It had begun to rain, and Marguerite balanced precariously on the gunwale, clinging to her typewriter with hands slippery from ocean spray.

Finally aboard, she approached the wardroom eagerly, her spirits lifted by the smell of hot coffee. Once inside an unpleasant surprise awaited her. It was Captain Duffy, angrily demanding to know what the hell she was doing there. Marguerite pulled out the now very damp orders that he had issued himself verifying that she could board any navy ship in pursuit of press duties. For a moment he was speechless—but only for a moment.

Finally it was agreed that Marguerite could write her invasion story and file it from the ship. She was assigned a stretcher in the dispensary—despite the fact that an empty cabin complete with "facilities" was available—and allowed to spend one night on the ship.

The next day she was banned from the ship. From then on she slept on the dock or with the troops as she had before. One of Keyes Beech's memories of the Inchon days was of waiting impatiently on the dock while Marguerite typed out her stories, which he would then take with him to the ship to file, her wistful face fading from view as he headed for a warm shower and scrambled eggs aboard the *McKinley*.

Within a month the navy amended its rule and allowed Marguerite to board any ship she wished as long as she was chaperoned at all times by a navy nurse. By that time it no longer mattered. The great gamble at Inchon had paid off, and Marguerite was headed east away from the beach. She was about to fulfill a promise she had made to herself. She was going to walk back to Seoul.

Sixteen

Korea was brown, an ex-soldier recalled.

Trucks, tanks, and jeeps were muddy. Tents were a washed-out tan. The terrain was ochre from having been churned up by artillery. The dull rice paddies enclosed flooded areas that were an even darker shade.

The young soldier had been wounded and was being taken by jeep to a tent hospital immediately to the rear of the fighting. In the distance, luminous in the midday sun, he glimpsed a patch of bright yellow gold. The spot of glitter in a sea of drab brown drew closer as their vehicles approached each other. He was dumbstruck: A blonde! She was headed toward the lines! As her jeep passed his he caught the sound of a woman's laughter, wonderful and unbelievable in Korea. Later he learned that it was Maggie Higgins, but he never saw her again. He had just that fleeting patch of gold.

Keyes Beech, who very likely was driving the jeep that day, never quite lost the habit of automatically waving back at the soldiers who enthusiastically cheered his companion. Viewing Marguerite as a frequently combative colleague, he would forget that she was becoming a kind of folk heroine to the GIs. Jimmy Cannon of the *New York Post* once complained, "Riding in a jeep with Maggie is like being a jockey on Lady Godiva's horse."

Other correspondents were less philosophical. When *Time* cabled Frank Gibney in Korea, suggesting a feature on the woman reporter with the innocent face, Gibney promptly cabled back, SHE'S AS INNOCENT AS A COBRA. The very presence of a woman there as a reporter infuriated him, and the idea that his own publication thought it newsworthy was too much.

Keyes Beech explained, "Maggie was not the most popular press member, but then she wasn't out to win popularity contests. All she really cared about was getting her story. It's hard today to understand the kind of prejudice that she endured, but somehow in spite of it Maggie became part of the Korean landscape, and I was the guy driving the jeep. The association didn't enhance *my* popularity in some areas, but there were compensations. Maggie and I worked well together most of the time. We covered the war as well as any and better than most. We were mobile and we took a lot of risks."

Working with Marguerite was certainly never dull. Beech remembered driving along a very bumpy road and noticing that she was hunched over. "What's the matter—stomach cramps?" he asked, wondering if he should begin looking for what Marguerite referred to as a "friendly bush."

It was an entirely different problem. "I forgot my bra and this road is shaking me to pieces," she muttered, her arms hugging her chest as they hit rut after rut. "Holding herself in took some doing," Beech said. "She was stacked; well endowed with stand-up breasts."

The night before they were scheduled to recross the Han River in the offense of Seoul, Marguerite startled him with another disclosure: "I've got the goddam curse."

"I wondered why she was complaining to me about it and asked tentatively, 'Don't you have something for that?'

" 'No.'

"Her voice was bleak.

" 'Well, what are you going to do about it?' I asked, still trying to sound casual; lightly conversational. It turned out that there was only one thing she could do and that was drive thirty miles to Inchon, where a hospital ship was anchored. Presumably some of the nurses menstruated. 'Okay, let's go,' I said very disagreeably.

" 'No, I'll drive myself. Just give me the keys,' she insisted. There was really no way I could let her. Besides the fact that we were under strict blackout conditions with about ten thousand trigger-happy marines between us and Inchon, the jeep had developed a very stubborn character. It was permanently locked into second gear.

"She put up quite an argument but we finally set off together. Fortunately it was a moonlit night. We reached Inchon in one piece. Maggie got a launch and went out to the ship to collect what are commercially known as sanitary napkins. I sat in the jeep cursing my fate. This would never have happened if I'd been covering the war with a man.''

More pleasantly but with rueful amusement, he remembered another time when they pulled the jeep over next to a clear, running stream. ''The appeal of being clean and cool was so overwhelming that we pulled off our clothes and jumped in without even thinking. Later when I cast an eye around for hostile people I didn't see any. Instead I spotted twenty GIs with binoculars sitting on a nearby hill. They certainly weren't looking at me. Maggie was very cool about it. 'You'd think they'd never seen a woman before,' she sniffed. She splashed around a bit more and then got out of the water and into her clothes.

''The GIs were far less sophisticated under similar conditions. Another day I drove into camp and found Maggie in a state of total frustration. 'They've captured a North Korean commissar,' she said. 'They're interrogating him right now! You've got to go right over there.'

''I looked at her in complete surprise. 'Why don't *you* go?'

''Her face was red with annoyance. 'There's a bunch of goddam men swimming naked near where they're holding him. They won't even let me walk by.'

''I think it's significant that she was only interested in getting the story and could have cared less about the naked men. It was *they* who were concerned about propriety. It all seems pretty silly now, but remember we're talking about nineteen fifty. Maggie Higgins was at least thirty years ahead of her time.''

On September 17, the *Herald* ran a Page One story by Marguerite Higgins that began: ''I returned to Kimpo Airfield tonight just eighty-three days after I landed here on June 27, two days after the invasion of South Korea.'' She went on to relate how she and Beech had advanced on Kimpo with a battalion of marines.

Although they were frequently pinned down for as long as a half hour at a time by machine gun and small arms fire, the real crisis didn't come until midafternoon when the battalion got lost.

The day and the situation were saved by a pretty, pigtailed South Korean girl, Kim Sung Yung, age seventeen, whom Marguerite and Keyes had met in a liberated village and brought along as an interpreter. She had been the sweetheart of an American soldier in the days when the United States Army occupied South Korea. In honor of the appearance of the Americans she was clad in all her finery: American sporting shoes,

American stockings, an American skirt, and an American blouse from the post exchange.

"Unfortunately she had to spend a good deal of the afternoon along with the rest of us dodging bullets in a muddy ditch," Marguerite wrote. "This was a poor reward for her very great help after the tanks spearheading our advance had got[ten] hopelessly tangled in a side trail. It was Kim Sung Yung who pointed out to the battalion executive officer the road down which the tanks and other vehicles could go.

"Somewhat unhappy over the responsibility we had indirectly taken on ourselves by introducing our protégée into battalion affairs, Beech and I kept asking as we traveled swiftly down the road she had pointed out: 'Now, Kim, are you absolutely sure this is the right road? Do you recognize it for sure?'

"Weary of questions, Kim finally stated simply. 'You may kill me if I am wrong.' " Fortunately for all concerned, she was right.

As they drove along the shell-pocked road, Kim told them of her own experiences. She had had a child by her American soldier, a baby that had been shot by Communists as the two attempted to escape from Seoul. "They looked at her eyes and saw that they were blue," Kim said matter-of-factly. "I have a picture of her at home. She was a very pretty baby."

They were riding confidently along just behind the lead tank when it was ambushed and blown up. "Kim, Beech, and I dove for the ditches," Marguerite wrote in her dispatch. "Kim kept her head down like a veteran and spoke not a word about the mud that was ruining her finery. 'I am so happy I don't care,' she finally exulted."

The skirmish eventually ended, and the battalion was able to move on, reaching Kimpo Airfield before dark. Immediately bulldozers began to fill in the holes in the runways. "When the American planes come in tomorrow it will seem like old times," Kim said.

Marguerite's long-anticipated walk back to Seoul was a virtual toe dance. The marines blazed a bloody trail to the city along a path that had been heavily mined. She attached herself to Charlie Company, which at one time was intent on capturing a Catholic church on a strategic hill. As they pressed forward a medic's jeep raced past. A few seconds later it blew up directly in their path. Two of the passengers were killed instantly. The driver was still alive, although his body looked as though it had encountered a buzz saw.

It would have been impossible to send more vehicles up the road until the engineers had cleared it, but the infantry had to go on. The men and Marguerite were warned by the company commander that freshly turned dirt could cover a land mine. It was a typically rough Korean road but the mounds and bumps made it suddenly look suspicious. They stepped forward gingerly on their toes, an advance that Marguerite likened to a macabre ballet.

The fighting continued day after day. On September 26, Marguerite wrote: "Flames and smoke wreathed downtown Seoul today as marines battered and burned their way forward in slow hour-to-hour fighting. . . . American flame-throwing tanks stabbed at the flimsy Korean houses, igniting whole blocks but still the enemy fought on, bringing tanks, grenades, and self-propelled guns to support their last ditch fight.

"By late this afternoon no place in the western part of Seoul was free from the hum of sniper bullets or safe from sudden attack by riflemen or machine gunners hidden in cellars or hillside buildings. Creeping behind the forward marine troops this correspondent entered the downtown area by the main Seoul railroad station. Most of the houses on the hillside directly behind the station had been razed by crossfire."

Marguerite and Keyes climbed the hill to survey the situation. Not far off they could see the historic Chosun Hotel, a combination of German and French wedding-cake architecture. The famous landmark was a sentimental favorite of Beech's, and he determined to see how it had fared against the Communists. Taking off through an area encircled by smoke and flame, Beech reached the big wooden gate to the compound. It was closed but not barred. He paused. The Chosun was built more like a fort than a hotel; it had once housed the king's concubines. What better place was there for a Communist defense post?

With carbine ready, he put his foot against the gate and pushed. Crouching low, he charged forward, braced for a burst of machine gun fire. Instead he heard the sound of cheers. The entire Korean staff of the Chosun stood at attention in the hotel courtyard. They had been waiting for hours for someone to come and "liberate" them.

A few moments later Marguerite rushed in, flanked by six spear-carrying Korean home guardsmen. She found that Beech had the situation well in hand.

On September 29 Marguerite was present when General MacArthur handed over the keys to the city of Seoul to President Syngman Rhee.

The occasional crash of glass and debris from the torn roof of the capitol punctuated the necessarily brief noontime ceremonies, a grim reminder of the battles that had gone on only hours before and were still continuing only a few miles away.

Assorted admirals and generals—French, British, Korean, and American—had flown in from Tokyo for the momentous occasion, which culminated in the solemn intonement of the Lord's Prayer by the general. Marguerite thought MacArthur's manner very much in keeping with his usual role of man of destiny. "The dome of the building had been badly battered in battle," she explained in her story. "As the wind rose, down came piece after jagged piece of glass to the consternation of us lesser mortals in the audience who, with thoughts riveted on safety rather than dignity, rushed to get under a beam or an arch. MacArthur and Rhee, who were both near misses, never flicked an eyelash.

"After the ceremony, MacArthur headed for the bedraggled audience of officers and men of the First Marine Division who had been plucked from the Seoul battleground to attend. Since only a few hours before I had been busily burrowing in a dusty foxhole to escape a fire fight, I was among the most bedraggled of all and had no desire to be seen by the general. But the surge of those eager to congratulate him carried me to a spot almost directly in his path. Catching sight of me, MacArthur, affecting an air of mock astonishment, called out: 'Hello there, tall, blonde and ugly. Come up and see me sometime.' "

The faces of the dignitaries around him were reflections of astonishment, an emotion shared by Marguerite; but as a reporter she wasn't about to let the invitation go by. About a month later, when summoned home to address the *Herald Tribune*'s annual forum, she stopped in Tokyo and presented herself at the embassy to request an interview. The request was made six times, and six times the answer came back, "Not now."

Marguerite called the general's office a seventh time and asked the aide, "If I give you a message will you promise to give it to the general *exactly* as I give it to you?"

The aide agreed and Marguerite instructed him: "Please tell the general that I consider that invitation to come up and see him sometime a military order."

Some five minutes later the aide called to say, "The general will be glad to see you as soon as you can get here." From then on she had only to ask once.

Marguerite found MacArthur's desk piled high with telegrams from President Truman and others congratulating him. She suggested that the messages must be especially satisfying since Washington had such grave doubts about the Inchon invasions.

Smiling somewhat ruefully, MacArthur said, "I'm afraid I can't take these messages too seriously. I learned long ago that it's best to be wary of praise, because it can turn into the opposite very quickly the moment that circumstances change."

After a moment of silence and a few puffs on his corncob pipe, General MacArthur added, "I learned that lesson at West Point. I was a pretty good baseball player once, and I can remember my excitement at the approving roar of the crowds when I was a star of the team and we were running up a string of victories. Then, one game my knee was twisted, but they decided to keep me in. In the middle of the game, I ran for a fly, and, as I reached, my knee gave way and I fell. No one would believe I had a bad knee. They thought it was just an excuse. The boos of the crowd were louder than the cheers had ever been. And so I have never forgotten how quickly cheers can turn to boos."

On January 3, 1951, Marguerite was on hand for the third fall of Seoul. The circumstances were tragic. She had been part of the heavy advance forward across the thirty-eighth parallel. Suddenly without warning the picture changed. The Chinese had entered the war, surging across the Yalu River and driving south.

In the face of the numerically superior Chinese, Seoul was ordered abandoned. This was politically expedient, but for all directly involved it was a bitter moment.

The withdrawal was orderly, and by nightfall the city was largely deserted. Fires had broken out but did nothing to relieve the dreadful cold. In the distance Marguerite, Keyes, and two other correspondents from the Associated Press and *Time* could hear the boom of artillery. That and the crackle of flames were the only sounds. All Americans had been ordered to leave, but no one wanted to go.

Keyes pointed out that his beloved Chosun was located nearby. Despite the advancing Communists and the wishes of the United States Army, they decided to go there, driving through the fire-lighted streets, through the wooden gate, and into the compound. This time there were no welcoming cheers, but there were clean sheets and the four correspondents slept well that night. When they awakened early the next morning the Chinese artillery was closer but there was still time to catch up with the American army.

Once hot and dusty, Korea became unbelievably cold. Often the temperature dropped to as low as twenty below zero. Plasma froze, men's feet stuck to the bottoms of their boots, and some men who would have died from loss of blood didn't because their blood congealed. Marguerite stuck it out. The extent of her complaints was a characteristically understated admission in her memoirs *News Is a Singular Thing* that the war made her "tired."

"Physical condition has a lot to do with whether your mood is bold or cautious. Beech and I used to refer to the mood that accompanied physical exhaustion as the 'I'm-going-to-get-killed-today' feeling. The opposite was the 'nothing-can-touch-me' mood. It happened that on many of the occasions when I was having an 'I'm-going-to-get-killed' mood Beech would be buoyed up in a 'nothing-can-touch-me' phase. And vice versa. This probably affords one explanation of why we both managed to spend so much time in the war's hottest spots. If one of us wanted to press on, the other wasn't going to be left behind, no matter what his forebodings."

That's one explanation.

Keyes Beech wrote, in *Tokyo and Points East*, "She was a good man under fire. When we drove through sniper country to and from the front, Higgins rode 'shotgun' and counted the enemy bullets while I pushed the accelerator to the floor and fought to keep the jeep on the road. She never panicked."

For almost a year the war had been Marguerite's life. With her flea powder, toothbrush, typewriter, lipstick, and towel, she experienced all the war's hardships. "She's either brave as hell or stupid," one war correspondent complained. "Her energy and recklessness make it tough on all the others."

Undoubtedly Marguerite never considered her actions reckless. "If you worried about being shot at, you'd never get a story," she insisted.

In 1951, she was awarded the Pulitzer prize for overseas reporting: the first woman to be so honored.

PART V

TROUBLE
IN PARADISE

Seventeen

Nineteen fifty-one was one of the richest years of Marguerite's professional life, yet as one award followed another so did a major disillusionment. On the day she was named Woman of the Year by other women newspaper reporters, she learned that Bill Hall was involved seriously with someone else.

All her life Marguerite had heard the expression, "You can't have everything." Very likely she had used it countless times—in regard to others. For herself Marguerite secretly expected a special dispensation —if not everything then almost everything. Why not? Hadn't she always been lucky? she must have thought, reflecting on her eleventh-hour acceptance to the Columbia School of Journalism; her hiring by the *New York Herald Tribune*; her being assigned overseas in time to cover the last momentous days of World War II; her promotion to bureau chief; and finally Korea: How many journalists had been sent against their own wishes to an assignment they viewed as the low point of their professional careers only to have the situation explode immediately into the most dramatic story in the world?

Later Marguerite speculated that luck was really too limited a concept for the miracle of surviving war after so many near misses. In her 1955 autobiography, *News Is a Singular Thing*, she philosophized that it didn't "express the wonder at survival after those times when all seemed lost and you were sure that you could not escape the fate of those around you. . . . Whatever it was—fate, destiny, Kismet—I had perhaps more than my share in Korea. And perhaps this is why, in the period directly after I went home from the war, fortune was so often absent."

Her surprising candor provided embarrassing moments for Bill Hall and raised eyebrows. She wrote: "In the first eleven years of my adult professional life I had an exciting career. Now, in my conceit, I had thought I would top it all off with something far rarer: a love both true and deep; a man to whom I could be both friend and lover; a man who would need no other love than mine. It is in just such moments of overconfidence that you stride blithely ahead, not bothering to look where you are going. And just at this point fate with her inevitable sense of timing sticks out the foot that sends you sprawling headlong."

With the exception of her association with George Millar, Marguerite had been as lucky in love as she had been in battle. From high school on she had left a trail of saddened or disgruntled suitors. A man who disliked her said, "Maggie uses men like Kleenex." Now it was Marguerite who suffered the humiliation of rejection, or so the situation appeared in the light of her own somewhat unrealistic expectations.

Self-analysis had never been Marguerite's strong suit. Love for Bill Hall could never have stopped her from pursuing her career goals in Korea; it could not quench her drive for experience or her thirst for adventure. It didn't even preclude a relationship of convenience with Keyes Beech. Yet she was totally devastated by Hall's infidelity.

This intense personal problem couldn't have come at a worse time. For months she had shared the pride and the passion of war as well as the hardships and heartaches. Now the Chinese invasion of Korea had turned the tide of the conflict. The men who had fought so valiantly and successfully against the North Koreans in places like Seoul, Yudamni, Chingdongni, and Hagaru now saw these critical battle sites swarming with Chinese. Hopelessly outnumbered and ordered to retreat, the company of the Fifth Marines with whom Marguerite had made the Inchon landing invited her to walk out of Koto with them. Very proudly she marched beside the foot soldiers down a narrow mountain pass. It was a dreadful ordeal for all concerned, with fierce winds and stinging frost almost as deadly as the mortar fire. Trucks, half-tracks, bulldozers, and jeeps bounced and jolted their way down the road. Sometimes the convoy was halted for hours while engineers filled in the crevices in their path. It was a struggle to keep from freezing during these long intervals and some of the men lost hands, feet, and even legs to frostbite. Finally Marguerite reached the harbor of Hungnam with the fighting unit, which brought with them, as they had vowed to do, all their wounded and newly dead.

With the war now relegated to a "holding action" and men dying while politicians, generals, and finally governments jockeyed for position, Marguerite had been called home. The six-month sabbatical was her first long leave in twelve years. Emotionally drained by her war experiences and the tragic sacrifice of so many lives negated by cynical political maneuverings, Marguerite needed only the knowledge of Bill Hall's other involvement to land in the hospital. The list of her ailments was formidable: bronchitis, acute sinusitis, a recurrence of malaria, dysentery, and jaundice, as well as an attack of nervous tension that in her own words rendered her "a social menace."

Over the next few months Marguerite received the George Polk Memorial Award, the Overseas Press Club of America citation for "courage, integrity and enterprise," the Marine Corps Reserve Officers Association presentation of the *Non Sibi Sed Patraiae* (Not for Self but for Country) award, the Veterans of Foreign Wars Gold Medal, the Poor Richard Citation presented by the Poor Richard Club of Philadelphia, and a special award from the New York Newspaper Women's Club. There were some fifty prizes and awards, crowned by the most exciting and prestigious of all: the Pulitzer prize. Marguerite's stunning triumph was undimmed by the fact that she shared the honor with Keyes Beech and Homer Bigart. She was the first woman to receive the prize for stories on actual combat.

It was a proud moment, but it did not relieve her longing for Bill. The contrast between personal grief and professional triumph, she admitted later, was a spectacular and permanent reminder of life's role as a leveler.

In June 1951, Marguerite's book, *War in Korea*, was published, to critical acclaim. In a personal note of congratulations, President Syngman Rhee wrote: "I have just finished your gripping and illuminating book and know it will appeal to many as it has to me. While you were here you and I did not always agree on how certain problems should be handled. I am delighted to learn from the text of your book that you have set forth the facts in such a way that few can misunderstand. You have accomplished wonderfully your objective of making the meaning of war in Korea clear to all those who remain far from the scene."

S.L.A. Marshall, a political historian for the War Department, wrote: "This Maggie's eye view of the Korean police action is downright irresistible in its candor, in its simple expression of the things which many of us feel strongly but can't say very well, in its change of pace between the tragedy of the battlefield and the high comedy of much human behavior in close relationship to it. . . . Many of her word pictures are remarkable for their ability to convey much in little; where she philosophizes at all about men in battle her style is almost epigrammatic, and many of her observations have such a true ring that they deserve to be remembered and widely quoted.'' This was high praise, indeed, for one who was considered even by her strongest admirers as far more a reporter than a writer.

Unfortunately Marguerite was not always this successful in other areas of her new public life. Still ailing, she embarked on a lecture tour that was greeted with mixed reactions. One unfortunate weekend she struck out twice. On Friday the women of the Century Club in Amsterdam, New York, although impressed by her words, found Marguerite's manner cool and were stung by her refusal to attend a reception planned in her honor. The following night the members of the Woman's Civic Club of Glens Falls were so disappointed in her talk—''a rehash of Korea'' according to the chairman of the Ways and Means Committee— that they refused to pay her agent. This action added fuel to a series of disagreements she had with the agent that ultimately ended in a lawsuit.

Making money was new to Marguerite, and it introduced her to a whole new set of problems. She had returned home to find herself a superstar. Within thirty days there were more than two thousand requests for public appearances as well as offers for articles and endorsements. One endorsement offer she accepted was from the makers of Hermes typewriters. Soon pictures of Marguerite, in battle fatigues, sitting at her typewriter (with Charles Payne's prized pen-and-pencil set sticking out of her pocket) were featured in all the leading magazines. For the sum of twelve hundred dollars, she earnestly proclaimed that Hermes had proved indispensable in front-line coverage: ''Despite the rough treatment, exposure to soaking rains, jolting jeeps, dust and dirt, it never let me down.''

She flatly rejected a film offer to dramatize her life; she regarded the characterization of herself as inane and an insult to the journalistic profession. Later, when lack of money was critical, she had reason to regret her high-handed rejection of the script.

Home leave, rather than a time of rest and relaxation, was a frenzied round of activity intended to leave little space for thoughts of Bill. Marguerite went to Washington, planning to make the capital her home away from home. She had spent most of her savings and prize money on the purchase of what had once been a guest "cottage" on the fabulous Evalyn Walsh McLean estate. Fred Shaw, a former lover from the early Berlin days and a lifelong friend, was working for the State Department at this time. "It was a charming place," Shaw remembered. "Maggie was still in the process of furnishing it. I spent most of my weekends hauling furniture and hanging pictures. I remember the house was filled with letters from parents of soldiers in Korea, often pathetic, nearly always asking impossible questions.

"One night Maggie asked me to be her escort to a lecture she was giving at Lissner Auditorium. She was very effective as a speaker and made a big hit with the audience. At the end of her talk she announced: 'If any of your have any more questions you can come backstage.' I thought we'd never leave! The auditorium was packed and it looked like everybody there had someone in Korea to ask about. Maggie did very well. If she couldn't recall the guy himself, she had at least visited his unit and could tell them something about that. She really knocked herself out. It was after one when the management finally insisted on closing up."

The round of luncheons, lectures, banquets, and receptions did little to assuage Marguerite's pain. The time came when she was anxious to return to her duties at the *Herald*. The question now was what the *Herald* would do with her. If Marguerite had not been a team player before her rise to prominence she was even less so now. No one at the *Herald* or its bureaus wanted to work with her. The answer seems to have been to keep her out of trouble by sending her on a round-the-world tour of trouble spots. Whatever the rationale behind the assignment, Marguerite was delighted.

Just prior to her departure, a private interview with President Truman was granted. As Marguerite entered Truman's office, she found the president seated at his desk poring over a map. He rose, stretched out his hand, and observed with a smile, "Well, young lady, you certainly had quite a time of it in Korea. I read all about it." Whether by design or accident, the president couldn't have found a quicker way to make a friend. Marguerite immediately spotted *War in Korea* on his desk, open and turned face down.

As they talked about Korea, Marguerite said, "In the urgency of war you are bound to find out a great deal about yourself and your countrymen. You form very close bonds."

The president agreed. "Let me show you something," he said, pulling out a drawer and pointing to a card index file. "There are two hundred and thirty names there, veterans of my outfit in France. They are men I'll never forget. I've kept track of them for more than thirty years. I've even made a character sketch of every one—whom they've married, what businesses they're in, how many daughters or sons they have. It's something I like to be up on when we get together for reunions."

Only the month before President Truman summarily had fired General MacArthur from his Far Eastern post, one of the great controversies of the era. When Marguerite brought up the subject the president said, "If MacArthur had not done so much strutting around and had tended more to business, I would not have had to fire him."

The president's use of the words "strutting around" applied to MacArthur was at first incredible to Marguerite. "Then," she wrote later in her column, "it dawned on me that a man from Missouri might well regard as empty posturing the psychological style that MacArthur practiced with a skill that was just right for Asia, newly emerging from chaos and feudalism, even if it would not sit well in some parts of Midwest America."

A few days later Marguerite began her tour with a transatlantic crossing aboard the *Ile de France*. Two days out to sea Marguerite awakened one morning to find that a square white card had been pushed under her door. The name Bernard M. Baruch was engraved on the outside.

Quickly she bounded out of bed and tore open the envelope. Inside was a handwritten note: "Mr Baruch will be in deck chair twenty at eleven o'clock and will be happy to have a talk with you at that time if you are free."

Since it was then one minute of eleven—she had danced until four that morning—there was a mad scramble. Marguerite claimed to have arrived only two and a half minutes late. In an article written for *Women's Home Companion*, she wrote: "Baruch has made several fortunes in Wall Street and probably knows more about war financing and production than any other living American. Equally impressive to me is the fact that Mr. Baruch is a wonderful, gracious human, selflessly devoted to his country's welfare.

"Since I have passed so much time behind the Iron Curtain I could not help comparing Mr. Baruch with the official Communist portrait of the big bad capitalist. If I ever tried to express the personality and motivations of Mr. Baruch to even the most intelligent of the Communists I learned to know behind the Iron Curtain, I simply would not be believed. I am glad of this Marxist incredulity. It forms part of their miscalculations about the power and nature of the west. The more the Communists miscalculate, the more likely we—the galaxy of anti-Communist nations—are likely to defeat them in the long run."

In Paris, Marguerite paid her first visit to General Dwight D. Eisenhower's supreme headquarters and had a pleasant reunion with John Michaelis, who was serving there. Now a brigadier general, Michaelis looked "spick and span, beribboned and generally shiny"—a far cry from the weary, mud-bespattered colonel who had led the Twenty-seventh (Wolfhound) Regiment in Korea. But then Marguerite, too, was a contrast from the sweaty, dusty correspondent who had worn nothing but dirty army uniforms for nearly a year.

That evening Marguerite and her former lover from Berlin days, Edward Morrow (now working at the *New York Times* Paris bureau), had dinner with Michaelis and his wife, Mary, at Tour d'Argent. It was her first meeting with Mary, and as the two women sat chatting at a window overlooking the Seine a close friendship was formed. Later there were long conversations about war with the general, and even longer ones about life, love, and marriage with his wife. "Marguerite was a lonely, unhappy girl beneath the facade of self-confidence," Mary remembered.

Don Cook, now back at the *Herald*'s Paris bureau, found that facade still very formidable. "Maggie would literally steal the trousers off you for a story and had to be watched constantly. *Herald* writers were competitive but not with each other. Maggie was different; out there by herself. She was like a figure skater twirling and whirling—a journalistic accident that she herself helped to create."

Marguerite launched a series on world leaders with a journalistic coup, an exclusive interview with Franco of Spain. She then went on to talk with Tito of Yugoslavia, Nehru of India, Liaquat Ali Khan of Pakistan, Chiang Kaishek of Formosa, the shah of Iran, and the king of Siam. Entrée to these notables was easy, she soon discovered. The dignitaries were as curious to meet her as she was anxious to interview them.

Apparently a little of Daisy Mae remained in Marguerite beneath the cosmopolitan veneer. Don Cook's wife, Cherry, remembered that Marguerite set off on her tour in a specially purchased Christian Dior ensemble and returned weeks later wearing the same dress, which was scarcely recognizable under all the wrinkles and spots. "I don't think she gave much time or thought to things like dry cleaners," Cherry said. "Don was out of town when Maggie returned. Though we'd known each other casually for several years, this was really the first opportunity we'd had to spend any time together. As it turned out we spent the better part of two days. Despite her glamour trip, Maggie was depressed, reluctant to be alone for a minute."

Throughout these long months Bill Hall remained conciliatory. "Everybody knew that I was a man who liked to work hard and play hard, too," he says today. "I liked parties and I liked a good time. I was in the San Francisco area by myself, and I didn't let any grass grow under my feet. There were ladies whose company I enjoyed, but there was never any doubt in my mind that Marguerite was the one I loved. The hard part was convincing her of that."

In November she came home to Oakland to give a lecture. It was the typical hometown girl-makes-good script: The Gamma Phi Betas elected to forget the sins of the past and greeted Marguerite as a returning heroine. Bill Hall crossed San Francisco Bay to escort her to the lecture and afterward to a reception sponsored by the sorority.

A few days later the Higginses gave a large party for their daugher. Once again Bill Hall was present. "I remember it all so well," Jean Craig, her childhood friend, said. "Maggie was beautiful. She wore a blue-green dress, oriental style, with a slit up the side to show those beautiful legs. To us, she was the golden girl again."

Larry Higgins didn't approve of Hall or the fact that Marguerite was sharing accommodations with him at the Claremont Hotel. After a few drinks he no longer cared who knew it. "I know what you're doing with my daughter," he roared. "Now I want to know what you're going to do about it. What are your intentions?" There was no answer from Hall, and no one else spoke either. Time seemed to stand still as guests stared at one another in embarrassed silence.

A. A. Marchant, an old family friend, looked across the crowded room at Jean. "Shouldn't somebody get the show on the road?" he urged. Jean hurried into the kitchen and began making gravy. "That wasn't such a good idea after all," she recalled. "Marguerite Senior was furious at the idea of anything as mundane as flour and water being mixed in her kitchen. Her cooking was strictly French. She was so exasperated that she began throwing things. What a mess! Pretty soon everybody was in the kitchen cleaning up and carrying out what was left of the food. Of course Marguerite Senior didn't stay angry long. She adored drama. If things got quiet or she felt neglected you could count on her to pull a tantrum or faint, but her recovery was always swift.''

Bill had just a few months left of his tour of duty at Hamilton Air Force Base. He was eager to convince Marguerite of his sincerity and urged her to remain in California. Well aware that her romantic competition was in San Francisco, she allowed herself to be persuaded. She obtained a temporary West Coast assignment and sublet the apartment of the popular *San Francisco Chronicle* columnist Herb Caen.

Jean Craig remembered visiting at the apartment. "In the San Francisco area Caen is almost as essential as hot water and coffee in the morning. I was almost as excited at seeing the great man's inner sanctum as I was in seeing Maggie again. She very proudly gave me the grand tour before we sat down to talk. Soon it was like old times; we were kids again. Maggie fixed an elegant dinner just for me—rare leg of lamb with natural gravy; fresh peas. Marvelous!

"People kept calling and finally she just took the phone off the hook. She talked a lot about Bill Hall. She seemed happy, hopeful, in love. I remember her singing along with a recording of *I'm Just a Girl Who Can't Say No* and calling it her theme song."

On an April afternoon in 1952 Bill Hall received his divorce in Reno. A few minutes later he and Marguerite were married. "I was thirty-one years old," she recalled later. "It seemed too late in my life to start turning back. Also, I was in love."

Eighteen

A picture of a smiling Marguerite and Bill flashed over the wire services. The accompanying story listed the bride's accomplishments and stated that the bridegroom, then forty-four, was one of the youngest generals in the air force and had been the American army intelligence director in Berlin during the Soviet blockade of the city and the Allied airlift.

Among the hundreds of congratulatory cables that flooded in from all parts of the world were messages from King Paul and Queen Frederika of Greece, General MacArthur, Norman Cousins, President Syngman Rhee, Chiang Kaishek, General Lucius B. Clay, General Mark Clark, Governor Earl Warren, and Bernard Baruch.

The newlyweds' first guest upon returning to the small cottage Bill had rented on Indian Valley Road in Novato, a few miles north of San Francisco, was a stray dog waiting on their doorstep. The animal gave an enthusiastic, tail-wagging welcome. It seemed an omen. The abandoned dog was named Reno in honor of their marriage place and became the first of a large and varied animal family.

For a time Marguerite enjoyed playing house. "Bill is the most exciting thing next to war," she told Dick Demerest, an old friend from the *Daily Cal* and now a *San Francisco Chronicle* editor. Marguerite shopped at the commissary, cooked gourmet dinners, danced and attended receptions at Hamilton Field. The typical life of an officer's wife—with a difference.

One day Bill undertook to give Marguerite a lesson in marksmanship. Carefully setting up a target, he handed his bride a rifle and methodically explained how to use it. She listened intently, watched as he fired the gun, accepted the weapon from him, took careful aim, and fired.

"I can't believe this!" Bill exclaimed.

Bill had fired five shots; Marguerite, two. Both of hers had hit the bull's-eye. Three of his missed the target entirely; the other two hit the outer rim.

Marguerite was innocent: "I only did what you told me to." She didn't mention her days of riding shotgun for Keyes Beech in Korea. They made a copy of the target with its telltale holes. Marguerite treasured it for years.

Dave Perlman, who is now an associate editor of the *San Francisco Chronicle*, had also returned recently to the area following several years at the Paris bureau of the *Herald Tribune*. He and his wife had known Marguerite during the postwar days and renewed the friendhsip. "The four of us had dinner fairly often," Perlman remembered. "Maggie and Bill seemed very pleased and proud of each other. They were typical newlyweds, the only difference being that we all knew Maggie wouldn't be staying in one place very long."

A temporary diversion was offered when she was invited by the San Francisco affiliate of CBS to do a television series. Marguerite's baby voice had taken on a more authoritative note after a twenty-four-city speaking tour. "Marguerite Higgins News Close Up" was a twelve-part series that triggered an avalanche of mail, most of it positive. Her television presence was simple, direct, and sometimes uncertain. Much of her fan mail contained advice. "Don't smile even if you do have a beautiful smile," a man wrote. A woman felt that she showed some bias toward General Eisenhower, then a presidential candidate, and urged her to "be more objective."

Marguerite's manner was so appealing to the San Francisco writer Albert Ujcic that he sat down and wrote the kind of person-to-person communication that most of us fantasize about sending but never quite get around to writing. He said:

Dear Miss Higgins:

I begin not unlike the guy next to you at a bar but with the disadvantage of not being able to offer you a drink. My advantage though is that I have observed you while you have not observed me and I know your name.

Since we can't have a drink together (which means you can't refuse me no matter how graciously) at least I can talk. And I can talk about you.

I didn't realize at first that you were local or that the program was being broadcast from San Francisco, so I judged it on the basis of my concept of *top* national news reporting and remarked to my brother what an exceptional program and person we were watching.

When the lady in the convent collar got jittery I was especially glad because it seemed an honest response. It's very nice to meet anyone—and particularly a woman—with cerebral fulfillment who is still an honest-to-God human being and yet not maudlin.

I have every expectation that your shaky but pretty knees will steady. But as they do, don't get Walter Winchelish. Stay Miss Marguerite Higgins (or Mrs. Something Else, if you prefer). And when your director, agent or crew chief tries to coax you to glibness or a "dynamic, hard-hitting style"—you resist, you fight, you give 'em hell. Now please forgive my tone if it sounds patronizing. I know you know all the things I've said, but maybe you'll be reassured to hear them again from a stranger. Now! Touch my glass. Here's to you. Drink up and good luck.

The mental toast from an unknown well-wisher was treasured by Marguerite until her death fourteen years later.

Although the series was a success, television commentary was not Marguerite's forte. She was anxious to be back on regular assignment at the *Herald Tribune* and had written its owner, Helen Rogers Reid. Once again Marguerite was appealing to the woman who once demonstrated her confidence by sending a young reporter with scarcely two years newspaper experience off to cover World War II. Actually two days prior to her marriage Marguerite had outlined the situation with surprising candor:

Since I consider the *Herald Tribune* a kind of second family, I wanted to be sure and inform you, before the columnists did, that I am marrying General Hall.

I also wanted to tell you that the marriage will not, so far as we are concerned, affect my plans for resuming my work with the *Herald Tribune* very shortly. I see no point in being coy about our problems. Briefly they stem from the fact that Bill's alimony leaves him with less per month than I used to earn per week. So even if I wanted to stop being a reporter—which I don't—I couldn't.

Despite all the manifold problems, we decided to go ahead with our marriage on the theory that it was better to face the difficulties as a team than apart.

I'm looking forward to being back in New York. I detest California, but I'll have to admit the weather has been wonderful and at last I appear to be completely cured of all my ills including sinus. This bout with the bugs has been quite an exhausting one and I'm glad that particular battle is over.

When Bill was transferred at the end of the year it was Reno who was his companion on the long drive east. Marguerite was once again in

Korea. It was the first of many separations that would become a way of life for them.

Jeeping to the truce talks at Panmunjom she passed through scores of devastated villages that were twisted, burned-out specters. The dry hills, which might have been brilliant with autumn foliage, were blackened by forest fires caused by bombs and artillery fire.

In Panmunjom Marguerite faced one of the strangest reporting obstacles of her varied career. Western liaison officers attending the talks were forbidden to speak to the Western press, whose members were reduced to getting their stories from the Communist press. Thus it may have been the only occasion in history when Communist and anti-Communist newspaper people gathered daily to interview each other.

Marguerite's communicant was Wilfrid "Peter" Burchett, an intimate during the Berlin days. Although Burchett had represented the ultra-conservative *London Daily Express* in Berlin, his leftist leanings were known. Now he was covering the truce talks for *Ce Soir*, a French Communist paper. It was a strange and bitter reunion for Marguerite. In Berlin she had been tolerant, considering Burchett a misguided idealist. In Panmunjom, she discovered that her former colleague and companion —the man with whom she had once traded information nightly regarding happenings in the American sector of Berlin for that of those in the British—was now helping the Red Chinese to question and influence American POWs to "confess" to germ warfare in Korea.

Marguerite recently had interviewed French consular officials who had fled to Hong Kong. They had described mass executions they had witnessed in Shanghai. Members of the upper middle class, clergymen, and intellectuals had been dragged into the streets, where ropes were placed about their necks. Loudspeakers on all major street corners blared kill-by-kill accounts of the massacre.

"Even the Nazis tried to hide most of the facts about the concentration camps," she reminded Burchett. "I don't see the purpose of all the fanfare. Millions of Chinese hear the unpleasant facts whether they want to listen or not."

Contemptuously he replied, "You seem to have forgotten an elemental fact: The purpose of terror is to terrorize."

As the truce talks dragged on so did the fighting. "SOMEWHERE IN KOREA" was Marguerite's frequent dateline. Tightened security often forbade mention of specific locations. She wrote:

The war in Korea is today, as in the past, the victim of the military orders that were not placed, the planes that were not produced, the shells and bombs that were not manufactured, the ships that were not built, and the civilian economy that could not afford to be much "disturbed."

This far-off and nearly forgotten war is the victim of halfway mobilization, which when it finally started was many months late. It is the victim in this writer's opinion of false politics based on the belief that the American people at home cannot be told the truth and asked to take the discomfort and to exercise the self-discipline required to finish the job in Korea . . . I wish those who talk about "not disturbing the economy" would come to a Korean air base sometime and explain why our production of first-rate jets isn't sufficient to permit the fulfillment of requests for reinforcements. . . .

Her plea was eloquent; but, like the program chairman of the Woman's Civic Club of Glens Falls, most Americans were not interested in a "rehash of Korea." The general public, unless involved through family ties, had grown bored with a war that ground painfully on and on, a war that was no longer even called a war but rather a police action or conflict. The deaths of men who were now known as Harry Truman's police force were no longer considered hot copy.

When Marguerite was instructed by the *Herald Tribune* to continue her round-the-world tour, she discovered that a new front had been added to the old war. Curiously she had returned to Vietnam, the beautiful land where she had been taken as an ailing baby, the country where her grandfather, the young Count de Godard, had died fighting with the French colonial forces in the 1890s. She found that although colonialism had ended, the country's troubles had barely begun. Having been granted autonomy and the right to create its own army, the new nation was now gripped by civil war.

"Continuous road and rail transportation is impossible," Marguerite wrote. "This is a country of air communication only. To make a rough comparison, the Communist position in Vietnam if duplicated on the West Coast of the United States would show the Communists occupying northern Washington with additional groups of Reds holding key villages and cities in Oregon. San Francisco's position would equal that of Saigon if the former's suburbs of Palo Alto and San Jose were occupied and administered by Red mayors, policemen, etc." She described Vietnam as "a place where the enemy is an elusive guerrilla whose favorite trick when cornered is to masquerade as a peaceful farmer tending his rice paddy."

She went on to describe a journey out of Hanoi when she "had happened by chance upon a beautiful and apparently forgotten Confucian temple located in a faraway village at the end of an enclosed courtyard, its stones covered by moss and shaded by tall, tall trees which were reflected in a pool filled with water lilies and goldfish. I am not a member of any particular religion, but even as an agnostic I have been drawn to temples and churches and found beauty and an inexplicable sense of rapport to I know not what—but a sense of magnetic quality that draws me back again and again."

Not only its temples but Vietnam itself would call Marguerite, causing her to return again and again as though ensnared in an enchanted web that would one day become her shroud.

Nineteen

WHICH FACTOR WAS MOST IMPORTANT IN HELPING YOU
BECOME THE SUCCESSFUL PERSON YOU ARE, RATHER THAN
THE FAILURE YOU MIGHT HAVE BEEN?

The question was one that had been mailed to Marguerite in advance
of a lecture. She took time to ponder analytically and answered carefully:

"People are always looking for gimmicks and gadgets with which to
achieve success, and there aren't any. There are usually an awful lot of
failures involved in any successes. In journalism, you have to be completely in love with your job and put it ahead of anything else. You can't
think in terms of working five days a week and then taking two days off
or keeping regular hours and going home for dinner at the same time
every night.

"From 1944 to 1952 there was nothing in my life except journalism.
There wasn't any time for fun and social life and I didn't go to any parties
except those at which I might meet sources for stories. I had an overwhelming desire to do my job well and this was complicated by the fact
that because I was a rarity so much attention was focused upon the
lonely, struggling girl that I was."

Whether she chose to acknowledge it or not Marguerite was still very
much a rarity, a woman at odds with an era that placed its highest
premium on domesticity. Against this child and home-centered standard, Marguerite struggled to find and maintain her own sense of
balance. It wasn't easy. "My home is where my typewriter is," she
explained to Ellen McCann, who interviewed her for the *Richmond
Times-Dispatch*. She added, "I like to cook." (Although it was true that
Marguerite was considered a superb cook such concessions to domes-

ticity were almost mandatory in women's features during the fifties. Success was scary; ambition, in a woman, suspect. Both could be injurious to the health of the family.)

The short article continued, "In three years I've been around the world twice, to Korea seven times and gotten married." Both this story and another in *Mademoiselle* neatly sidestepped the controversy implicit in Marguerite's pregnancy by not even mentioning it. Working mothers (unless they really *had* to) were probably the ultimate no-no of the decade.

In the *Mademoiselle* article, guest editor Anne Shawber quoted Marguerite as advising aspiring journalists to "get a job on the best big paper you can find. Journalism school is a stepping-stone but it's like training to have a baby—there's no substitute for experience." She rated brashness and perseverance high, adding, "A woman must convince an editor that she has something the average male reporter lacks, then in times of crisis, she can get to the top. Otherwise there's no magic formula for success, just sheer slaving."

While the issue of Marguerite's pregnancy was avoided in print, her colleagues greeted the news with much speculation. All wondered what its effect would be upon her life-style and personality. One story, possibly apocryphal but told and retold into legend, involves a group of journalists dining at the Stork Club. When a latecomer greeted them with the news, "Hey, did you hear Maggie Higgins is expecting a baby?" Homer Bigart looked up. "Wonderful!" he said. "Who's the mother?"

As she had once pleaded with the *Herald Tribune* to send her overseas, Marguerite now begged for a longer time at home. The demands of her life had not diminished, nor had the tensions they evoked. "Bill and I are getting along pretty much as one would expect," she confided to her friend from Korea days, Carl Mydans.

In February 1953, Marguerite wrote to General MacArthur, who had returned to private life in New York declaring himself off limits to the press. She appealed frankly to him for an interview.

"My newspaper, after many months of unflattering hesitation, has finally decided to give me a chance to work within the country," she admitted. "This is only a temporary break in my foreign corresponding but an important one to me personally since my husband is stationed here. I'd like to begin the series with an interview with you."

MacArthur agreed and a new phase of Marguerite's career began; but as she had said, "the break" was only temporary. Three months later she was back in Vietnam where she met and interviewed a rising leader, Ngo Dinh Diem. Her own views of the man were shared at the time by Justice William O. Douglas. Douglas, also touring the country, reported: ''Ngo Dinh Diem is a hero in Central and North Vietnam with a considerable following in the South, too. . . . Ngo Dinh Diem is revered by the Vietnamese because he is honest and independent and stood firm against the French influence. There are few officials in the Vietnamese government who have that reputation.''

Home again, Marguerite was plunged into a round of projects that included articles and lectures in addition to her *Herald Tribune* assignments. She and Bill, on a brief holiday in Jamaica, had fallen in love with a small resort near Montego Bay, which was developed on a time-sharing basis. Marguerite had called her investment a ''pleasant insanity.'' Less pleasant was coming up with the money to cover it. It was the first of many close-to-the-vest business speculations.

As the summer drew to a close Marguerite was busy with an article for the *Saturday Evening Post* on CIA techniques. She was excited about the assignment, which would be challenging as well as lucrative. Then on October 2, 1953, she wrote a brief message to Marty Summers, the foreign editor of that magazine.

> Just a note to report that I was hauled off to the hospital last week. I hope the timing won't be too important in that piece on intelligence. I'll be out of bed and on my feet no later than the middle of the week, I hope.
>
> I'm pretty pleased on one point. W. H. Jackson, the man who did the psychological warfare survey for Ike and the person who carried through the organizational streamlining of CIA when Bedel Smith came in, has volunteered his services. He sent me his original report on our intelligence services as a whole and is filling me in on some work he's currently doing, (kind of, but not very secret) whereby a group of private citizens meets each month with CIA analysts to challenge their conclusions, fact gathering, etc. Jackson is Ike's advisor on intelligence matters.
>
> I'm also double-checking my own ideas and anecdotes with Dulles, C. D. Jackson, and the head of intelligence, department of Soviet affairs, who is an old friend from Berlin days.
>
> I'm awfully anxious to get going on the piece as is everybody concerned with it, which is unusual, as so often these intelligence people adore the cloak-and-dagger attitude just for its own sake.
>
> So if I can just get my health and the doctors under control, perhaps I'll have something.

The actuality was not as Marguerite had planned at all. Six days later

Sharon Lee was born two months prematurely, a fact the distraught mother later blamed on her frantic pace, which had never slowed as her pregnancy advanced.

Marguerite and Bill watched Sharon anxiously through the glass partition that separated the premature babies. Describing those precious moments to her friend, Helen Lambert, Marguerite told how Sharon had laughed, waved, and kicked up her pink heels, wriggling enchantingly. ''She did all those things that young babies do to make you their devoted slaves,'' she recalled, adding, ''so far as looks were concerned, she had a special advantage. Premature babies don't have that extra fat that often leaves newborns so puckered and red. Sharon's skin was smooth, her profile adorable, and her disposition remarkable.'' Although under four pounds she began eating at once while the other premature babies were fed intravenously.''

Although the new parents longed to hold her, Sharon, in her antiseptic little glassed-in crib, remained off limits to all but doctors and nurses. Marguerite had been promised that after ten days she and Bill would be allowed to hold their daughter for at least a little while.

Dawn was just breaking on the morning of October 13 when a young woman doctor awakened Marguerite from a sound sleep. Stale cigarette smoke lingered from the guests of the night before, mingling with the scent of roses on the table beside her. Marguerite knew instinctively that something was terribly wrong.

As an aide helped her into a wheelchair, the doctor explained, ''The baby vomited a little while ago and then stopped breathing. We are administering oxygen and she seems to be improving a little. But I think you had better come now. With premature babies things can go wrong very suddenly.''

When they arrived, a nurse was giving Sharon artificial respiration, gently pressing down on the baby's little bottom, lifting her legs up and back toward her head. ''Incredibly Sharon was still waving her arms, and once she smiled,'' Marguerite recalled. But she was gasping hard, emptying her lungs with every breath and then on the intake pulling her skin taut against her ribs.

''Sharon's death stunned Marguerite as nothing had,'' Helen remembered. ''She had never invested so much of herself. I'll never forget her describing the child's gallant battle to survive. 'I have seen many wounded soldiers on the battlefields of Europe and Korea struggling hard to live,' she reminded me. 'None struggled harder than Sharon. It was two more hours before she gave up the fight for breath and life. After she died, all I could think—and it went through my head like a chant—was, I never even held her in my arms.' ''

"In the terrible moments of Sharon's dying I thought inevitably of how familiar—and yet how unfamiliar—death had been to me. And yet, as Sharon died, I made the discovery that I had seen death and yet I had not known it. Certainly I had been sorry for the thousands I had seen dead and dying—so sadly, wearingly, many thousands. But sorry in a detached sort of way. I had not comprehended the tears of the bereaved. I had not known how the death of another could be the death of a part of yourself. I had not known many things, for I had never understood the meaning of compassion."

Seeking some kind of catharsis from the pain, guilt, and bewilderment that followed her child's death, Marguerite undertook the writing of her memoirs. Not yet thirty-five, she had a great deal to tell. Marguerite spared no one, not even herself—laying bare the story of her parents' stormy marriage, her aborted love affair with George Millar, her disappointment over Bill's infidelities, the couple's precarious financial situation, and her concern about their future.

A third trip to North Vietnam to record the death rattle of Dien Bien Phu interrupted the enterprise. She was only a few feet away when Robert Capa of Magnum Photos, a close friend, stepped into a rice paddy to take a picture and was blown to bits by a land mine.

While still in Vietnam, Marguerite received word that a visa had been granted to her for a trip to Russia. She would be the first American correspondent to be allowed entrance to the country since Stalin's death. Marguerite was excited, for she had fought hard for the opportunity; but there was also some trepidation—her anti-Communist stance was well known. During her coverage of Korea a Russian paper had singled her out as a "hyena of the press."

Yet this was nothing compared to her concern about the activities of the man she was leaving behind. She seriously questioned whether, once the lengthy assignment was completed, there would be a marriage to return to—it was a risk she had to take.

Before leaving for Russia, Marguerite went home to finish her memoirs. The book ended with the prediction that her life, not only professionally but personally, would be as it had always been—"rough but interesting."

She was quite right.

PART VI

WORLDWIDE
COLUMNIST

Twenty

Marguerite wrote the brief letter in her Helsinki hotel room just prior
to departing for the airport. It was mailed to a friend in the State
Department pending her safe return from behind the iron curtain.

Whether such a drastic measure was necessary or not, it certainly
made for a dramatic introduction to her next book, *Red Plush and Black
Bread*. Marguerite's 13,500-mile sojourn through Russia took her to
remote areas that were open for the first time. "With the lively curiosity
of a wide-eyed tourist and the knowing eyes of a reporter" (the book
jacket's description) "she frequently bypassed government spokesmen
to talk to Russia's little people." She photographed everything she saw
while traveling from one end of the country to another and, as a result,
was detained sixteen times by the police. Often without guide, interpreter, or companion she traveled thousands of miles through Siberia.

The whole adventure was yet another journalistic coup. Marguerite
was the first American correspondent to get a visa after restrictions
against visitors were relaxed and was therefore the first roving news
representative to enter Russia since the Stalin era.

The initial idea of the Russian trip had come at a time when Marguerite's spirits were at their lowest ebb. Sharon had been very much a
wanted child. Once at a small gathering attended by close friends, she

had begun to cry softly. "I've had so many abortions," she confided. "I *want* a baby." Again Marguerite had determined to have it all; once again fate had tripped her up.

The child's premature birth and her own long illness that followed resulted in a loss of twelve thousand dollars in lecture fees and other commitments in addition to the medical bills themselves. Marguerite's lengthy convalescence gave her an opportunity to review her finances and consider her future. Bill's extrication from his first marriage necessitated his turning over all property to his first wife and paying out more than eighty percent of his yearly earnings. For Marguerite it was a Catch-22 situation. Her contribution to their mutual finances was essential, yet this necessitated travel outside the country with subsequent long separations, the likes of which almost separated them permanently.

By now she had few illusions. Many of the qualities that she admired in her husband also made him extremely appealing to other women. He was not going to change. It remained for her to continue with her own life. Possibly it would have been her choice under any conditions.

The idea of Russia was one more challenge to be overcome. She not only applied for a visa but a Guggenheim Fellowship for Russian study as well. Chances of receiving either were considered impossible. Journalists were simply not admitted to Russia in those days when the cold war was at its most frigid. Nevertheless she persevered.

She began by taking a Berlitz course in Russian, poring over her grammar while flying to and from other overseas assignments. If she was surprised to be granted the visa or receive the award she didn't show it. She had been getting ready for months.

At the time of her departure in September 1954, she was reaping the flowery harvest of her first full-scale garden. The author Ruth Montgomery, who was then a syndicated columnist, lived around the corner from the Georgetown house and had become a close friend. She remembered the garden well. "It was a showplace and Marguerite was so proud of it. She loved to arrange flowers and knew each by its Latin name. I was astounded. 'How did you ever learn all those Latin words?' I asked.

"Marguerite laughed. 'That's how I rested up between Russian lessons.' "

The crash course stood her in good stead. Marguerite's Russian experiences frequently were frightening and easily could have accelerated into something worse if she had been unable to express herself.

"If I'd known in advance that during my travels I'd be arrested sixteen times I might never have left Moscow," she admitted in *Red Plush and Black Bread*. "That would have been a mistake. I was lucky, amazingly lucky, when you consider how another American woman was later manhandled by the police during her detention. While I was being held and questioned by the Russian police I was treated correctly and always released within a few hours. I would not want to relive the moments of anxiety while the question of my release was being debated, but my detentions were always educational. One can learn a lot by sitting around police stations talking to the militia, or even to the other people in police stations."

With photographs of Russia so rare at that time, Marguerite felt that a few hours in prison were a small price to pay. The arrests invariably followed the taking of pictures, although she had never been instructed not to take them. "Of course," she acknowledged, "I'd be less than honest if I didn't admit that each time I was arrested I was scared. There was always the possibility that the stay in the police station might be unpleasantly long."

Once, while taking a picture of a tomato vendor, Marguerite was accosted suddenly by an apparent civilian. Placing himself squarely in front of her, he began to cry out, "Spy! Spy!" Soon a large and aggressive crowd had formed about her. When she tried to leave they became hostile and pressed closer. A woman tried to grab her camera. There seemed no way out and Marguerite was badly frightened.

Then a policeman appeared, ordering the crowd back and taking her firmly by the arm. For once she was glad, even grateful to be arrested. Marguerite felt so relieved that she was emboldened to turn on her original tormentor and level a verbal attack. After weeks of reading *Pravda* she was well aware of the state's emphasis on *kulturni*. Although few really were certain what culture meant, they knew it was a disgrace to be without. Another word that cropped up with increasing frequency was *piani*, meaning drunk.

Now that the policeman was leading her firmly away, she turned to the troublemaker and gave him a piece of her half-Irish temper. "I am a stranger to this country. It is very *nye kulturni* to behave this way to a stranger; and furthermore, I think you're *piani*."

The noisy crowd grew silent, considering. Then as Marguerite departed with the policeman, they all began to speak at once, shaking their fingers at the man and chorusing, "*Nye kulturni! Vui piani.*"

Marguerite's detention at the police station lasted three hours.

Weighed against her possible fate with the angry crowd, the wait was not nearly so tedious as usual.

Nearing the end of her departure, Marguerite wrote a memo to her editors summarizing her frustration at having to frequently censor herself. Russian suspicion and propensity for blackmail placed highly unique self-imposed restraints on foreign correspondents. No one could forget that reporters behind the iron curtain had been condemned as spies for asking questions that would be routine anywhere else in the world.

Just before leaving Moscow, Marguerite had a vivid personal experience that brought home exactly how these self-imposed inhibitions affected her own reporting performance. She had ordered lunch to be sent to her room, but well aware by this time of the slowness of room service, she decided to take a bath while waiting. She had hardly settled into the tub when there was a brisk rap on the door.

Slipping into a robe, she hurried to the door and opened it a crack. There stood two uniformed men. She slammed the door. Her emotions balanced between fear and annoyance. If she was to be arrested once more, the final indignity was not to even have her clothes on.

She called to the men through the closed door: "*Kak vui hottiye.*" A burst of masculine laughter caused her to realize that she had in her nervous confusion substituted (How do you want?) for "*Shto vui hottiye*?" (Who do you want?).

As the three attempted to communicate through the locked door, Marguerite learned that the two men were actually air force pilots whom she had met casually in Kiev. They had apparently decided to pay her a social call while passing through Moscow.

Anywhere else the event might have been a pleasant, relatively commonplace occurrence. In Russia, Marguerite was at a loss to know how to play it. Were they in reality merely officers out on the town or were they actually agents of the secret police instructed to place her in a compromising and dangerous situation? A scene was easy to imagine— two Russian officers alone with a woman in a hotel room. She could imagine the headlines: AMERICAN WOMAN SEEKS TO PRY MILITARY SECRETS FROM RUSSIAN OFFICERS DURING DRUNKEN ORGY. The situation did seem ripe for blackmail.

Marguerite took no chances. Quickly she called Alexis Shiray, a Russian-speaking representative of Agence France Presse, and urged him to join them immediately. Asking the officers to wait, she leisurely slipped into a dress. When Shiray arrived the Russian floor administrator tried her best to persuade him that Marguerite wasn't in. Fortunately he was insistent, making certain there was a witness to the afternoon's seemingly lighthearted interlude. Whatever the intent of her guests, Marguerite found it difficult to behave normally. When the pilots began to speak of an upcoming aerial parade, her natural response would have been to ask, "What do you fly?"

Knowing that any questions about airplanes could be construed as prying into military secrets, she merely said, "Hmmmmmmmm, interesting."

When the Soviet captain confided that his friend the colonel had many decorations, had been a bomber pilot in Manchuria, and had there developed techniques that even the Americans didn't know, Marguerite's reply was still, "Hmmmmmmmm."

"We often fly to Berlin these days," the bomber pilot commented. "We can get there very fast in our new planes."

Marguerite smiled demurely. "They have interesting nightclubs in Berlin," she offered helpfully.

The pilots then seemed determined to get everyone drunk. They had brought a large bottle of Russian cognac and poured the contents into water glasses, insisting that all drink it down, bottoms up. Marguerite and the French correspondent rebelled after the first toast.

Finally the bomber pilot asked, "If I came to America would I be stoned on the streets because I'm a Soviet citizen?"

"Not if you came by *boat*," she told him.

He got the point and ended the questioning.

Marguerite found the Russians particularly suspicious of a woman traveling alone. Several times when she was arrested and taken to the police station crowds would gather. "*Odna*?" they would ask, which meant "Alone? Why are you alone?" She would carefully explain, "I'm here as a correspondent and there isn't any reason to share my information with a competitor."

Although the Russians remained mystified, it was a very characteristic explanation, one that Marguerite's colleagues at the *Herald Tribune* and elsewhere would have easily recognized.

Marguerite returned to Washington and a fresh controversy. This one centered on a novel, *The Iron Maiden*, by Edwin Lanham. Lanham, an

slipped into a dress. When Shiray arrived the Russian floor administrator
cub reporter days. His narrative centered around a group of macho
editors and reporters whose wildest nightmare came true when Carolyn
Brown, ''a woman of iron,'' married the young publisher of her newspaper. As might be expected, heads rolled as Carolyn, with a few nasty
scores to settle, began her reign of terror.

Once past the ''she left her legend in the city room'' and the descriptions of her walk that reminded one ''that every muscle of her body had a
function,'' the story ceased to be banal and became revealing. The
parallels drawn must have amused the Reid family, who owned the
Herald Tribune and frequently benefited from the rivalry that Marguerite sparked: ''Carolyn was a catalyst going from bureau to bureau to
raise the bubble in the brew. . . . Where Carolyn went, something usually
happened . . . [and most telling] ''She was always looking for an exclusive. She wasn't trying to beat the other bureaus—she was trying to beat
the guys in her own bureau.''

The timing of this roman à clef was unfortunate. Once again Marguerite was locked into a power struggle, matched against a more senior
correspondent, Walter Kerr. Marguerite was determined to spend at
least part of the time with Bill Hall in Washington and had succeeded in
wangling the assignment against everyone's better judgment. It was not
a compatible arrangement. Kerr was the elder statesman, and having
received the plum assignment of Washington bureau chief, was considered the flagship of the paper. Marguerite was a newcomer to the
Washington scene, brash, determined, and something of a prima donna.
The association ended with Kerr's resignation. The backlash was not
pleasant.

Marguerite was happy to receive an assignment to return to Russia. By
now *News Is a Singular Thing* had come out, and not even her parents
were speaking to her.

Twenty-one

On January 6, 1956 Marguerite Higgins, then thirty-five years old, was interviewed by *U. S. News and World Report* as an expert on Russian affairs. In a lengthy question-and-answer article she discussed views gleaned from two successive trips behind the iron curtain.

In contrast to her first trip when she had been arrested sixteen times, the second time around Marguerite easily gained entrée to Khrushchev, Bulganin, Mikoyan and Zhukov. For once being a woman had proved an advantage. "I think they were so surprised to see a woman reporter that it overcame their hostility and suspicion toward anything American," she explained. "They were so curious about this strange person who'd come so far from home to ask them questions that they answered those questions—at least some of them."

Despite their heavy-handed courtliness toward her, Marguerite saw little indication of a lessening of international tensions but did discern a willingness to at least meet with non-Communist leaders. It was a prophecy that bore fruit and would provide some of her most dramatic moments as a political writer.

Red Plush and Black Velvet, dedicated to William E. Hall, had been published the previous fall. Sales, timed for the holidays, were brisk. Readers proved as curious about the adventures of a lone American woman behind the iron curtain as they were about Russia itself.

Vice Admiral Leslie Stevens, who had served after World War II as a naval attache in Moscow, writing in *Saturday Review*, described the book as "clear-sighted and direct without a hint of malice, naivete or punditry." The book, he found, primarily focused on the conditions of life in Russia and what people thought of them and why. "It answers many questions and there isn't a dull page in it," he promised.

Marguerite had established the *Herald Tribune* bureau in Moscow but, anxious to return to Bill, had not wanted to remain as its chief. At the insistence of Helen Rogers Reid, she had been assigned as a correspondent to the Washington bureau. The main office directive had meticulously spelled out the terms of Marguerite's salary and sick leave, but it left the guidelines of assignments up to the bureau chief.

Characteristically Marguerite wanted the biggest, most sensational, or most significant stories—stories traditionally the chief's to write or assign at will. After deciding ''She's going, or I'm going,'' Walter Kerr had gone. Then another staff member resigned in protest. The next bureau chief left for health reasons.

When author and veteran newsman Robert Donovan stepped into the chief's slot, morale was at an all-time low. ''I'm in charge or I don't take the job,'' were his conditions. The head office agreed; Donovan, true to his words, called the shots. But Marguerite had an uncanny faculty for turning up at key times and places, claiming to be there on magazine assignments. Her stories, frequently hard-won exclusives, could scarcely be dismissed or discarded by the bureau.

Marguerite simply could not relax. ''There's no such thing,'' she told a group of college interviewers, ''as saying, 'I'm sick, I'm going home.' Maybe your editor would understand but the story you got the day you wanted to go home may be the one that will win a prize for you and you don't dare miss getting it. If you don't have that kind of dedication, you settle down into a groove of mediocrity where you do all right, you don't get fired, but you don't win any prizes either.''

She was not about to settle into a groove of mediocrity whatever the personal consequences. As always Marguerite sought love through achievement, forgetting the other side of the coin was envy. In addition to continuing friction at the office, a growing rift with Bill, and financial pressures, Marguerite had developed a weight problem.

John Michaelis, now returned from Paris, was shocked to discover that Marguerite had gained an unflattering amount of weight. ''At that point I think she and Bill had a marriage in name only,'' he recalled. ''Bitter about Bill's women and concerned about office rivalries and home finances, she indulged herself with food.''

Some of Marguerite's attempts to solve her monetary crises bordered on the humorous. The pompous reactions of her colleagues were predictable.

"Oh, God! Not another controversy!" was Marguerite's response when she returned from a brief assignment in Europe in November 1957 to find the journalistic community in an uproar. This time her dignity was under fire rather than her determination.

In August she had dashed off a bit of advertising copy under the headline ONE BILLION UNFILLED CAVITIES MUST BE WRONG!, which appeared in *Reader's Digest*. Having already endorsed typewriters Marguerite saw nothing immoral about toothpaste and happily pocketed the five hundred dollars. (The money was spent on a surprise for Bill: a motorcycle intended as a sentimental reminder of Berlin days.)

The matter was unremarked and would have been forgotten if a malicious colleague had not clipped the ad and sent it to the Committee of Correspondents Governing Capital Press Gallery Membership. Marguerite's homecoming was enlivened by a letter from Daniel M. Kidney, the committee secretary. "By a unanimous vote of the membership, the committee instructed me to call your attention to Section B, Rule 4 of the rules governing the press galleries . . . 'that [correspondents must not be] engaged in paid publicity or promotion work.' "

Marguerite fired a salvo in return: "I regretfully withdraw (or forfeit) or do whatever is necessary to relinquish press gallery membership. P. S. The fact that I have appeared on sponsored television shows, would not, it seems, disqualify me?"

The postscript added to the furor as she knew it would, for most who had voted to oust her had also appeared on such programs. Still, the committee unanimously accepted her withdrawal.

Marguerite's comment, to *Newsweek*, was flip. "The committee action doesn't affect me. I go after exclusives. As for the toothpaste, it's *really* very good."

"Do you know why we stay together?" Bill Hall remembered Marguerite asking one day. "It's because we never are."

Marguerite had written once of desiring a "man who could be both friend and lover, a man who would need no other love than my own." She had not found this paragon in Bill, a lack she saw fit to share with her reading public in *News Is a Singular Thing*. In or out of print, Marguerite was not one to suffer in silence. She intrigued and confused her friends with glowing accounts of Bill ("Isn't he the most marvelous, exciting man you've ever met? Isn't he wonderful?") only to follow a few days later with lurid tales of violent arguments and blatant infidelities. Both pragmatism and idealism were included in Marguerite's character and contributed to the dramatic mood swings that dominated her complex personality.

It seems inevitable that two ambitious, competitive, and at least in Marguerite's case, driven people would evolve their own marital guidelines. At a time long before the term "open marriage" came into vogue, the ventilation afforded by separation may have been necessary for both Marguerite and Bill. Constant challenge may have been a prime ingredient in their relationship. A need for variety and experience would have been essential, a need that neither could have denied indefinitely.

In light of Bill's amours, it's not surprising that Marguerite would form a close association of her own. His name was Peter Lisagor, and he was considered the dean of journalists in Washington circles. Everyone admired the much published correspondent who had attended Harvard on a Nieman Fellowship and was now the bureau chief of the *Chicago Daily News*. Soon the two were collaborating on a series of articles. Many thought Lisagor had a mellowing effect on Marguerite. Certainly he had a cosmetic effect: The excess weight came off. Soon the busy correspondent was enlisting the aid of a crew of saleswomen at various fashionable Washington stores, who kept a wary eye out for the perfect styles for her. Daisy Mae disappeared into history. Many who had once been appalled at Marguerite's lack of grooming were amazed and amused to read an article quoting her fashion tips for world travelers.

At about this time Marguerite's Georgetown house was becoming a mecca for the young movers and shakers of the capital. Among the most frequent guests were the young senator, Robert Kennedy, and his wife, Ethel. Marguerite had first met him in 1953. Then newly returned from Korea and Indochina, she was fascinated by Washington dispatches on the important roles being played in government by Roy Cohn, David Schine, and Robert Kennedy, all members of the Senate Investigating Committee then headed by Senator Joseph McCarthy. Assigned to do a piece on young men in government, she first called Roy Cohn because he appeared the most flamboyant, and then she tried David Schine. As fate would have it, both were out. Robert Kennedy was available, though, and enthusiastic about her project. He suggested they have lunch to discuss it. Marguerite noted with amusement that he was not overly anxious to place her in touch with Cohn or Schine (he was soon to break with McCarthy) but did offer to introduce her to another young senator whom he was certain she would find interesting—his older brother. Marguerite had not even heard of John Kennedy but enjoyed meeting him at a party hosted by Robert. The friendship ripened when the younger Kennedys and Marguerite and Bill became Georgetown neighbors and dog walkers.

Both brothers were frequent party guests. Marguerite, increasingly impressed by Jack's abilities, was one of the first journalists to spot his presidential potential. She was excited by his prospects and eager to introduce him to people who might be influential.

Ruth Montgomery, in *Hail to the Chiefs*, recounted a dinner party at the Higgins-Hall home. "Jacqueline Kennedy arrived on time as did an assortment of senators, but dinner cooled on the back burners while we waited for Jack to appear. Jackie became increasingly agitated, as she tried vainly to telephone him at his office; but he finally arrived with the casual explanation that he had been detained. Being the bride of a man accustomed to carefree bachelorhood was not all tea and crumpets."

Jim O'Donnell, Marguerite's longtime friend from Berlin, who then had recently returned to Washington, remembered another occasion when Jack was on time but the man that Marguerite had sought to connect him with—Walter Cronkite—was not. When the newsman finally made his tardy arrival dinner was ruined and Senator Kennedy had left. As Cronkite stood in the doorway Marguerite angrily grabbed a bouquet of flowers, vase and all, and hurled it at him—a crash heard round the house.

Marguerite's next pregnancy coincided with the advent of the "sack" or "tent" dress. Although many deplored this free-flowing line that ignored the waist, the fashion seemed divinely inspired for the busy mother-to-be, who continued to be very much in the public eye. The healthy baby boy arrived a few weeks short of his mother's thirty-eighth birthday. Excitedly Marguerite called her friend Ruth Montgomery from the hospital to relay the happy news. "I want to name him for my father, but I just hate the name Higgins," she complained.

Nonplussed, Ruth asked, "Why?"

"It isn't really our name. My grandparents changed it. They thought O'Higgins sounded too Irish."

"Why don't you set the record straight by calling him Lawrence O'Higgins Hall?"

Marguerite thought Ruth's suggestion a marvelous idea and did just that.

Possibly influenced by her growing intimacy with the Kennedy family, Marguerite had returned at least nominally to the Catholic faith. At any rate she decided that Lawrence was to be baptized a Catholic. A special dispensation was required to allow Ruth, a Protestant, to be his godmother at the christening. Ambassador Robert Murphy, a friend from Berlin days, served as godfather.

In July 1959 the whole world was talking about the Nixon-Khrushchev confrontation, but among the press contingency in Russia, Marguerite Higgins and Peter Lisagor were the primary topics of conversation. The two were inseparable.

Seemingly oblivious to the gossip, Marguerite, in the last stages of another pregnancy, was mainly concerned with getting the story. Once again she had wangled her way onto the press junket without the consent of Bob Donovan, who had assigned David Wise to cover the Nixon tour. Now she was determined to justify her presence there.

Ruth Montgomery, also among the press corps, recalled that Marguerite was eight months pregnant during the Russian trip and had difficulty outsprinting the bevy of *New York Times* reporters. In Sverdlovsk, Siberia, she made a waddling dash for the nearest telephone, miraculously arrived there first, and made an equally incredible quick connection to the *Tribune* office in Paris. Delighted to have bested her *Times* rival, she pantingly explained that she had an important story to dictate, only to be told, "Sorry. Everyone's out to lunch now. Call back in an hour."

Marguerite's story, when it finally made its way to Page One, read:

> Vice President Nixon today swept through two widely separate areas of Siberia in a hectic schedule marked by an unprecedented turnout of friendly crowds, some heated verbal free-for-alls, and inspection of everything from dams to formerly secret science centers and giant heavy industries.
>
> In the midafternoon the Vice President flew nearly 1,000 miles by Soviet jet from Novosibirsk westward to Sverdlovsk, the Pittsburgh of the Soviet Union. He was greeted here by throngs whose uninhibited enthusiasm even exceeded that of his welcomers yesterday at Novosibirsk.
>
> Politically speaking the most fascinating part of Mr. Nixon's morning in faraway Novosibirsk were the virtually identical, well-rehearsed, sometimes belligerent questions put to him by so-called average workers, obviously intent on straightening him out on American foreign policy.
>
> Although Mr. Nixon kept his temper, even when accused, in effect, of

hypocrisy, his hard-hitting answers pointedly reminded the Russians of some unpleasant facets of communism. For instance he publicly and for the first time on this trip brought up the matter of Soviet imperialism in Hungary and added some frank talk about Soviet-inspired aggression in Korea. . . .

Marguerite was to witness a replay of the Nixon baiting later that day when she followed the two world leaders into what she later described as "the moist, brown gloom of a Russian copper mine." Sverdlovsk may have been a more trying ordeal for Marguerite than for the vice president.

The highlight of the Russian trip occurred in Moscow at an exhibition of American products. Later to be known as the Kitchen Cabinet Debate, the exchange erupted unexpectedly as Nikita Khrushchev and Vice President Nixon were walking through a model American kitchen. Unexpectedly challenged by the bombastic Russian leader in the fascinated presence of newsmen and the general public, Nixon quickly rose to the occasion. Marguerite described the spirited debate: "Standing toe-to-toe with Mr. Khrushchev for fifty minutes with the crowd pressing in, Mr. Nixon capped a long argument on relative living standards and freedoms by saying: 'Mr. Khrushchev, you would at least agree that it is better to be discussing such things as the comparative merits of washing machines than to be arguing over the comparative merits of rockets.

" 'In modern times,' the vice president added, 'any argument on comparative military strengths misses the point in any case, for if war comes we both will have had it.' "

While in Moscow Marguerite had an opportunity to spend some time with her friends from Korea, Tom and Helen Lambert. Lambert was now Moscow bureau chief for the *Herald Tribune*. He and Helen had long been friends of Peter Lisagor's as well. Helen recalled the circumstances of the visit. "Though married, no one would ever have called Peter a womanizer. He was a gentle, kindly man, rather studious looking, who was much admired by everyone. It was good to see Marguerite looking so well and happy. We thought he was good for her."

The exhausting excursion across Russia was not the end of the Khrushchev marathon for Marguerite. During the Soviet prime minister's subsequent trip to the United States she was once again part of the press entourage accompanying the dignitary from coast to coast. Angered when a lack of security made an impromptu visit to Disneyland impossible, Khrushchev staged a tantrum at what Marguerite described as "the most lavish and expensive luncheon spectacular ever staged in Hollywood."

Fortunately the prime minister was in a better mood a few days later in Coon Rapids, Iowa, where he was the guest of Roswell Garst, a pioneer hybrid-corn developer. "Here," Marguerite wrote, "Khrushchev engaged in a cornfield debate that was a unique talk for the folks down on the farm considering his oft proclaimed posture of a leading atheist. The Russian leader claimed that God was on his side in the Soviet-American agricultural race. It was the human interest highlight of a frantically busy day in which Mr. Khrushchev tramped miles and miles through the rich black earth having himself a wonderful time, perhaps possible only to a former peasant from the Ukraine propelled by an inquisitive zest.

"The Soviet chief was obviously in his element despite the mob scenes that sometimes made his inspection tour dangerous. The only occasion on this tour when Mr. Khrushchev felt concern for his safety occurred when a tractor intended to scare off the surrounding reporters and photographers seemed instead to be heading irrevocably toward him. Mr. Khrushchev—and everybody else—jumped just in time."

At one point Garst became so angry that he threw silage at the press in an attempt to drive them away. "Guards mounted on horseback were even told at one point to charge the press," Marguerite wrote, "but somebody thought better of it before any damage was done. The fact that not one of the spectators got the back of a hoof is a tribute only to horse sense for the police, in their eagerness to clear a path for the prime minister, pushed many onlookers into unwanted and nerve-racking proximity to the horses' rears."

The arrival of Linda Marguerite Hall was a joyous occasion. Even Khrushchev appeared pleased. His first question on spotting the newly slim Marguerite at a reception was, "Was it a boy or a girl?"

Robert and Ethel Kennedy were godparents at the christening, a happy and elegant affair enjoyed by all but Linda, a usually sunny-dispositioned baby who surprised everyone by crying throughout the ceremony.

Robert M. White, president and editor of the *Herald Tribune*, was among the first to send a note of congratulations to the new arrival. It ended with the wish, "What I don't know is whether you will become a great newspaperwoman or the first lady general in the air force, but you can be sure that you have all my good wishes for your great happiness and success."

Never one to allow any opportunity to slip by, Marguerite's answer was prompt and characteristic:

Many thanks from Bill and myself for the letter to Linda which has duly been given a place of honor in her scrapbook. Thoughtfulness is especially welcome to an old *Herald Tribune* hand of nineteen years even if, in making the point, she has to give away her age.

While I haven't taken this up with Linda yet (formally, that is), I'd also like to express the hope that the new arrangement between myself and the paper will work out.

In this connection, I was particularly glad to hear that it was merely uncertainty over Linda's arrival that kept me from going to the Paris Western summit meeting this last December rather than a retrenchment or change of past policies toward me (since my return from Korea I've always helped to cover such diplomatic summits).

I do hope, therefore, that I can look forward to covering the forthcoming "April in Paris" summit and the Ike-Khrushchev summit.

I hadn't intended, really, to inject a professional note, but it just goes to show that the old habit of putting newspaper business first is still with me.

As to Linda, my bet is on a newspaper career. After all, not many babies have had such a newspapery prenatal conditioning as Linda gained in all that time she passed in July and August following Mr. Nixon through Russia and Siberia, and then whistle-stopping across the United States in company of Mr. K.

Do you suppose her first word will be *Nyet?*

Twenty-two

In May 1961, Bill Hall, then commander of Continental Air Command (CONAC), gave an interview to a *Macon Telegraph and News* reporter following his transfer to the new CONAC headquarters in Georgia. Hall, then occupying an apartment in the officer's quarters at Robins Air Force Base, explained that he and Marguerite had the same problem that many married people must have when nearing the tops of their professions.

"With each of us traveling a great deal and drawing assignments all over the globe, we don't see each other as much as we'd like. We solve this by trying to meet in Washington or New York as often as possible."
It was an uneasy compromise that allowed both to advance in their careers.

The article referred to the fifty-four-year-old Bill as one of the "top brains in America's military department" and explained that he held two key positions in the nation's defense posture. As top man in CONAC, he had the responsibility for the entire Air Force Reserve program, a worldwide organization with more than fifteen thousand military and civilian employees. In addition, Hall served as a senior member and air force representative of the United States delegation to the Military Staff Committee of the United Nations, which necessitated his being at UN Headquarters in New York every two weeks for conferences as well as serving as a military adviser to the United States Ambassador to the UN, Adlai Stevenson.

The reporter was obviously impressed with Bill, a command pilot with, by that time, more that twenty-five years of flying experience. "The general is a soldier's soldier," he wrote, "a tall, lean man whose handsome rugged appearance gives ample evidence of an active interest in athletics.''

At about the same time on the other side of the world, a *Newsweek* correspondent speculated in print: ''Is it courage, initiative or sheer blind luck that gives Marguerite Higgins her exclusive stories from the Congo?''

Once again there was an international crisis; once again Marguerite was at the scene. After seventy-five years of colonial rule, King Baudouin of Belgium had granted independence to the Congo. The result was chaos. The Congolese army and police suddenly became outlaws brutalizing blacks and whites alike. Their much longed-for ''independence'' became a license to loot, rape, torture, and murder.

Within two weeks nearly eighty percent of the 180,000 Europeans in the Congo had fled the country. With them went the technical and managerial skills required to maintain the economy. The void was soon filled by hundreds of Russian ''technicians'' invited by the new prime minister, Patrice Lumumba. For a time the Congolese leader and one-time beer salesman became deliberately hostile toward Americans. Then, as his rule began to teeter, he frantically sought the aid of UN forces. Through it all the rampaging Congolese soldiers continued their own bloody reign, burning plantations and factories, slaughtering whole families for no apparent reason.

Perhaps Marguerite had reached an ''another opening, another war'' rationale, for her arrival upon the scene was not without a certain show biz flare. Discarding the battle fatigues that had been her trademark in Korea, she stepped off the plane in Leopoldville wearing what was later described as a ''posy printed dress.'' It was past midnight and the dark continent seemed very dark indeed. Casually Marguerite picked up the phone and called the United States ambassador, Clare Timberlake. Before he realized it, the sleepy diplomat was en route to the airport to pick up the newly arrived correspondent.

On the way to the Memling Hotel, unofficial press headquarters, Timberlake, who had been at his post only eight days before the Congo erupted in his face, filled her in with the events of the recent past.

''The entire fabric of Congolese society disappeared before our very eyes,'' he said. ''I remember trying to think, 'Well, who can we call on the telephone to come and protect the American Embassy?' There was nobody. Those who were supposed to keep the peace were now the forces of lawlessness and disorder. It was like being in a situation where your house is being robbed and you call up the police station and they tell you very happily, 'Yes, our boys are doing it.' Even Patrice Lumumba had rocks thrown at his car and was forced to take refuge in a house in the suburbs.''

A few nights later John Starr and John Bidley, British correspondents, were struggling to repair the telex machines at the Leopoldville post office. Atmospheric conditions were clogging the lines, which cleared just as a colleague called from the airport to report the arrival of UN troops from India. Both men were able to relay the story to their London papers. ''While I was watching my story go through,'' Starr remembered, ''some dame came up and leaned over my shoulder, 'How do you work the telex machine?' she asked, and I gave her a quick lesson.''

Other writers found the unreliable telex line down again when they arrived from the airport, but Marguerite had received more than a lesson. She had gotten the facts and filed her story, an exclusive in the United States.

The chaos continued as faction fought faction and coup followed coup. Lumumba was ousted and with him every single Russian official in Leopoldville, but this had little or no effect on the general deterioration of the country. Nor was the situation improved by the autocratic attitude of the reigning UN commander, Rajeshwar Dayal of India, a man foisted onto the Congolese against their will. Marguerite found the Congolese in Leopoldville friendly and helpful, once it was established that she had no connection with the United Nations.

Wild and weird as the days of crisis in Leopoldville had been, they were now surpassed in raw, grisly terror by events in Stanleyville, the capital of Oriente Province in the north. Months after Lumumba had been ousted from power, Antoine Gizenga, his self-appointed heir, continued in the name of the Lumumbist movement to serve Russian interests and to conduct a rebellion against the Central Government, using Stanleyville as his base. Here, as opposed to other parts of the Congo where black and white were indiscriminately brutalized, racist terrorism focused on whites.

The city was the site of the *Herald Tribune* reporter and explorer Henry Morton Stanley's jungle encounter with Dr. Livingstone. When Marguerite climbed wearily from the vintage DC-3 that had taken nine and a half hours to fly the seven hundred miles from Leopoldville to Stanleyville, she was the first *Herald Tribune* reporter to visit the city since Stanley was there in 1877.

More importantly, she was to be the first non-Communist correspondent accorded an interview by the terrorist leader, Gizenga, who had declared himself off limits to "imperialists." Marguerite succeeded where all others had failed by carefully studying her quarry. Sensing that Gizenga was essentially timid, suspicious, and indecisive, she overcame his objections with a challenge: "People believe that you've been overthrown. Some say that you are dead. Wouldn't it be to your advantage to talk with a Western reporter?" The rebel leader admitted Marguerite to his orange stucco house covered with flaming bougainvillaea and talked for over an hour.

"What kind of press does America have anyway?" he asked her during the course of the interview. "All those atrocities they write of; has anyone beaten you?"

Marguerite happily allowed that no one had. But others, both white and Congolese, in Stanleyville had suffered a nightmare of sudden arrests in the night, beatings, and worst of all, unnerving uncertainty as to when, if ever, their precious exit visas would be granted.

At one point Gizenga had ordered the mass arrest of all Europeans in Stanleyville and held them for twenty-four hours in a single enclosure without food, water, or toilet facilities. Once released, they attempted a mass exodus. But Gizenga, belatedly realizing what a brain drain this would be, used every means at his disposal to force them to remain.

Most of the Europeans, Marguerite found, had taken refuge in the Stanleyville Hotel. Many, totally demoralized by their experiences, spent the day in the great cavernous lobby with its noisy whirring fans, commiserating with one another. In a Casablanca-like setting, the political elite, the riffraff, and the hostages gathered in the scruffy bar to gossip with and about each other. Marguerite washed her dysentery pills down with Primus (the beer made famous by its former salesman, Patrice Lumumba) and listened. Here at last was a war that could, at least in part, be covered from the bar.

"I never thought the day would come when I'd look on Leopoldville as paradise," a European businessman confided to her, "but that day has finally come." His visa had been granted after a six-month wait. He was scheduled to leave the next day.

The man was arrested just as he placed his foot on the first step leading to the open door of the Congo airliner.

He was among the last of the casualties. The Communist foothold in Stanleyville was too precarious to maintain. When the inconvenience of supplying the landlocked province proved too difficult, the futility of Gizenga's attempt to take over the Congo became obvious. Eventually even his most devoted supporters began to drift away to the true power center, Leopoldville, where a modicum of order was being restored. A new political figure was emerging, Cyrile Adoula, who promised to be an important force for moderation and would become premier later that year. The story was nearly over and it was time for Marguerite to go home.

Among the correspondence waiting for her was a letter forwarded from the main office. A young naval officer serving in Italy who was a regular reader of Marguerite's column had a complaint:

"Miss Higgins' picture has a tendency to indicate to the reader that he is in store for anything but a sound political or intellectual discourse. Though it is unfortunate, one of my friends said that he actually had to cover the picture before he could read the column.

"Miss Higgins is an attractive woman and she should use this more for her benefit. May I suggest a new picture, one indicating more maturity and perhaps without the smile. Personally I cringe when members of our mess make statements such as 'Don't tell me you read that grinning, featherbrained, female gossip column.' Do you think that you might tactfully pass on this suggestion?"

The forty-year-old Marguerite acted immediately, and the old photograph was rapidly replaced.

Once the children had arrived, Marguerite and Bill found their Georgetown home too small for a ménage that now included a baby nurse and a housekeeper. Marguerite had her heart set on a house that had once been the residence of the famous bandmaster and march king John Philip Sousa.

Although dilapidated, the house was in an elegant neighborhood. Marguerite bought it for under twenty thousand dollars but ultimately spent one hundred eighty thousand dollars on remodeling. W. J. Anderson, the contractor who did the job, remembered Marguerite well. "She knew exactly what she wanted; wallpaper made from metallic-plated tea papers from Japan, for instance. It had to be applied by static electricity, then varnished. The process was painstaking and expensive, but the effect was sensational."

Marguerite would, Anderson recalled, meet the crew each morning with coffee and donuts, then present them with a list of things to do that frequently included redoing things she wasn't happy with from the day before. "I remember her as attractive, interesting, opinionated, not the easiest person to work for, but at least she knew exactly what she wanted. Sometimes it seemed to me that she put on airs a bit more to reassure herself than to impress us. I think she felt a lack of control over her own life. Occasionally she'd say rather outrageous things just to hear herself talk or to stir up a little controversy. It was a job I never forgot."

Marguerite had been partially financing her renovation project by renting out the Georgetown house—one of her most celebrated tenants was Madame Nehru—but when she and Bill decided to buy a weekend home in the country, it became necessary to sell their original home. "Marguerite had the French desire to own land and the Irish flare for risk," Bill recalled. "We'd had an offer of ninety-five thousand dollars for the Georgetown place. The couple who owned the country house in Middleberg, Virginia, were asking twenty-seven thousand dollars. Both prices were fair enough, but I remember the expression on Marguerite's face when she considered. Finally she said, 'If the Sawyers will pay ninety-five thousand dollars, why not ninety-seven thousand five hundred dollars? And if the Carrolls will take twenty-seven thousand five hundred dollars, why not twenty-five thousand dollars?' She made two phone calls and got exactly what she wanted. Marguerite was lucky like that, but she took a lot of chances. She gambled with money like she gambled with her life. It was all a part of that general spirit of adventure that powered her whole life."

Besides lectures and magazine articles, Marguerite continued to augment her finances with endorsements. The slap on the wrist from her Washington colleagues had not deterred her in the slightest. Once again *Reader's Digest* carried an ad with the Higgins by-line: "... Recently I zipped across the U.S.A. on American Airlines' latest little number, the 707 Jet Flagship. L. A. to New York, four hours and three minutes. Look it up if you don't believe me. . . ."

Despite the fact that ad copy was considered beneath a journalist, Marguerite put more enthusiasm into her paean to the 707 than she gave to another, more dignified project. Her fourth book was a biography for juveniles. The choice of subject, Jessie Benton Fremont, a woman whose main claim to fame was her colorful and controversial husband, was strange. Author and subject appear to be the antithesis of one another, yet Marguerite had sought the assignment.

In her proposal to Stanley North, the general editor of North Star

Books, Marguerite wrote of having worked her way through school as a waitress at Yosemite and Lake Tahoe. Perhaps Marguerite was fascinated by the grandeur of the Sierra Nevadas, which Fremont explored. The short proposal focused entirely on Marguerite's California years with no discussion of the biography itself. *Jessie Benton Fremont* was not one of Marguerite's finest efforts. One wonders if she would have fared better with *Young John Kennedy*, a biography still on the drawing board at the time of the president's assassination.

Marguerite had maintained close ties with both John and Robert Kennedy. During John's presidential campaign she had given generously of her time in attempting to introduce the senator to potential backers. Her files were filled with warm, friendly notes from both men and copies of her own memos commenting on, and sometimes suggesting, appointments.

One significant incident was recalled by Jim O'Donnell. By August 1961 pressure between East and West Germany was again building up. When John Kennedy had announced in a speech that he would defend West Germany, he had by omission written off West Berlin.

O'Donnell, who was working then in the State Department, had learned that the chief of the Soviet army had secretly arrived in Potsdam. East German police had begun to string the barbed wire that was the forerunner of the Berlin wall. "Morale among the West Germans, who believed that the U. S. had sold them down the river, was at an all-time low," O'Donnell recalled.

"Maggie had gone up to Cape Cod with Bill and the children for a holiday. When I saw things coming to a head, I called her. She informed me that her neighbor was General Lucius Clay, former American military governor of Germany, now retired. 'May I tell him?' she asked. I said yes, knowing that she would anyway.

"A few moments later Clay called. The thought of all his postwar efforts and the Berlin airlift going down the drain was sickening to him. 'I want to help,' he said. 'I'm a Republican but I can take John Kennedy. Bob is an anathema to me.' "

O'Donnell admitted that he felt the same but reminded the general that both Kennedys, particularly Robert, were close friends of Maggie's. "Why don't you let her arrange it?" he suggested.

A few minutes later Marguerite was on the phone to Bob, who immediately called his brother. Both Kennedys were overjoyed to have this great leader who had been the symbol of American strength and loyalty ten years earlier back in the ball game. An agreement was quickly reached and General Clay was dispatched to Germany as a special presidential envoy, his job being to pull the pieces together.

It is clear that the Kennedys valued her judgment and welcomed her friendship. Trouble in paradise erupted with the presence of Pierre Salinger, who appeared to have a personal vendetta against the *Herald Tribune*. When the often officious press secretary attempted to interject himself into the preparations for the biography *Young John Kennedy*, Marguerite appealed directly to the president:

> As you will see from my enclosed letter to the attorney general, my firm agreement with him has always been that anything involving material made available by the Kennedy family would be cleared by him and the Kennedy involved. I would prefer therefore not to work with Pierre but, as before, clear directly with Bob and yourself, if you have the time. Bob and I understand each other. Besides, it is more rewarding to cooperate with someone who has a measure of confidence in my judgment and integrity which I believe Bob has and which Pierre obviously does not.

The president agreed, granting special dispensations to "Maggie." The project continued to simmer on the back burner, work frequently delayed by both their hectic schedules. In the meantime, as a result of a charming profile for *McCall's*, Marguerite was approached to ghost-write an autobiography of Rose Fitzgerald Kennedy, an enterprise eventually shelved by the escalation of the Vietnam war and Marguerite's subsequent involvement there.

Besides the obvious salability at the time for anything having to do with the Kennedy family, Marguerite was prompted to do the article by curiosity. It had always been a part of the Kennedy legend that they played for keeps, whether it be touch football or politics, and that they played to win. How did they get that way? she wondered. Was Rose the key?

Scholastically at least, Marguerite discovered, it was Mrs. Kennedy who set the family's intellectual pace. Not only had the former Rose Fitzgerald been voted the prettiest high school senior in Boston; she may well have been the youngest and smartest. Rose had graduated with honors from Dorchester High School at age fifteen.

Marguerite admired the panache of the former debutante who set off for Communist Russia in the early 1930s with only her young daughter as a companion. The two women laughed together over a letter that Mrs.

Kennedy had written to her other eight children during the trip. Marguerite included it in the article:

> My dear children, Kathleen and I went to Leningrad where the czars used to live, and now we are here in Moscow for a few days. It is very different from New York or Paris. All the people go to the opera or the ballet in their old working clothes, because they have not anything better to wear. The government gives them their tickets. Every time Ambassador Bullitt goes out, the secret police, called the GPU, follow him, so that is all very exciting. Everyone wears berets on their heads instead of hats, and everyone has to take their coats off when they go into a museum so they will not take something, I suppose. So you can see that it is quite exciting and we love it. However, I shall be very glad to arrive home with all you eight little darlings. Much love and many kisses to you all.

The woman, who at seventy, had attended her son's inaugural ball wearing the same gown she had worn twenty-three years before when presented to the Court of St. James's, ended the interview with concern for the president. "There are still so many problems, but I know he will find a way to overcome them, too. . . . We are so very proud and yet in some ways it seems unreal," Mrs. Kennedy admitted. Even this proud, politically sophisticated woman found it difficult to reconcile the awesome role of president of the United States with the little boy whose bruises and joys she had softened and shared not so very long ago.

In another *McCall's* article, which appeared February 1962, Marguerite was able to draw on personal observations of close friends to describe the private world of Robert and Ethel Kennedy. "It's as demanding as a time clock, as casual as a picnic." "Their strenuous life might have made Teddy Roosevelt feel like an armchair idler. Relaxation to this lively young couple is a series of sportive challenges: Foolhardy indeed is the guest who is unprepared for a test of nerve, wit, and even muscle."

Admiringly she wrote of Ethel's manner of coping. "If Ethel had a handbook on life with the attorney general, it would include such items of great and little moments as these: Be casually cool when hoodlums threaten your children with kidnaping or acid throwing or when your house is stoned. In the Kennedy lexicon, courage is grace under pressure, and this does not permit getting excited about a few rocks. Be ready on thirty minutes notice to serve lunch to twenty guests including a couple of Cabinet officers and an ambassador or two. Master the art of politics and keep your eye on the latest world crisis or you won't have a conversational chance at Kennedy clan gatherings. Remember that the Kennedy in-laws are as competitive and observant as they are loyal and warm and that they'll comment on everything you do, from how you bring up your children to how your party compares with the last one Jacqueline gave.''

In official Washington where legends thrive like crabgrass, Marguerite thought it inevitable that a family such as the Kennedys, which shunned public displays of sentiment, would acquire a reputation for unalloyed toughness. This she believed was particularly true of the man who, as chief counsel to the Senate Rackets Committee, tilted with such labor toughies as the Teamster Union's boss Jimmy Hoffa. It had also required grit and inflexible purpose to direct the campaign for the presidency of a forty-three-year-old Catholic, a religious persuasion that had once, many people believed, defeated the presidential candidate Al Smith.

But Marguerite had been among the very first to read Robert Kennedy's book, *The Enemy Within,* and to observe the dedication, ''To my wife—whose love through this long struggle made the difficult easy and the impossible possible.'' More revealing, she had seen the copy of *The Enemy Within* that John and Jacqueline Kennedy had had bound in red leather and presented to the author. The president's dedication, scrawled directly under Bob's tribute to Ethel, read, ''To Bobby—the brother within—who made the easy difficult.'' This family joke was treasured by Bob as was the accompanying card, signed ''Jackie and Jack'' and written by the first lady, which said, ''To Dear Bobby—How can anyone give you a present when they think of all you've given them?'' On the book's flyleaf Jacqueline had written what Marguerite believed John F. Kennedy, the public figure, would have been the first to affirm but what the studiously unsentimental brother Jack would be the last to admit: ''To Bobby—who made the impossible possible and changed all our lives.''

Whatever conclusions one might draw then or later regarding the Kennedys, Camelot was a classy place to visit. As one who had frequent entrée there, it was inevitable that Marguerite would one day write home about it. It's hard to believe the little girl in Marguerite didn't hope that the big girls back in California (particularly those snooty Alpha Phis) read every word when the article, ''R.S.V.P.,'' appeared in *McCall's*.

At one White House affair described in the article, Marguerite had an opportunity to renew her acquaintance with the shah of Iran, a potentate she had already interviewed several times. The dinner, she commented, was truly fit for a king: trout en chaud-froid doria, guinea hen Santa Carla with wild rice and asparagus, sauce mousseline, mousse de foie gras en gelée rustique, assorted pastries. After dinner the guests moved to the strains of a string ensemble into three adjacent rooms for coffee and tall glasses of champagne, following which they were shepherded into a large room where they watched a spirited performance of authentic American ballet on a stage especially assembled for the purpose. The dancers for this one-and-only night performance had been plucked from several top Broadway musicals to reenact numbers that had fascinated the hostess when she had seen them some years before in Europe and New York. When the shah and his empress had taken their leave, the young hosts mingled with their other guests and the performing dancers in an easy, informal exchange of pleasant conversation.

That was only *one* party attended by Marguerite and Bill that was recapped by the Washington correspondent.

Despite many professional successes, Marguerite, during these months, was coming increasingly into conflict with the *Herald Tribune*. On one occasion, stung by the paper's questioning of her expenses, she fired off an angry letter to the business manager:

> Concerning taxi fares, the cheapest thing—and the easiest thing for me—would be to sit in the office all day. We all agree that's not in the paper's best interests. My taxi bills are high because I get around a lot and work seven days a week because some appointments must be made for weekends. I'm certainly not going to turn down an interview with Dillon because it falls on Saturday or refuse to go to a Herter background meeting because it's held Sunday evening.
>
> Concerning entertainment, the only criterion is whether it pays off in news stories. The State Department is a funny place. In Congress everybody wants to be quoted, but at the department the best sources won't even be seen with a newspaperman at a restaurant. He has to be entertained at my home. Some examples of stories 'mined' in this way include the exclusive on Khrushchev's New Year's Eve threats to Ambassador Thompson in Moscow, the exclusive on the Khrushchev disarmament exchange, the exclusive on de Gaulle agreeing to cooperate in European air defense, the exclusive on Chessman, etc.

The matter of the expense account was resolved for the time being at least but tension continued to mount as the months passed. The nagging feeling that the *Herald Tribune* was treating her badly became a conclusion. The final straw came when the editor Jim Bellows dropped her editorial-page story ''due to lack of space.'' Marguerite believed the move was prompted by conservatism. She had taken the State Department to task for its stance on Berlin.

Marguerite summarily ended a twenty-two-year association with the *Herald Tribune* by signing with *Newsday*. According to the agreement, Marguerite was to do three columns a week. For this she would receive twenty thousand dollars a year plus a percentage of material syndicated. There would be a five-thousand-dollar travel allowance in addition to an ample expense account.

Although Marguerite would be based in Washington, the understanding was that she ''go to places that other columnists were either too lazy or too fearful to go.'' In describing her new job to Ray Erwin of *Editor & Publisher*, she said, ''Writing a column adds a point of view to reporting the news. A reporter writes what other reporters write and all he can do is try to write it better. A columnist can give something extra special to writing and can draw some conclusions.

''As a columnist, you have time to think. During the Hungarian and Suez crises I was at the typewriter and the telephone from nine to twelve hours a day. The sheer volume of all that made thought virtually impossible. Now I can study what developments mean. I try to make my column a combination of firsthand, on-the-spot reporting and thoughtful interpretation rather than just armchair opinions from my office in Washington.''

No one could ever accuse Marguerite of armchair reporting. ''The lovely, slender, blue-eyed blonde girl''—as Erwin described the forty-three-year-old Marguerite—had just returned from a grueling three-month tour of Africa and South America and was about to set off for yet another trouble spot: Vietnam.

Twenty-three

In July 1963, Marguerite had just returned from an assignment in Europe, where she had contracted a bad case of flu. Her temperature had risen to 103 degrees when she was awakened from a feverish sleep by the ringing of a phone.

"How soon can you leave for Vietnam?" a voice demanded.

She felt a sudden and unexpected sense of apprehension. This was one "adventure" assignment that Marguerite didn't want. The reason had nothing to do with illness. Something strange and inexplicable warned her to avoid the country.

Three days later on a plane bound for Saigon, Marguerite was still trying to shrug off the sense of foreboding. This would be her seventh trip to the place where her aristocratic grandfather had died of tropical fever while fighting with the French colonial forces.

She loved the rich and beautiful country that had struggled stubbornly for generations to oust France, its final achievement a triumph of will over power. Admiring the Vietnamese and believing that she knew them as well as any Westerner could, Marguerite should have felt confident of the outcome of her assignment but did not.

The bizarre sacrifice of a monk setting himself aflame in Saigon's main intersection two months before had shocked and stirred the entire world. As the weeks passed, the crisis had intensified, all the while growing more complex and complicated. The Buddhist contention of persecution remained the one constant factor in the swift march of events. The fact that Vietnam continued to be under constant attack from the Communists in the north was momentarily forgotten. The primary question concerning the reading public was the religious crisis. What did the Buddhists really want? What was President Diem doing to cause them to choose self-immolation rather than live in a country guided by him?

Marguerite was bewildered by the accounts of Buddhist monks rampaging through the streets, descriptions which conflicted totally with her own memories. In all previous contacts, Vietnamese Buddhists had seemed to sincerely practice the spirit of nonviolence and compassion that was the soul of South Asian Buddhism.

Predeparture briefings by government officials did nothing to illuminate the cause of the turbulence depicted so luridly in the daily press. The State Department was angered by President Diem's stubborn insistence upon running his country his own way. Ignoring the fact that demonstrations in the middle of the war were against Vietnamese law, Kennedy's New Frontier was concerned that its own liberal image might be tarnished by association. Was not the act of self-immolation indisputable proof of a massive offensive against the Buddhist religion by President Diem, a Roman Catholic?

In Saigon, Ambassador Frederick Nolting, Jr., told Marguerite a different story. The ambassador, who had been assigned to Vietnam for the past two and a half years, had accompanied the president on numerous trips into the provinces. In his opinion, Diem was a much misunderstood and often maligned man. Once a province chief under the French, the president was still familiar with and intensely interested in rural problems. "He was," Nolting said, "full of ideas and on-the-spot suggestions for improvements and especially interested in, and proud of, the agricultural improvement stations which his government had established, teaching many things, from fruit and nut-tree raising to fish ponds, manioc grinding, and even mushroom raising in rice-straw shacks."

Nolting represented Diem as a man "genuinely and sincerely seeking the truth about rural conditions and local government, inviting the airing of problems and complaints and settling many matters on the spot." Although Diem was not a good orator before large crowds, Nolting had found the president extremely effective with groups of peasants and villagers. "He frequently complained about the ceremonies laid on for him by provincial officials, preferring to eat simply with a few village elders, discussing real problems. Diem invariably spent the one holiday he allowed himself—Christmas—with his troops in the farthest province. The fact that he didn't shake hands and slap backs, but bowed instead, was of course the result of his country's customs, not a reflection of an aloof or disinterested attitude, as some members of the press profess to think.''

Nolting, who had a doctorate in philosophy, found a scholarly counterpart in Diem. In the course of their many theological and philosophical discussions, Nolting came to see the president as a man of deep moral convictions, compassion, and tolerance, a far cry from the narrow-minded, fanatical Catholic portrayed in contemporary news stories. Unfortunately Nolting was about to be replaced by Henry Cabot Lodge.

In the meantime, Marguerite wondered: If Nolting is correct, why the conflict? She was determined to find the answers for herself. The search took her to remote provinces far from the gossip and intrigue of Saigon.

Beside a tiny pagoda Marguerite encountered a wizened Buddhist monk, who was considered a saint by the local villagers. When she described the fiery Buddhist suicide in Saigon, the man shook his head disapprovingly. It was the first that he had heard of the incident that had shaken the outside world.

Later Marguerite would describe the interview with the provincial priest in her book *Our Vietnam Nightmare*. ''I do not understand it at all. I would not kill a fly myself. Buddhism does not believe in the taking of life in any form—even by suicide.

''White people do not understand the Vietnamese. They are very tolerant. There is no discrimination. There are many Cao Dai [a mixture of Western and Eastern religions] in this village, but they are our friends. So are the Catholics. Our village chief, a Buddhist, distributes fertilizer and rice seeds without asking anybody his religion. The Catholics don't get more than we do, nor than the Cao Dai do, nor do we get more than the others.''

In the arid coastal plains of Phan Rang province to the north Marguerite interviewed a Moslem leader. Standing beside the village mosque with its blue mosaic dome, he, too, shook his head in puzzled dismay. The villagers who crowded around appeared equally confused.

''We know nothing of any religious persecution,'' said the Moslem priest. ''President Ngo Dinh Diem was province chief here. He may be a Catholic, but he helped our people build mosques and did more for us than any other province chief has ever done. Now he sends us rice, seed, and water [a large dam was being built in the area]. So we are grateful to President Diem.''

In the Mekong delta, Marguerite stopped at a whitewashed Cao Dai temple. Inside, a priest with a half-dozen followers beside him was burning incense before a painting portraying a group of favorite Cao Dai saints: Joan of Arc, Jesus Christ, and Victor Hugo, as well as Sun Yat-sen, Buddha, and Muhammad.

When she found that the Cao Dai priest couldn't read, Marguerite asked her interpreter to tell him the key points of a newspaper clipping describing the suicide and subsequent demonstrations.

He registered surprise and then turned to Marguerite, asking: "Aren't these demonstrations against the law?"

"Yes," she replied, "they are illegal."

"Disregard for authority is bad," he said, "especially in time of war. The Vietcong are very clever. They could get into a mob and make trouble. We would not permit this kind of thing in our village."

Later Marguerite was to write, "Wiser than the West in the ways of their countrymen, the villagers to whom I showed my newspaper clipping never fell into the trap of equating voluntary self-burnings with a deliberate policy of persecution on anybody's part.

"One Buddhist monk, fingering his brown beads, said firmly, 'No true Buddhist would commit suicide. It is written in the verses of Buddha that suicide is wrong. Buddha says that a man's responsibility is to mend his own life, not to meddle in politics. So these men who are, according to your newspaper article, marching in the streets are not Buddhists. They betray Buddhism.' "

When Marguerite reminded him that the demonstrators were believed by the Americans to represent Buddhism, he replied, "White men have brought many things to Vietnam. But white men have not brought much understanding to Vietnam."

"Why do the American correspondents insist on calling my government Diem's Catholic regime?" President Diem demanded angrily. "I notice they never say Kennedy's Catholic regime."

Marguerite found President Diem clearly torn by his desire to please the Americans and his conviction that the Buddhists were determined to keep things stirred up and topple him. Even to placate the Americans, she realized, he was not about to take steps he felt might weaken his personal power and so begin the liquidation of his regime.

Marguerite wrote, "The Buddhist capacity to keep things stirred up stemmed directly from their public relations skill. But while this skill skyrocketed the 'Buddhist cause' to world attention it was also part of the reason for their current plight, including arrests during the brutal police raid on the Xa Loi pagoda. Equal to Diem's fury at the Buddhist political agitation was his fury at the attention it received from the world.''

An example was the story of an eighteen-year-old girl ''found'' on the steps of the Xa Loi pagoda, her right arm slashed and bleeding profusely from a self-inflicted injury. Within ten to twenty minutes of the discovery, American photographers and reporters were at the macabre scene, summoned by the pagoda spokesmen. The Xa Loi monks maintained this grisly spectacle for at least forty minutes, allowing time for ample photographs and a tape-recorded message, before the blood-drenched girl finally was taken to the hospital.

A flashy feminist with a genius for saying the wrong thing, Madame Ngo Dinh Nhu, first lady for her bachelor brother-in-law, was outspoken in her denunciation of the demonstrators, whom she called ''provocateurs in monks' robes.'' To Marguerite, she bitterly attacked the anti-Diem American press, accusing Americans of being Ivanhoes perpetually in love with the underdog. In this case, she believed them confused as to the true identity of the underdog.

On one occasion when Marguerite, with a group of journalists, toured the Xa Loi pagoda, she passed through a crowd of several thousand Vietnamese who were standing before the iron-grilled gates while a monk with a loudspeaker harangued them from the roof of the pagoda souvenir shop. Older members of the crowd were impassive but the young people roared back enthusiastically when the monk-cheerleader gave the signal to shout ''Buddhism Forever'' or ''Down With Madame Nhu.'' Inside the shop other monks were doing a brisk business selling postcards of the flaming monk Thich Quang Duc, who had first set the tragic precedent of suicide by fire.

A young saffron-robed monk welcomed the journalists, greeting each by name. Inside the ornate pagoda with its peaks thrusting three stories high, Marguerite could smell the mixed aroma of burning joss sticks and jasmine. Ceremonial services were being held for Thich Quang Duc.

The young monk, Thich Duc Nghiep, the assistant secretary of the General Buddhist Association and a spokesman for the pagoda, handed out mimeographed sheets of new allegations about government repressions against Buddhists. Almost as an afterthought, Marguerite noted, he suggested that it would ''be very interesting'' for the journalists to go to Hue (four hours flight time from Saigon) ''right away.''

''Is it another barbecue?'' a photographer asked.

Thich Duc Nghiep appeared undismayed by this irreverence. "Ahhhhhhh, I cannot say, but I recommend going to Hue, and it would be a good idea to take your cameras."

Learning that Marguerite was newly arrived, the young monk asked, "What kind of play are we getting in New York?"

She looked at him blankly. "Play? Did you have some particular play or drama in mind?"

"No, Miss Higgins." He elaborately gestured to indicate the front page of a paper with headlines across it.

Although she hadn't anticipated this degree of public relations sophistication at a pagoda, Marguerite got the point: "Yes, a very good play. That's why I'm here."

When Thich Duc Nghiep learned that her stay would be limited to four weeks, he lamented: "You're making a great mistake. When [new ambassador Henry Cabot] Lodge arrives, there will be many demonstrations that will make what went before look like nothing. And there will be many more self-immolations; ten, fifteen, maybe even fifty."

Later Marguerite received a message at the Hotel Caravelle where she was staying that "the highest monk" at the Xa Loi pagoda wanted to see her. She was to report to the pagoda immediately and not bring an interpreter as this was to be top secret.

Once at the pagoda, Marguerite was ushered past rows of politely bowing monks into the innermost sanctum, a small, cozy room in the residential wing of the Xa Loi. There sat Thich Duc Nghiep and an older, alert-looking monk who was introduced as Thich Tri Quang, "one of our most important leaders who ordinarily never sees correspondents but since you represent the White House. . . ."

Marguerite dug into her purse and pulled out her White House press card, which she had used earlier that day at the pagoda for identification. "You don't understand," she attempted to explain. "I am a reporter. I'm only *accredited* to the White House."

"Precisely." Thich Duc Nghiep took the card from her and showed it proudly to Thich Tri Quang. "You are accredited to the White House and we have a message for President Kennedy."

Marguerite gave up and took the message: "We the Buddhists have good information that President Kennedy sympathizes with our anti-Diem efforts and he no doubt has to maintain a certain public posture. But his last press conference was entirely too favorable to Diem. The time is coming when President Kennedy will have to be more outspoken because it would be hard to get rid of Diem without explicit American support.''

Marguerite later recalled, ''In response to my rather astonished questions, Thich Tri Quang indicated that the Buddhists felt Mr. Diem would be inhibited by American pressure from cracking down on them. So they thought they had a good chance of continuing their agitation to the point where the Americans would be embarrassed into withdrawing their support of Mr. Diem or getting rid of him. The Buddhists had no apparent doubt that getting rid of Mr. Diem would be Washington's choice.''

What the Buddhists wanted, Marguerite now realized, was not religious reform, but Diem's head, not on a silver platter, but neatly wrapped in an American flag.

Twenty-four

Returning to the United States in September, Marguerite wrote a note to President Kennedy. "I have just come back from Vietnam where I really got down to the hamlets—forty-two. Diem *does* have a lot of support in the villages, where peasants are getting more rice, seed, pigs, and fertilizer than ever before." She earnestly requested a hearing with the president, hoping to correct the record.

Had the meeting taken place, it still might have been too late to halt the forces already set in motion. Unknown to Marguerite, a cable had been sent from Washington on August 23, 1963, ordering the Vietnamese generals to proceed with a coup d'etat to unseat Diem. The generals at first hesitated.

In the meantime, Marguerite reminded the president in print: "Never in history has a Vietnamese paper carried an ad saying, 'No Buddhist need apply.' But, as President Kennedy's father and mother remember, advertisements saying, 'No Irish need apply,' were a fact of life not long ago. . . . The shock at police brutality has been profound but Vietnam is not the first nation whose police have gotten out of hand. And these days it's a bit delicate for an American to lecture because it is not impossible for a Vietnamese simply to reply, 'Remember Alabama.' "

As though the beleaguered Diem didn't have enough problems in the Pentagon and the pagoda, the gravest resided within his own palace. His brother and chief strategist, the ambitious, autocratic Ngo Dinh Nhu, was the scapegoat for everything that went wrong in the country. When the State Department strongly suggested that Diem fire his brother, the president was outraged. "What would you think if I suggested that John Kennedy fire Bobby?" he demanded. Besides being hard-working and dedicated, Nhu was an intellectual. These were the three qualities that Diem appeared to admire most.

"I am hated in Vietnam," Nhu had acknowledged to Marguerite in an interview. "Every government has to have a tough guy, the man who does the dirty, unpleasant work. Even Eisenhower had to have Sherman Adams, in a country as advanced and unified as the United States. In Vietnam, where violence and virulence are everywhere, I am the person who takes on the unpleasant jobs. It is I who am vilified, so that others may be spared."

Although strongly anti-Communist, Nhu was a political pragmatist. In early fall 1963, when American interference increased to a degree the brothers considered untenable, Nhu put out feelers to North Vietnam, hoping to effect some kind of coalition government. Although totally at variance with Kennedy policy, such an arrangement, had it been allowed to happen, would have saved the United States tens of thousands of lives and billions of dollars in addition to avoiding a tragic issue that split the United States as nothing had before or since the Civil War.

Nhu's wife, known at home and abroad as "The Dragon Lady," was even more controversial. Madame Nhu, vigorous, vital, and uncompromising, had a propensity for pressing the wrong buttons.

In *The Making of a Quagmire*, David Halberstam described her well:

> Madame Nhu was a strikingly beautiful woman, and she was well aware of it; yet she looked too perfectly manicured, too much like someone who had just stepped out of a beauty shop, to be leading a country at war. Her speeches rang with appeals to sacrifice, but there was nothing about her which gave any indication of sacrifice. To me she always resembled an Ian Fleming character come to life; the anti-goddess, the beautiful but diabolic sex-dictatress who masterminds some secret apparatus that James Bond is out to destroy. She liked power and it showed; once in an interview she told me, "People say I am a woman of intrigue, but that is not true. People who intrigue are people without means, and I am a woman of means."
>
> She hated the American press, but she loved all the trappings of the personal interview: the long list of American correspondents going through the elaborate procedure of requesting a private audience; the personal letters addressed to her explaining precisely what they wanted to ask; the correspondents finally arriving—and being kept waiting; her own dramatic entrance, and their paying homage before asking their questions; tea being served by little male servants who bowed and

scraped so low that the gesture resembled some form of medieval torture.

In contrast to Diem, who was shy and ill at ease in public, and Nhu, who often seemed indifferent, Madame Nhu had a real zest for the ceremonies of leadership. She was the only one of the family who walked the way a dictator should walk—with flair and obvious enjoyment, trailed by a line of attendants—turning first to the right, then to the left in acknowledging the crowd. It was always a virtuoso performance, and a reporter watching felt this was the way Mussolini must have done it.

Well aware of the journalist's feelings about herself and her brother-in-law's regime, Madame Nhu suggested: "Halberstam should be barbecued and I would personally be glad to supply the fluid and the match."

Although Marguerite secretly might have approved (she and Halberstam conducted a typewriter duel that would follow her beyond the grave), she was appalled by the first lady's use of the word barbecue, which she had also publicly applied to the Buddhist suicides. While in Vietnam that summer Marguerite had been eager to interview the notorious Dragon Lady and had been delighted when her request was speedily granted.

Now back in Washington, Marguerite had received a note from Madame Nhu indicating that she would be coming to the United States in mid-October. Recalling her initial interview vividly, Marguerite wondered how the don't-involve-me American public would accept this fiery, totally involved, brutally frank woman.

It couldn't.

Marguerite's initial interview with the first lady had gone quite smoothly. Madame Nhu had meant clearly to charm and disarm her. She was not only on time but flattering. "I read everything you wrote about the Korean War," Madame Nhu said. "I never thought I would be fortunate enough to meet you."

But Marguerite was not to be put off. As the two women settled into big overstuffed chairs in the center of the main hall of the Presidential Palace with its high ceilings and whirring fans, she got right to the point. "Why did you use the word barbecue to describe the Buddhist suicides?"

Madame Nhu was equally direct: "To shock the world out of this false vision of religious persecution that doesn't exist. If President Kennedy continues bowing to the unreasonable demands of the Buddhists, they'll keep right on taking advantage of his weakness to impose new demands. I would welcome a condemnation of Vietnam by the United Nations.

Then they will send a team here to investigate and finally discover the truth.''

Marguerite persisted. ''Don't you realize that your use of the word barbecue has hurt your country's image terribly and damaged Vietnam's relations with Washington at a critical time?''

''But,'' Madame Nhu argued, ''I would never have thought of the word barbecue if it had not been used first by the Americans.''

''The Americans?''

''Yes,'' she explained, ''my daughter was at the post exchange the other day. And she heard some American photographers talking about some new 'barbecue' that the Xa Loi monks were predicting.''

''Don't you see the difference between a photographer using such a term in a private conversation and the first lady of Vietnam using it in a television interview that will be carried into the living rooms of Americans and onto the headlines of the whole world?'' Marguerite asked.

She shook her head wordlessly, not even annoyed by Marguerite's bluntness. Her limited English simply didn't accommodate to the meaning of the word.

If Madame Nhu had hoped to enlist Marguerite's sympathies on feminist grounds she had chosen the wrong woman. Marguerite had been too involved in competing with men in their own world on their own terms to give much thought to the subjugation of women. She was puzzled by Madame Nhu's assumption that they were sisters fighting the same battle. The first lady talked enthusiastically about ''the struggle to wrest decent treatment of women from the reluctant, devious, and often hypocritical men of Vietnam.''

Among her efforts to achieve this goal was the establishment of the Women's Solidarity Movement, a sort of Oriental Junior League whose 1.2 million members supervised workers' nurseries and welfare centers and served as a political intelligence network throughout the country; and, more controversial, the Paramilitary Women, a parade-ground force of crack shots and jujitsu experts. ''If women have their own army, they have a better chance of obtaining their rights,'' she explained.

Prior to Madame Nhu's intervention, Vietnamese women virtually had no rights and could be discarded by their husbands at will. ''In these circumstances,'' she said, ''a woman was an eternal minor, an unpaid servant, a doll without a soul.'' While Vietnamese men merely sneered at Madame Nhu's women's groups, they were enraged by her family law, which not only made adultery a prison offense but outlawed polygamy and concubinage as well. Marguerite regarded Madame Nhu's zeal as commendable, her timing terrible. "A country in crisis can ill afford to have century-old social customs (and abuses) assaulted head-on by such controversial reforms," she wrote.

Looking at the tiny woman before her, Marguerite speculated on the train of savage events that had taken this fragile, superficially frivolous creature and forged her into a warrior. Marguerite knew a fellow survivor when she saw one. Born to one of the wealthiest families in Vietnam, Madame Nhu, whose maiden name, Tran Le Xuan, meant beautiful spring, had been waited on as a child by twenty servants. Despite the luxury, Beautiful Spring was anxious to escape her mother (another strong-willed, forthright woman). An early marriage seemed the only avenue open to the rebellious sixteen year old. Her choice was Ngo Dinh Nhu, then chief archivist at the Indochina Library, a frequent guest at her mother's salon. Madame Nhu admitted that her love for Nhu was not "a sweeping passion" but there had always been a strong affection and mutual respect.

In 1946 Ho Chi Minh had swept through the land, slaughtering non-Communists by the thousands. Provincial mandarins, because of their prestige and intelligence, were particularly sought out. Ngo Dinh Khoi, the elder brother of Diem and Nhu, was among the victims. He was buried alive with his young son. When Madame Nhu was taken prisoner with her infant daughter and her aged mother-in-law, her husband was in another part of the country. Her childhood of elegance and pampering was hardly training for captivity, but Madame Nhu was able to survive on two bowls of rice a day and somehow save her baby and keep her mother-in-law alive. Finally, as the French forces approached, the Communists retreated, allowing Madame Nhu to leave with her family. "The Communists did not seem to consider me much of a prize," she recalled.

In October 1963, when Madame Nhu came to the United States to plead her country's case, the State Department didn't think she was much of a prize either. Neither President Kennedy nor Secretary of State Dean Rusk would see her. Not one to suffer a snub meekly, Madame Nhu lashed out verbally against the Kennedy administration. Marguerite believed the first lady's atrocious English intensified her problems. A frequent mistake was to assume that English words derived from the French had the same connotation in both languages. One such disaster occurred when Madame Nhu declared to a group of American journalists that Buddhist monks were intoxicated. The French word *intoxiquer* means to poison, and her intent was to say that the minds of the monks had been poisoned against the Diem regime. Her misuse of English made it look as though she were slandering the monks, who are forbidden by their religion to touch a drop of alcohol.

Madame Nhu made no effort at conciliation on October 16 when she addressed the Women's National Press Club, where she described the Kennedy administration as "not red but pink." Looking deceptively demure in an unadorned sapphire blue gown, Madame Nhu, when asked her opinion of Henry Cabot Lodge, said, "I have not seen him yet, but he is becoming more mysterious than the Asian."

Marguerite invited Madame Nhu and her seventeen-year-old daughter, Le Thuy, to tea at her home. Ruth Montgomery, who was the only other guest, wrote of the afternoon in *Hail to the Chiefs:*

> During our two-hour chat her quicksilver moods ran the gamut from fiery anger to little-girl hurt. Her anger was reserved for the Kennedy administration, which had publicly snubbed the first lady of an allied nation who was also a member of its parliament.
> Marguerite and I gently tried to point out to her the mistakes that she had been making. We suggested milder synonyms for such inflammatory words as "liar" and "coward," which she so freely hurled at the U. S. officials, and we urged her to express more appreciation for the million and a half dollars a day that Americans were pouring into Vietnam's war effort, but she could not really grasp the point. Her daughter said, "I agree with you," but Madame Nhu proudly retorted, "They would think I was begging. Why should I beg?"

When reminded of her charges that the CIA had tried to promote a coup d'etat against Diem, an arrogant smile flitted across Madame Nhu's scarlet lips and her eyes burned fire. "It is true," she replied, "but they are wasting their time. After all, my husband has the youth with him and I have the women. How could a coup accomplish anything?"

Possibly even as the women sipped their tea, the newly appointed ambassador, Henry Cabot Lodge, informed President Kennedy of the time, place, and cast of characters of the coup d'etat that took place November 1. During the night President Diem and Ngo Dinh Nhu escaped from the palace through an underground passage. Early the next morning they took communion at a Catholic church in the suburbs where they had sought sanctuary and found death.

Initially there was an attempt to call it suicide but Marguerite knew better. Bill Hall remembered that the two heard the news on the car radio just as they reached their country home for a weekend holiday. "Marguerite ran into the house, grabbed the phone, and called the State Department. I can still remember the expression of fury on her face when she demanded: 'How does it feel to be a murderer?' " Eventually the true story came out. Both men were shot in the back while their hands were tied behind them. Nhu also had a dagger or bayonet wound in his chest.

Near midnight on November 2, Marguerite returned home to find an urgent message to call Madame Nhu at the Beverly Wilshire Hotel in Los Angeles; her speaking tour had by this time taken her to the West Coast. Adding to Madame Nhu's pain was the shock of learning of the sudden tragic events while watching television in a strange, hostile land.

Le Thuy answered the phone, explaining, "Mother wants to ask you about the children."

Marguerite instantly recalled the charming four-year-old daughter, the same age as her own Linda, whom she had met in the Presidential Palace. There were also two boys, eleven and fifteen.

When Madame Nhu came on the line, she spoke first of her husband and brother-in-law.

"Do you believe they are really dead?" she asked.

"I'm afraid so," Marguerite answered.

"I could spit upon the world," Madame Nhu answered.

There was nothing that Marguerite could say. It remained for Madame Nhu to break the silence. "Are they going to kill my children, too?"

A series of horrific pictures passed before Marguerite's mind. Anything was possible. "It's the last thing that President Kennedy would want," she insisted lamely.

"Then why doesn't the United States government do something to help me get them out?" Madame Nhu, demanded to know, her words barely audible through her choking sobs.

"I'll call the State Department officer in charge of Vietnam right away," Marguerite promised. "Please hurry," Madame Nhu begged, "and ask about Can." (Ngo Dinh Can was another brother.)

It was 2:00 A.M. when Marguerite aroused Assistant Secretary Roger Hilsman. He responded to her agitation with touching concern: "Revolutions are rough; people get hurt."

"What about Madame Nhu's children? Are they going to get hurt?"

"If you will find out from Madame Nhu where her children are,"

Hilsman said, "we will have General Harkins send his personal plane to get them. Find out where she wants them sent and we'll buy them tickets."

"What about Ngo Dinh Can?"

"He can have asylum if he wants it," Hilsman promised.

Within days Madame Nhu's three children landed at the Rome airport where their mother was waiting. The ending for Can was quite different. When the man sought asylum at the American consulate at Hue, he was urged to go to Saigon.

Ngo Dinh Can was reluctant. The American consul only persuaded him to board an American plane by promising that he would be taken to a 'safe place' in Saigon. The understanding was that this would be either the American embassy or exile, the only "safe" places possible. When the unfortunate man arrived in Saigon, the Americans turned him over to the Vietnamese police who were waiting for the plane to land. He was executed by a firing squad.

Ironically, almost three weeks to the day after the murder of Diem and Nhu, John Kennedy was killed. It was left to Lyndon Johnson to pick up the pieces resulting from an act he had strenuously opposed. To Robert Kennedy, Marguerite predicted: "Three coups d'etat from now, Lodge is going to go down on his hands and knees and say, 'God-Buddha-Confucious—please send me back Diem.' " In her column, she likened the removal of an effective ally to changing barrels in the middle of Niagara Falls.

Marguerite was discovering that it wasn't much fun to be a Cassandra. Washington, still reeling under the loss of President Kennedy, did not appreciate the added discomfort of egg on its face. Most preferred to ignore Marguerite's column, which asked:

"How does it come to pass that under the military junta, which seized power in the name of an end to 'persecution,' there have been more suicides by fire over a short period than had ever been the case under President Diem?"

Returning to Vietnam immediately after the assassinations, she encountered a whole new spate of suicides by fire, macabre protests virtually ignored by a Western press who had no ready perspective in which to place them. If Diem was the villain and that villain had been removed—one can imagine the State Department mentally addressing the Vietnamese dissidents like weary parents: "Look at all we've done for you. Now, damn it, be happy!"

No one was happy. There were more suicides and more demonstrations. The war escalated, and the military junta became so unpopular that within a month there were rumblings of another coup d'etat. To make matters really bad, Diem and Nhu were no longer around to blame. Saigonese society was truly desolate. With Madame Nhu an exile halfway around the world, who was there to gossip about?

While attempting to maintain a cheerful war-as-usual stance, the State Department and the military junta had to cope with the United Nations investigation prophesied a few months before by Madame Nhu. The 234-page report failed to find any evidence that Diem's policy was one of religious persecution.

It underscored, however, what Marguerite had written; and it was given a bizarre twist by a new incident. She and Peter Lisagor, coauthoring an article for *America*, described the damage dealt the morale of Vietnamese forces by the arrest of a war hero, Major Dang Sy. During the violent May riots when Buddhists had run rampant through the city of Hue, Sy had been ordered by the province chief, a Buddhist colonel, to protect government property with whatever means necessary. Major Sy had authorized the use of American MK 111 concussion grenades to dispel the crowd because they produce a spectacular pyrotechnic effect but little else.

Despite his moderation, Sy was arrested after the assassination and sentenced to life imprisonment. The lesson of Dang Sy had not been lost on the military rank and file. In Da Nang, Vietnamese paratroopers stood aside while Buddhists burned homes and murdered Catholics. Fearing that they, too, would later be denounced, the government troops refused to do anything without written orders from a superior.

If rule by mobocracy wasn't depressing enough to see and write about, Marguerite had yet another professional confrontation, this time a personality clash between herself and the *New York Times* correspondent David Halberstam.

Halberstam had been sent to Vietnam in September 1962. At twenty-eight, he was assigned to replace Homer Bigart, now a *Times* correspondent. Possibly Halberstam inherited the ancient Bigart-Higgins feud along with the assignment. For whatever reason, he picked up the cudgel and has never let go. By the time Marguerite had made her seventh visit to Vietnam in July 1963, he was an established member of the resident press.

Both shared an idealism about the calling of war correspondent and a romantic sense of the journalist in search of himself as a kind of Hemingway-like character. Halberstam, too, had been captivated by the camaraderie of war. When he wrote, ''Everything is so intense, everything so completely shared, and everyone so dependent upon everyone else that it defies all other relationships,'' he was unknowingly paraphrasing sentiments expressed by Marguerite years before.

Again like her, Halberstam had lost his political innocence. ''Ideals of egalitarianism were not easily exported and often the people in Washington most eager to export them were, in fact, those who most clearly failed to live up to them at home,'' he wrote in a *Parade* article. Marguerite long ago had reached the same conclusions. Halberstam was the purveyor of bad news: The war, in his opinion, was not going well and he was highly critical of the efficacy of the army. Presidents Kennedy and Johnson were, in turn, furious. Marguerite had encountered the same obstacles in reporting. Both fought the battle of military censorship.

From the vantage point of twenty years, there seems more similarity than disparity between the two, but the feud continues to sizzle even though one combatant no longer can defend herself. Marguerite may have felt resentful of the young upstart getting all the play; wasn't it only yesterday that *she* had occupied that position? Halberstam had only begun to prove himself. Perhaps he, too, was jealous and resentful of the world-renowned senior journalist who had seen and done it all and now was frequently treated more as a VIP than a member of the working press. Whatever the reasons, it appears to be a classic case of macho meets macha. The result, at least on Halberstam's part, was open warfare.

One article in a series on Vietnam written by Marguerite in the summer of 1963 seems to have triggered Halberstam's wrath. Although the article, an interview with General Paul Harkins, was merely a factual account of the general's viewpoint, it was contrary to Halberstam's viewpoint. When a *Times* editor queried him on the generally upbeat mood of the interview, which conflicted with the antimilitary tone of many of his own releases, Halberstam took it as a personal slight and fired off an angry cable threatening to resign. Two years later, in his book *The Making of a Quagmire*, Halberstam was still fighting the battle. He made a point of the ''briefness'' of Marguerite's stay (four weeks), choosing to ignore the fact that her familiarity with Vietnam had begun in 1951.

When Marguerite returned to Vietnam after Diem's death she found herself the center of a miniscandal. The story allegedly told by General Victor Krulak, a Defense Department specialist on counterinsurgency, to a reporter was that Halberstam had approached Marguerite in a bar and asked her if she had ever seen a dead man (in itself a curious question for a newly accredited correspondent to ask a veteran of two major wars). Halberstam was supposed to have pulled out a picture of some dead Vietcong soldiers and then burst into tears.

Not only did Halberstam indignantly retell the story of the alleged exchange in *The Making of a Quagmire* two years later, but he also brought it up again in 1982 in a Memorial Day article for *Parade*. In the latter piece, the thinly veiled put-down "brief tour" was again included in the anecdote to discredit her even though Halberstam by then knew that Marguerite had returned time and again to Vietnam long after his own transfer.

Leaving Vietnam for a time and returning to Washington via Berlin, Marguerite had an opportunity to renew her friendship with Jim O'Donnell. When questioned by Jim about the current wave of flak concerning Halberstam, she sighed. "I assume the inference in all this is that I'm supposed to think he's a coward. Why else would anyone get so worked up over a senseless rumor? How should I know whether he's a coward? How does he even know himself? He's never fought for anything. When a correspondent who's fought in World War II or Korea interviews a military man, he has some understanding of his problems. They may not agree at all, but they speak the same language. The trouble with Halberstam and the other young Rover boys is that they've never served one day. Naturally there's some resentment among the military and a lot of misunderstanding."

O'Donnell recalled that Marguerite, who although she had never actually fought had so eminently paid her dues, regarded Halberstam as symptomatic of a deeper issue. "Somebody has made the decision to let the blacks and the poor whites fight this war," she pointed out. "All things considered, they're doing pretty well. But more significantly, the middle class has opted out. The class Halberstam belongs to was able to avoid service merely by paying tuition, getting a student loan; college or counseling was the great escape. Once they removed themselves, they condemned the country to defeat in the field. When deep inside you've got a guilty conscience because you know you managed to evade an obligation then you must somehow prove that the obligation you escaped was evil anyway. In a sense you become a hero by being a coward."

Home again in December 1963, Marguerite tried to pull together the threads of her personal life. The Higgins-Hall ménage had expanded to include three cats, two parakeets, a dog, a rabbit, and a donkey.

Bill, who had retired one day from the air force and gone to work for an electronics firm the next, continued to commute. On Monday morning he would leave for New York, returning Friday afternoon to the Washington house. "Homecoming was something you wouldn't believe," he says today. "It was delicious. I'd come in the front door and right away I could hear the laughing and stomping going on above me. The living room of the four-story house was on the second floor. When I'd go up, there would be Marguerite at her typewriter, more often than not a parakeet sitting on her head. Linda and Larry would be playing all around her with the animals. I think Marguerite loved the pets as much as the children did. If she could have brought the donkey in she would have. The big buck rabbit was a special favorite. She cried when it died of paint poisoning from chewing on the furniture."

The rabbit's demise may not have been unanimously lamented. All the pets had free run of the house. Ruth Montgomery remembered that no one was exactly sure what might be encountered, but that both Marguerite and Bill were very cool and casual about handling unexpected surprises.

Despite the surprises and general air of informality (Bill's motorcycle was invariably parked in the foyer), parties at the Higgins-Hall home were very much the "in" thing. John Michaelis recalled that invitations were prized. "No matter how busy you were in that busy town you never thought of not going. The top people in every field would be there. Marguerite had a feeling for people, that Irish gift of gab; she knew how to make a party flow. A buffet for two hundred would become intimate and alive."

Ruth Montgomery likened her to Jacqueline Kennedy at that time. "Marguerite was very much a man's woman and didn't have many women friends; but to those of us who were her friends, she was warm and very generous. She had a faculty for picking up celebrities. Once in New York she invited me to have lunch with her at Bleeck's. I expected an afternoon of newspaper shoptalk. When I arrived she was sitting with Richard Rodgers and Lorenz Hart. Another time President Syngman Rhee was in Washington and seeing no one from the press. Marguerite invited me to lunch and there he was."

Marguerite's most exciting guest turned out to be a surprise even to her. She recounted the story in a column that appeared late in January 1964. "It all started out simply enough as a luncheon given at my home by myself and Peter Lisagor of the *Chicago Daily News* to talk politics and policy with Bill Moyers, twenty-nine-year-old White House aide, and Carl Rowan, new head of the United States Information Agency. Shortly after 1:00 P.M., Moyers telephoned to ask if he could bring along Jack Valenti, another White House aide. He was assured that there was a French ragout on the stove and more than enough for everybody.

"At 1:25 P.M., restlessly gazing out the window of my second-story living room, I noted a man with a walkie-talkie gazing up at my window and obviously casing the place. When I reached my front door, the walkie-talkie man turned, flashed a smile, a secret service badge, and the bulletin that 'they are five minutes away.'

" 'Oh,' I replied, turning to go back to my guests upstairs. 'But,' the walkie-talkie man called after me, 'aren't you going to stay here at the door to receive the president?'

" 'The president!' I echoed, fairly shouting (the cook heard it all the way upstairs). And, sure enough, when the black presidential limousine drew up, it produced, along with Valenti and Moyers, a smiling Mr. President. 'You didn't think I was going to let these young men come over here and chat with old friends and leave me out of it?' Johnson asked.

"It had been a hectic and harassing morning for Johnson, but he was a zestful, engaging, and responsive guest, full of stories and anecdotes, some serious, some funny. His informality had a wonderful way of making people relax. Even my cook, Mabel, began to calm down when the president shook her hand and said, 'Thank you for letting me come to this lunch, honey.' The president himself suggested saying grace, which he did with quiet eloquence."

The lunch progressed casually and easily. They had come to the French situation when an angry shout nearly drowned out LBJ's comments on General de Gaulle.

"Who left the door wide open?"

It was Bill. The secret service men were asking him what he was doing there and he was asking them the same thing. After a quieter exchange between the gentleman of the house and the gentlemen of the secret service, Bill bounded up the stairs expecting to find Marguerite lunching with the first lady. His first words upon entering the room were the astonished, "You're not Mrs. Johnson after all!"

"What an afternoon!" Bill recalled. "The president left us feeling that he'd really enjoyed himself. Marguerite ended up renaming the ragout 'Johnson stew.' "

In November 1964, Larry Higgins died of multiple sclerosis after a lengthy and debilitating illness. Marguerite, in Vietnam at the time, had just received long-sought consent to an exclusive interview with Prince Norodom Sihanouk of Cambodia. Prior to Diem's assassination, Sihanouk had received army training and half his country's financial support from the United States. After the murder he shocked the world by rejecting both. Marguerite decided to continue with the interview. In essence, the prince said: "Diem and Nhu had been friends of the United States. After seeing what your country did to them, I saw no point in having such 'friends.' "

The funeral was delayed one day to permit Marguerite to fly home to Oakland. Jean Craig remembered: "The church was packed. Larry had always been popular but there were many who came specially to see Maggie. She was marvelous, so strong and kind. As mourners passed from the church, she stood at the door shaking hands and thanking each for coming.

"I rode back from the cemetery with Maggie and Mrs. Higgins. It was the first opportunity that Maggie and I had had to talk. I mentioned that our old heartthrob, Carl Ferguson, had called to offer his regards. She smiled. 'It's always nice to be remembered.' Mrs. Higgins shushed us. I half expected her to say, 'Can't you girls think about anything but boys?' Maggie and I looked at one another for a long moment wordlessly, remembering so many things. I couldn't know that it was the last time that I would ever see her."

Back in Washington Marguerite received notes of condolence from *Newsday* executives that also congratulated her on the Sihanouk exclusive, expressing appreciation for fulfillment of a self-imposed assignment.

She replied: "I would be less than candid if I claimed to have stayed out there that extra day for *Newsday*. I did it for Dad. You see he was unconscious by the time I heard of his illness. When he died, I had to think—sentimentally perhaps, superstitiously even—of what he would want. He was a true man of adventure, from his earliest days in the French air force to the time in middle age when he parachuted into Formosa during World War II. In his declining years, his great joy was the journalistic adventures and achievements, such as they were, that I once had.

"I have returned depressed by many things, including me. I am really beginning to doubt that I have a place anymore in the newspaper business. In Washington, a columnist is nothing unless [he appears] regularly on the editorial page. I feel that I have failed and while I blame myself completely, I would appreciate knowing what the *Evening Star* has against my product."

Harry F. Guggenheim, the president and publisher of *Newsday*, replied immediately, referring to her column as a magnificent success as indicated by the number of papers eager to publish it. A Washington outlet would come in time, he predicted and reminded her. "You have so much that most columnists would envy. Your writing is tops and always full of interest. You have great powers of analysis. You have special entrée not only in key places of Washington but also in various parts of the world. To convince you that you must be mighty good, you make people mad."

Despite his words of encouragement, it was a sad and lonely Christmas for Marguerite. Larry's death had plunged her into a black depression deeper than any she had ever experienced and underscoring a growing dissatisfaction with her life. At forty-four, Marguerite felt even more keenly the sense of isolation that had characterized her entire life. Despite her international reputation, she still remained at bitter odds with many of her colleagues over her controversial stand on Vietnam policy. Syndicated now in seventy papers, there were significant holdouts among key papers. More than anything, she was deeply discouraged by her failure to win a continuing space on the editorial page of the *Washington Evening Star*. The paper's insistence upon running her stories in the news section was, in her eyes, a defeat.

Trying to forget her sadness, Marguerite threw herself into a round of holiday activities. A series of snapshots record bittersweet moments: . . . the house, never again so beautiful as in that year's Christmas trappings. . . . The tree glitters, a Fabergé-like creation. . . . The children beside a mountain of riotously wrapped gifts are aglow with excitement at having Mother home and Santa Claus, too.

The ghost of Christmas past and the specter of the one to come were unwanted drop-ins. A life that many considered "having it all" seemed to Marguerite at this time merely a succession of compromises and tacit concessions. Watching Bill playing with Linda, she must have thought often of Larry and another little girl who had dreamed of a life of high adventure in faraway places. Looking ahead, as one invariably does as one year ends and another begins, she wondered: *What next?*

Twenty-five

"What America wants in Vietnam," Peter Lisagor told Marguerite, "is a saintly Ataturk or a Simón Bolívar who understands the balance of payments and turns his paycheck over to charity."

What it got was quite different. General Duong Van (Big) Minh's junta had been in power less than three months before the takeover by Major General Nguyen Khanh. Khanh was so determined to show the United States that he was liberal and unlike Diem that he ordered his police force to look the other way while Buddhist and Christian factions literally hacked one another to pieces in the streets of Saigon. Still afraid of a repetition of the press campaign that had caused Diem's death, General Khanh resigned one day when Thich Tri Quang threatened to have two monks burn themselves the next morning. Following him was Tran Van Huong, who assumed the reins in October 1964 only to be ousted three months later. This time the Armed Forces Council, at the specific demand of Thich Tri Quang, selected Dr. Phan Huy Quat.

"Fortunately," Marguerite wrote, "even though Washington, for whatever reason, failed to recognize the fifth-column potential of the Buddhist minority, the Vietnamese people saw the danger. Anti-Communists of all persuasions reacted with increasing alarm against Premier Quat's violent purges of honorable Vietnamese." The heat proved too much for Quat and he voluntarily stepped down in June 1965, returning the government to the military.

The new coleaders were Major General Nguyen Van Thieu, a Catholic convert, and Air Commander Cao Van Ky, a Buddhist. They made an extraordinary pair. Thieu was calm, intelligent, mild-mannered; Ky, a daredevil pilot and flamboyant idealist given to writing poetry and wearing lavender scarves. The odd couple had only their anti-Communist sentiments in common.

Almost unnoticed amid this dizzying (if not dazzling) parade of premiers was a minicoup within the Xa Loi Pagoda, where Buddhist leaders expressed their disapproval of extremist violence and intrigue by expelling Thich Tri Quang. Visiting the former command post on her ninth trip to Vietnam, Marguerite found it now a haven of serenity and contemplation, with no switchboards, ringing telephones, or mimeograph machines in evidence. The trappings of riots and other earthly pursuits were gone and Thich Tri Quang had been forbidden to ever set foot in the building again.

The expulsion, although it vindicated the pagoda priests in their own eyes, had little effect anywhere else. The Machiavellian monk had moved to the newly created Buddhist Institute located five miles away on government-donated land, where he continued to stage-manage the riots of his extremist faction.

Marguerite found their tactics had changed very little since the anti-Diem days. She recognized many of the old professional agitators and waved in recognition. One waved back. "The demonstrating 'students,' " she commented, "included many who had seen thirty years of age many moons ago." She quickly learned to save time by calling the Buddhist Institute first thing each morning to learn the time and place of the day's riot. Information and directions were provided as courteously as though she were calling to inquire about church services.

Home again and working on a new project, Marguerite turned tour guide long enough to advise Crosby Noyes, the foreign editor of the *Washington Evening Star*, on a proposed trip to Vietnam. Her letter is significant because of what it reveals about her own familiarity with the country and methods of reporting.

Dear Crosby:

A quick and interesting way to see the diversity of Vietnam—important even though the State Department takes special pride in ignoring same—is to fly to Pleiku (magnificent country), have lunch with the province chief, then fly by helicopter to a Montagnard camp.

I usually ask one of the State Department youngsters who speak Vietnamese if they want to go along. Their sole duty is to circle the countryside and try to find out what's going on. They are rather timid souls and welcome going out with us bold and brash reporters because we ask questions they are scared of asking themselves.

From Pleiku fly to Quangnai—a historic and key province. Ask to go to the eleven strategic hamlets that have put up one hell of a battle when attacked. More interesting, visit Chu Hoi (amnesty) camps. These are filled with genuine live Vietcong who have come over (10,000 last spring and summer). The most interesting prisoners are the soldiers who are members of Ho Chi Minh's regular army in the north who came south with battalions designed as the backbone of forces to be created by "recruitment" and kidnapping of local Vietnamese.

A quick and easy trip to Cao Dai country can be made via Tai Ninh, also interesting because it borders Cambodia. The Cao Dai pope is worth talking to. The American advisor can take you to him. There are Catholic refugee villages in Tai Ninh also.

The Buddhists you should try and see are obvious: Thich Tri Quang and members of the Con So Mon (anti-Thich Tri Quang) Buddhist Organization.

Phan Rang is interesting because it is coastal and the people are spirited. The Cham (Moslems) with their beautiful women and lovely mosques are worth talking with.

Father O'Connor of the Catholic News Service in Saigon is the hardest-working and best-informed reporter. He doesn't sit in Saigon. He goes to the front lines and has long continuity. He is Irish and doesn't love Americans but has so much information at his fingertips that he is worth cultivating. He has some interesting contacts among the Orthodox Buddhists.

And by the way, dip into Graham Green's *A Quiet American* before going to Vietnam. When you get there, it will give you the creeps to see all those "quiet Americans" of today.

All the best,
Maggie

During this brief interval at home Marguerite had rallied her flagging spirits around a new goal. Approached by Harper and Row to do a book on Vietnam, she responded with enthusiasm, summing up in a proposal what would be the theme of *Our Vietnam Nightmare:*

We must find a balance between isolation on one side and intervention on the other. In this complicated, many-faceted world, Uncle Sam does not always know best. We are paying now in Vietnam for the arrogance of seeking to impose our own values on a country that resents our demands because it does not understand them.

A truly great country must resist the temptation to reshape an ally in its own image. What we did in Japan and Germany we did by virtue of our victory, our absolute mastery over those prostrated nations. Vietnam is not a conquered country. We reap disaster when we treat it like one. The only way America can reshape countries that are friends—not conquered enemies—is by example.

Marguerite was a woman with not one cause but two. Although she earnestly believed that American meddling in Vietnam was wrong and had to be stopped, she was also anxious to see her own judgments vindicated. Her view, she believed, was the balanced view, its carefully crafted presentation in book form a personal crusade.

That Americans might be tiring of an unwanted war was hinted by Harry F. Guggenheim, the publisher of the *Newsday* syndicate, who responded to yet another letter from Marguerite expressing discouragement at the *Washington Evening Star* column impasse:

> It would be interesting to count back and see how many columns you've written on Vietnam. You were right and our country's policy has been atrocious but after all, this is only one country. I'm afraid that most of our readers don't put it on top of the heap.

For Marguerite, who had come into daily contact with young American casualties, such apathy at home was incomprehensible. Vietnam had drawn her again and again like a moth to a flame. Now she strove to resist the awful fascination. Pragmatically—or intuitively—she attempted to reorder her reporting priorities.

The refusal of the *Washington Evening Star* to run her column on the editorial page on a regular basis cut deeply into her always shaky self-esteem. To her, far more than policy was involved. It was a measure of her worth as a writer, the sum total of everything she had worked for all her professional life. Placing her stories ROP (run of the paper), as the editor Newbold Noyes chose to do, merely threw her into competition with regular newsmen, a battle that she had fought, in her opinion, long enough. She felt that rough-and-tumble reporter days were behind her now. Marguerite considered herself a political pundit and wanted to be treated as one.

Once again back in Wasington following a trip to another trouble spot, Santo Domingo, she took her case directly to Noyes:

> I am assuming that the *Evening Star* prefers columnists that have a national impact and are provocative and controversial rather than bland. Unfortunately, it's a fact of journalistic life that it's impossible for any columnist to have national impact, meaning among other things, quotation in national magazines, publication in the Congressional Record, etc., unless he or she appears regularly in a New York City or a Washington paper.

> One of the problems of being ROP is that the *Star's* editors are very

sensible men and, naturally and understandably, must give priority to the journalists they work with day by day. If I write about Santo Domingo there is competition with O'Leary. If I write about Russia, there's Gwertzman. . . .

I was particularly regretful that most of my really controversial stories out of Santo Domingo didn't get printed. Being a journalist yourself, you will understand my feelings after wresting an exclusive interview with John Bartlow Martin in Santo Domingo (not used), I saw articles about him in the *Star* by colleagues who had no firsthand information.

A columnist loses face with a source when information or attitudes have been "leaked" and the source does not see them in print. Regular exposure on the editorial page would eliminate this problem as well as that of competition with your regular staff.

I was wondering if a trial run might be possible? Could you take the gamble of running me in a regular slot for six to eight months? If there are no dividends, I'll take my lumps and you can put me back on ROP.

Could you have lunch with Peter Lisagor and me one day next week at the International Club? Pete has a couple of things he wants to talk to you about, and as father confessor to my professional problems, he is privy to my hopes and aspirations with regard to the *Star*.

Newbold Noyes promised to "think about it."

In the meantime, Marguerite's work on *Our Vietnam Nightmare* had been interrupted by a trip to Puerto Rico that triggered yet another professional brouhaha. While on the island, Marguerite raised the ire of Carl Levin, a public relations man employed by the Puerto Rican government, by reporting Communist-linked arson cases involving damage to close to ten million dollars' worth of commercial property.

In an effort to discredit her, questions were raised as to what interest group had paid her way. The rumor found its way into print when Pat Munro, a Washington correspondent to the *San Juan Star* and *El Mundo*, wrote: "A controversial woman columnist who wrote some critical articles about the growing threat in Puerto Rico denies her trip to the island was paid for by antigovernment forces. Propagandists for the government have quietly rumored it to newsmen that Miss Marguerite Higgins, the newswoman in queston, was actually being subsidized by Republicans."

The whole thing was later smoothed over as a joke, which Marguerite considered very unfunny. The trip was a routine one paid for, as usual, by the *Newsday* syndicate.

In a letter to P. Vargas Badillo, the editor of *El Mundo*, she privately commiserated:

Since my return I have learned something of the efficacy and powers of harassment of the public relations people employed by the commonwealth government. Never in my experience have people tried so hard to prevent publication of news and facts that I consider pertinent.

I am beginning to wonder how *El Mundo* manages to print as much as it does about the arson cases, Red penetration into schools, etc. I assume that if they put this much pressure on a stranger from the continent of the United States, the efforts must be even more difficult for an editor inside Puerto Rico. Keep up the good work.

This unpleasant episode had barely blown over before Marguerite was taken to task by associates for "compelling" Robert Kennedy to risk his life. It all began when Franc Shor, an editor of *National Geographic* and close friend of Marguerite's, told her that *Geographic* planned to sponsor an expedition to explore and map Mount Kennedy. Since the previously unclimbed thirteen-thousand-foot-high Canadian mountain had been named for John Kennedy, Shor thought that possibly the senator might like to join the expedition and be the first to reach the peak.

At Shor's insistence she arranged a meeting and the mountain climbing idea was greeted with immediate enthusiasm. Marguerite duly wrote in her column that "Robert Kennedy was planning to accept an invitation to climb Mount Kennedy."

Reaction was anything but favorable. Some writers accused Robert of seeking publicity and trying to cash in on his brother's name. Others chided a father of nine for taking such risks. Kennedy began to have second thoughts. He was pretty busy just being a senator.

The next thing she knew Marguerite was approached at a cocktail party by Arthur Schlesinger, former aide to President Kennedy. He poked a finger disapprovingly at her. "Bobby would have been able to get out of it gracefully, if you hadn't frozen him into a position," he chastised her. "After all, he has never climbed a mountain, suffers from vertigo, and has a bum leg. Now he's stuck with it."

Fortunately for Marguerite, Bobby survived the climb.

Both typewriter tempests spent, Marguerite enjoyed the unusual lull. While putting the finishing touches to her book, she taught her parakeet, Fred Friendly, to drink martinis and gave moonvine parties. Helen Lambert remembered the moonvines well. "Joe Alsop had given cuttings to Marguerite and she'd planted them all over the back garden.

They were like morning glories except that they opened only at night. It took twenty minutes for them to slowly unfold their petals, a magical, mystical sight. Marguerite and Bill loved to invite people over for drinks. We'd sit in that fragrant flower-filled garden and watch the moonvines open. It was beautiful.

"There were tensions between them. Bill's indiscretions couldn't always be ignored. Marguerite and I had many late-night conversations. 'Why can't he just be satisfied with me?' she'd ask. At the same time, I know she was intellectually stimulated by Peter Lisagor and did, I think, enjoy his friendship fully. Many of the problems between Marguerite and Bill were aggravated by absence. When they were together they enjoyed many happy times.

"I remember Bill built a fiberglass boat to use on the river near their summer place. Marguerite loved to go out on it with him. Their country house was a beautiful place with a garden that Marguerite had planned and planted herself, a show garden really. Sometimes twenty or thirty of us would drive out for the day. The children were always there, beautiful and very good. I remember Linda was just learning to swim. The dog was so protective, he'd keep pulling her out of the water. There was another dog in the family, too, a blind dalmatian. The children had a donkey, called In the Way, and, of course, a donkey cart. It seemed as though everyone had fun."

Larry recalled that both his parents were gone a great deal but always managed to maintain a sense of family continuity. "The only TV [shows] we were allowed to watch were 'Flipper' and 'Lassie.' Mom and Dad always watched them with us with what seemed then to be great interest and enthusiasm. The parties they gave stand out vividly after all these years. We were supposed to be seen and not heard but still managed to have fun."

Linda, too, had clear recollections. "At the time I couldn't always appreciate Mother's motives but now I recognize her basic idealism. I remember once I had a big Easter basket with one very gorgeous candy egg. Mother organized a large Easter egg hunt and I was supposed to give my prize egg to the winner. I resented it terribly, but now I understand the values she was trying to impart. She wanted me to respect and reward achievement. Attachment to a possession was much less important than that.

"Mother never allowed us to give her anything for holidays. Instead, Larry and I were supposed to learn a dance, memorize a poem, or draw a picture for her. I can still remember those poems. They seemed so long to me—four whole lines. One in particular—about travel and adventure —remains with me still. I remember Mother swimming out with me into the big waves. She taught me not to be afraid of anything. I was sitting on a horse when I was only two.

"People didn't always understand Mother, she was so far ahead of her times. Much of what she did may seem ordinary now because everybody does it, but then she was an original. I wonder if anyone can really be a heroine anymore—at least in the sense that she was. Anyway I know that my mother continues to be my ideal."

In August, with the book at last completed, Marguerite and Bill decided to take the children and their nurse, Sver Trolley, to France. "Sometimes I wonder if Marguerite didn't have some kind of premonition," Bill says today. "It's easy to think that now; she was so eager to have the children see and do the same things that she'd enjoyed in France as a child. It seemed very important to her that they know and understand their roots. Then, too, I think she was also a very proud mother, wanting to show off her children to their French relatives."

Larry recalled the visit to their vintner cousins. "It was dark and musty where they kept the wine barrels. They let us taste the wine. I didn't like it very well but pretended it was quite good. It was more fun to sit and talk with Mother in the warm sidewalk cafés."

There was a sun-drenched interlude at a hotel overlooking the sea at Antibes before they went their separate ways. Bill, the children, and Trolley returned to Washington. Marguerite went on to Rome to interview Madame Nhu.

Two years had passed since the two women had last met. Marguerite looked about the modest villa where the former first lady lived in almost total seclusion and remembered the wild stories once told of her. It was curiosity about those tales that had partially motivated her first interview. One day at breakfast she had been told that Madame Nhu had a new lover among the generals. By noon the general, according to a later rumor, had been sent to prison. Marguerite had considered that very fast work even for a "dragon lady."

Listening to a replay of the rumor, Madame Nhu laughed softly and then sighed. "I suppose it was inevitable that they would attack my sentimental life and, finding none, invent it." She was even more amused by a story General "Big" Minh, leader of the first post-Diem junta, had told Marguerite. Madame Nhu, he claimed, was one of the richest women in the world. It provoked the only hearty laugh in the five-hour conversation.

"When I left California I had exactly three thousand dollars in my pocket. In Vietnam I owned only one piece of property, a house in Dalat that was confiscated. When I came to Europe I did not know how I would live or bring up my children." It was largely due to Archbishop Ngh Dinh Thue, one of Diem's two surviving brothers, who shared the house with her, that she and her children had a home.

At the time of the interview, Madame Nhu lived a reclusive life, contenting herself with her children, her garden, and some political writing. As they parted, she further confirmed Marguerite's original "survivor" impression. "I have discovered an important secret of life," she confided. "I have learned how to land on my feet."

Although Marguerite had planned to continue on to Vietnam, she unexpectedly had to fly back to Washington. In a note of explanation to the *Newsday* editor Tom Dorsey, she complained, "The hassle over the book has only just been settled. The censors took out a dismaying amount but I think the basic picture has been salvaged."

Now resuming her plans, this time heading westward, Marguerite stopped in Oakland, where her mother was in the process of selling the Chabot Court house. She returned to the University of California for the first time in more than twenty years to find the activity around Sather Gate as inflammatory as in her own days. But now the scene was reversed. Where she had been one of a noisy minority, the dissenters were now running the show.

If Marguerite recalled her own impassioned speeches as she stood at Sather Gate listening to the protesters, she offered no evidence in her columns. She saw posters comparing President Johnson to Hitler. Studying the angry young people, she wondered if there were any among them who even remembered Hitler.

In an interview, Steven Smale, a mathematics professor and key figure in the Berkeley antiwar movement, explained to Marguerite the rationale behind the much publicized demonstrations. "We want the Vietcong to defeat the United States for international reasons. If the United States is defeated in Southeast Asia, this will break American power elsewhere, giving new impetus to revolutionary social change (wars of liberation) in such places as Africa and Latin America. If [we are] surrounded by radical social change, it will make it easier to achieve similar action here."

Long ago Marguerite had watched the brutal means by which the Poles were beaten into submission. It had left her feeling outraged and betrayed by a system that she had once fervently believed in. Years of covering the terrorist takeover of Czechoslovakia, the effort of the Russians to starve the West Berliners into submission, and the atrocities of the North Koreans and of Ho Chi Minh had left their mark. As a former Communist sympathizer these events had been far more shocking than to one whose political beliefs were more middle of the road. The result was a 180-degree turn. Her *Newsday* column showed no understanding at all of the idealism of many of the young people taking part in the demonstration. It was as though she had never stood in the same place, saying many of the same things.

Sadly, she boarded a plane for Vietnam. It was her tenth and last trip. Traveling the length and breadth of the country for about a month, often herself a target, she once again interviewed spear-carrying Montagnard chiefs, peasants in their villages, monks in their pagodas, and American and Vietnamese soldiers in the field. '' 'Instant Democracy American style—or else' used to be the cry of the American,'' she gibed at Lodge. ''Now the cry is for stability, instant or otherwise.''

Sophisticated Saigon seemed to wilt helplessly in the tropical sun. At night there was sin of every kind, tailored to every budget. Returning from the hinterland, where the astonishingly enduring peasants continued to labor with a war going on all around them, she could understand why the American soldiers called the city ''the twilight zone.'' The moist air was heavy with unreality.

Her mood was not lightened by a British correspondent who described his feelings to her. ''Sometimes,'' he said, ''in my nightmares, I liken Vietnam to water in a giant bathtub out of which the drain has been pulled. Periodically as the water silently ebbs away, a tough-voiced American says: 'We will never let Vietnam go under.' Louder and louder he says it until his voice rises to a shout. At this point, there is a glug, glug, glug sound. The American turns around. And lo and behold, the bathtub is empty.''

All through that interminable final flight back to Washington Marguerite was violently ill. Her body ached, her fever flaring to a frighteningly high 105 degrees. At home, though, a happy surprise awaited her that raised her spirits immeasurably.

Newbold Noyes had at last capitulated. Her column would be run three times a week on the editorial pages of the *Evening Star*. The first appeared the day of her arrival. "I'm having it framed," she wrote him in a quick note.

Yet as always there were hassles. *Newsday* was complaining about telex charges. Which were hers? Which theirs? A salary check had been lost in the mail. Worse yet, the IRS had announced an audit for 1961, 1962, and 1963. Throughout it all the illness continued and Marguerite went from bed to typewriter and back to bed. A key interview with Ambassador Tran Thien Khiem was reluctantly canceled.

Our Vietnam Nightmare was out and she was too ill to help with the promotion. The strain of three columns a week was becoming unbearable and Marguerite was panic-stricken that she might lose her long-sought forum. Soon Peter Lisagor was coming to the house every day to help her. When the pressure, added to his own responsibilities, proved too much for him, he brought in another close friend, Mike O'Neill of the *New York Daily News*. It was O'Neill who said what they all were thinking: "Maggie, you're going to die if you don't go to the hospital."

Reluctantly Marguerite agreed. She was too sick to resist any longer. Lisagor and O'Neill would write the column under her by-line. Mrs. Higgins, who had flown in from Oakland, would supervise things at home.

Marguerite entered Walter Reed Hospital on November 6, 1965. A room filled with blossoms awaited her. Tom White, air force chief of staff, and also a patient, had ordered all his flowers sent to her. As the tests began, Marguerite felt slightly better. Something was being done. Surely her stay would be a very short one.

"I want to talk to Ruth today," she insisted. Poor Ruth Montgomery, when she got the word, was in a quandary. She was supposed to be on television that morning and had a column due that afternoon and not a single idea for it. "At first I thought I couldn't go," she said, "but somehow I managed. I remember the long ride out to Walter Reed and all those miles of corridors. Then her room was empty; they'd taken Marguerite to the solarium in a wheelchair. She was sitting at the window watching the gently falling snow outside.

"I'd brought her a bright red bed jacket and she put it on right away. I think it cheered her a little. 'Did you think I was going to die?' she asked and I answered, 'I wouldn't let you die.' She looked so wistful when she said, 'I wish I'd paid more attention to the things you're into (psychic phenomena) and talked with you about them.' I tried to reassure her that there was plenty of time, but she looked doubtful.

" 'I'm supposed to be on the "Today" show to talk about my book.

Should I do it?' she asked. My heart ached for her. We both knew how terribly important that kind of exposure is. 'If they'll *let* you,' I said, knowing all the while they wouldn't.''

It was as if Marguerite needed *somebody's* permission. She knew she wouldn't get it from her doctors or family. Secretly she arranged with her children's nurse, Trolley, to wheel her out of the hospital to a waiting taxi and then from the taxi to a plane. They flew to New York where she was taken in another wheelchair and taxi to the television station. Marguerite did her show, trying desperately and feverishly to sum up everything that she believed about Vietnam and sought to encompass in her book. Then she returned to the hospital.

The impact of the protest had been softened by time. The irony of the situation was described by one reviewer who wrote: "Two years ago this would have been a very controversial book. By now the consensus is pretty much with Miss Higgins. It is generally agreed that the 'Buddhist leaders' who claimed persecution by Diem were not Buddhist leaders, nor had they been persecuted. . . .''

It had been obvious from the beginning that Marguerite was desperately ill, but no one could find the cause. Doctors at first thought she had picked up the drug-resistant malaria that had reached epidemic proportions in Vietnam. Later they suspected that she had cancer. An exploratory operation uncovered nothing while Marguerite developed uremic poisoning and began to hemorrhage internally.

It was terribly painful. Ruth said that on one occasion she could hear Marguerite screaming all the way down the hall. She was calling, "Larry! Larry! Help me!" Once again she was a child calling her father. Finally there was a diagnosis: a rare tropical disease called leishmaniasis, in which the protozoa from the bite of a sand fly enters the bloodstream and attacks the liver and spleen.

A few days before Christmas her condition seemed to suddenly improve. As the pain lessened, Marguerite's optimism returned. When Ruth dropped by with a tiny tree and announced plans to cancel a trip to Egypt previously scheduled for the day after Christmas, Marguerite was adamant: "Don't you dare cancel! Have a wonderful time. We'll have so much to talk about when you get back.''

Helen Lambert overheard Marguerite apologizing to one of the nurses: "I'm so sorry, I must have yelled terribly. I just had to, it hurt so much." The nurse was reassuring. "*Everybody* yells." Marguerite was full of plans for a hospital Christmas party and enlisted Helen's aid. "She went to so much trouble planning the gifts and food," Helen recalled. "I think it gave her a great deal of pleasure. The staff really seemed to love her. You could tell by the way they spoke and the tender way they'd lift her.

"Marguerite had been doing a lot of thinking. One afternoon she said, 'I'm much better and I'm so grateful. I see my life quite clearly now. I've always been so driven. It doesn't have to be that way. I'm going to change. I'm not going overseas all the time. I'll spend much more time with Bill and the children. Things are going to be different. I'm going to be different.' "

But on Christmas day Marguerite took a turn for the worse. Bill recalled that President Johnson and Lady Bird had called from Texas. "Marguerite talked for a while and then her voice got so weak," he said. "Her last words were 'Thank you so much for calling, but I'm awfully tired, Bird.' "

The following day Helen came with a spring bouquet. "There's an old proverb that if you give an ailing person spring flowers they get better," Helen explained. "I told Marguerite the story and she said, 'Helen, let's not kid. Don't try to cheer me up. I'm facing it.' She was in great pain and her kidneys didn't sanitize. They'd functioned during that short period but now failed again. She was on a dialysis machine almost constantly and had to be moved from her private room to a laboratory."

Despite her pain Marguerite calmly set about making final arrangements. She called her brother-in-law, Scott Hall, in Paris where he was stationed and asked him to fly home. The two of them very carefully went over finances. "She was fully aware that she was going to die," Scott recalled, "but talked calmly, intelligently, sometimes even humorously about the future of the family. Their finances were complicated. Marguerite carried it all around in her head but was able to explain it to me so that I could help Bill later."

Bill remembered, "She even thought about what was going to happen to the pets. 'You take care of Blue Kitty,' she instructed our cook, who loved the animal. Sure enough when Mabel went back to Louisiana she took the cat with her."

Helen recalled the afternoon that Trolley brought the children to see Marguerite. "I think she knew it would be the last time she would ever see them. I expected Marguerite to be sentimental and just go to pieces, but she was wonderful, so brave. Larry was telling her about his grades and Linda interrupted him. Marguerite spoke to her just as she normally would. She said, 'You must remember not to interrupt when someone else is talking. Wait always until it's your turn.' I thought that took such courage. I really can't think of anything more difficult than saying good-bye to one's children when they're so young. They had no idea how sick she was. It must have taken tremendous will and control to act that natural.

"But then she was wonderful with everyone. I remember coming in when she was so sick and a young nurse was sitting beside her. The nurse looked up, her face flushed with embarrassment. She'd been telling Marguerite about her boyfriend and asking advice. Marguerite was so sweet to her. She seemed to be hanging on every word as though it was the most fascinating subject in the world. When Marguerite looked up and saw me, she said to her, 'We'll talk some more about this later.' The nurse looked happy and relieved."

Tom Lambert stopped in to see Marguerite on January 2. "I was shocked to see how she'd changed. She looked so wan and her hair was damp. I was standing next to her and she took my hand and said, 'Tom, I'm just not going to make it.' I said, 'Of course you are!' I just couldn't believe it. I kept thinking of that brave kid I'd known in Korea. Well, she was still brave and wasn't about to fool herself or anyone else."

Peter Lisagor and Mike O'Neill had continued to faithfully turn out columns. Lisagor is no longer alive, but O'Neill remembers how lucidly Marguerite followed the issues to the very end. "She always *cared*, even when she knew it was over for her," he said.

On January 3, 1966, Marguerite died quietly while in a coma.

Helen and Tom were with Bill and Mrs. Higgins when they looked at her for the last time. "Mrs. Higgins was so volatile, I really expected hysterics," Helen admitted, "but she was very calm. She went over to the casket and said, 'Oh, Marguerite, I never meant to beat you those times. I never meant to hurt you. I just wanted you to grow up to be a good little girl.'

"Bill bent over close to Marguerite and looked at her with such love in his eyes. 'I never had so much fun with anyone in my life,' he said. 'This was a girl I had more fun with than anyone I ever knew.' "

The decision to bury Marguerite at Arlington National Cemetery seemed appropriate. Not only was she a soldier's daughter and a soldier's wife, but also she was a woman who had often risked death to record the quiet, day-to-day heroism of soldiers.

On the day of the funeral the *Washington Evening Star* carried a drawing at the top of its editorial page. It showed a row of cemetery crosses. A plot of freshly turned earth indicated a new one in their midst. Beneath it were the words, "AND NOW SHE IS WITH HER BOYS AGAIN."

Bibliography

BOOKS

Beech, Keyes. *Not Without the Americans*. Garden City: Doubleday & Company, 1971.

———. *Tokyo and Points East*. Garden City: Doubleday & Company, 1954.

Bennett, Lowell. *Berlin Bastion*. Frankfurt: Fred Rudl, 1951.

Ellyson, Spuds. *Anchors in the Sky*. San Rafael: Presidio Press, 1978.

Gun, Nerin. *The Day of the Americans*. New York: Fleet Publishing Corporation, 1966.

Halberstam, David. *The Making of a Quagmire*. New York: Random House, 1965.

Higgins, Marguerite. *Jessie Benton Fremont*. Cambridge: Houghton Mifflin, 1962.

———. *News Is a Singular Thing*. Garden City: Doubleday & Company, 1955.

———. *Our Vietnam Nightmare*. New York: Harper & Row, 1965.

———. *Red Plush and Black Bread*. Garden City: Doubleday & Company, 1955.

———. *War in Korea*. Garden City: Doubleday & Company, 1951.

——— and Peter Lisagor. *Overtime in Heaven*. Garden City: Doubleday & Company, 1964.

Howard, Toni. *Shriek with Pleasure*. New York: Prentice-Hall, 1950.

Lanham, Edwin. *The Iron Maiden*. New York: Harcourt, Brace and Company, 1954.

Millar, George. *Road to Resistance*. London: Arrow Books, 1981.

Montgomery, Ruth. *A Search for Truth*. New York: William Morrow & Company, 1967.

———. *Hail to the Chiefs*. New York: Coward McCann, 1971.

O'Donnell, James P. *The Bunker*. Boston: Houghton Mifflin, 1978.

Selzer, Michael. *Deliverance Day*. Philadelphia: Lippincott, 1978.

Sevareid, Eric. *Not So Wild a Dream*. New York: Atheneum, 1976.

Springs, Elliot. *War Birds: Diary of an Unknown Aviator*. New York; Grosset & Dunlap, 1926.

ARTICLES

Clack, Jean Craig. "Marguerite Higgins '41." *California Monthly*, October 1950.

Erwin, Ray. "Marguerite Higgins Breaks the Cuba Story." *Editor & Publisher*, August 15, 1964.

Halberstam, David. "A Letter to My Daughter." *Parade*, May 2, 1982.

Higgins, Marguerite. "At Home in the Ruins." *Mademoiselle*, August 1964.

———. "Berlin—City of Women." *Mademoiselle*, December 1945.

———. "Foreign Correspondent." *Mademoiselle*, February 1945.

———. "Germany—the Lesson of Belsen." *Mademoiselle*, November 1945.

———. "Miss Higgins Speaks." *Newsweek*, August 7, 1970.

———. "New to Britain." *Mademoiselle*, March 1945.

———. "Night Raiders of Berlin." *Saturday Evening Post*, June 17, 1950.

———. "Paris—Heartbreak and Hope." *Mademoiselle*, September 1945.

———. "Paris in the Spring." *Mademoiselle*, May 1945.

———. "Paris—Youth in the News." *Mademoiselle*, January 1946.

———. "Private World of Robert and Ethel Kennedy." *McCall's*, February 1962.

———. "Rose Fitzgerald Kennedy." *McCall's*, May 1961.

———. "Round the World Diary." *Women's Home Companion*, November 1951, December 1951, January 1952.

———. "Saigon Summary." *America*, January 4, 1964.

———. "Terrible Days of Korea." *Saturday Evening Post*, August 10, 1950.

———. "Thoughts on the Death of a Five-day-old Child." *Good Housekeeping*, August 1954.

———. "Two Who Knew the Enemy." *Mademoiselle*, June 1945.

———. "Ugly Americans in Vietnam." *America*, January 4, 1964.

———. "Voices of the Defeated." *Mademoiselle*, August 1945.

——— and Peter Lisagor. "R.S.V.P.—The White House." *McCall's*, August 1962.

Martin, Harold H. "The Colonel Who Saved the Day." *Saturday Evening Post*, September 9, 1950.

Mydans, Carl. "Girl War Correspondent." *Life*, October 2, 1950.

Newsweek. "Maggie in the Congo." April 3, 1961.

———. "Powder Keg Ignited by Red Match." July 3, 1950.

———. "Significance of Korea: We Have to Put Up or Shut Up." July 3, 1950.

————. "This Time, Korea." July 10, 1950.

————. "U.S. Flexes for a Bitter Struggle." July 17, 1950.

————. "What Vietnam Did to Us, Special Issue." December 14, 1981.

Time. "Man of the Year." January 6, 1941.

————. "One Star for Mike." March 5, 1951.

————. "Pride of the Regiment." September 25, 1950.

————. "South Vietnam's Madame Nhu." August 9, 1963.

————. "The Bowling Alley." September 12, 1950.

————. "The Fine Print."November 5, 1957.

U.S. News and World Report. "Soviet Games." (an interview with Marguerite Higgins). October 12, 1955.

NEWSPAPERS

Chicago Daily News. Keyes Beech. July 9, 1950; December 5, 1965.

Communist Campinile. March 17, 1939.

Daily Californian. September 1937–June 1941.

Honolulu Advertiser. October 19, 1950.

Houston Post. December 8, 1964.

Indianapolis News. June 5, 1963.

London Daily Express. George Millar. May 3, 1945.

Korean Herald. October 2, 1981.

Macon Telegraph and News. Wallace Reid. May 14, 1965.

Newsday. October 1963–January 1966.

New York Herald Tribune. November 1941–October 1963.

New York Times. January 4, 1966.

Oakland Tribune. February 4, 1930; May 17, 1942; November 21, 1942; February 3, 1946; May 25, 1947; June 18, 1949; April 30, 1951; May 1, 1951; March 18, 1959; November 28, 1964; January 4, 1966.

Reno Evening Gazette. April 26, 1952.

Richmond Times-Dispatch. Ellen McCann. October 20, 1953.

San Diego Union. Ettilie Wallace. April 12, 1952.

Stars and Stripes. April 20, 1945.

Index

For a complete list of books available from Penguin in the United States, write to Dept. DG, Penguin Books, 299 Murray Hill Parkway, East Rutherford, New Jersey 07073.

For a complete list of books available from Penguin in Canada, write to Penguin Books Canada Limited, 2801 John Street, Markham, Ontario L3R 1B4.

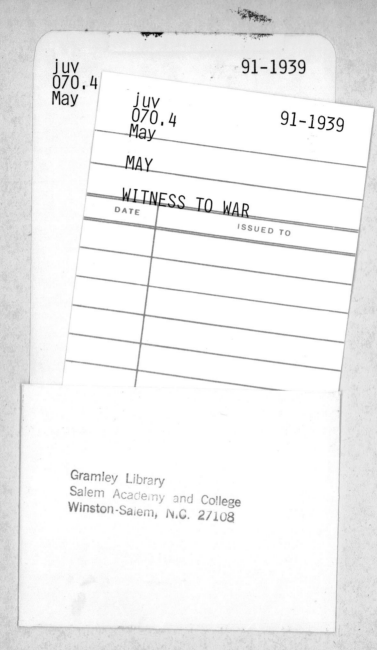